WILDFLOWERS
OF THE
TEXAS
HILL COUNTRY

From

matt + Julia

January 2017

# WILDFLOWERS
## — OF THE —
# TEXAS
# HILL COUNTRY

BY

MARSHALL ENQUIST

Lone Star Botanical
Austin, Texas

Library of Congress Catalog Card Number  87-80788

ISBN 0-9618013-0-1

Typesetting by G & S typesetters, Inc., Austin, Texas

# Contents

Introduction .......................................................... vii
Notes ............................................................... x
Acknowledgments ..................................................... xi

Araceae (*Arum Family*) .............................................. 1
Ephedraceae (*Ephedra Family*) ....................................... 2
Commelinaceae (*Spiderwort Family*) ................................ 3–5
Liliaceae (*Lily Family*) ......................................... 6–11
Amaryllidaceae (*Amaryllis Family*) .................................. 12
Iridaceae (*Iris Family*) ............................................ 13
Orchidaceae (*Orchid Family*) ........................................ 14
Moraceae (*Mulberry Family*) ......................................... 15
Rafflesiaceae (*Rafflesia Family*) ................................... 16
Polygonaceae (*Knotweed Family*) ..................................... 17
Amaranthaceae (*Amaranth Family*) .................................... 18
Nyctaginaceae (*Four-O'Clock Family*) ............................ 19–20
Phytolaccaceae (*Pokeweed Family*) ................................... 21
Portulacaceae (*Purslane Family*) ................................. 22–23
Caryophyllaceae (*Pink Family*) ...................................... 24
Ranunculaceae (*Buttercup Family*) ............................... 25–31
Berberidaceae (*Barberry Family*) ................................ 32–33
Lauraceae (*Laurel Family*) .......................................... 34
Papaveraceae (*Poppy Family*) ........................................ 35
Fumariaceae (*Fumitory Family*) ...................................... 36
Cruciferae (*Mustard Family*) .................................... 37–42
Capparidaceae (*Caper Family*) ....................................... 43
Crassulaceae (*Stonecrop Family*) .................................... 44
Saxifragaceae (*Saxifrage Family*) ................................... 45
Hamamelidaceae (*Witch-Hazel Family*) ................................ 46
Rosaceae (*Rose Family*) ......................................... 47–53
Leguminosae (*Legume Family*) .................................... 54–78
Krameriaceae (*Ratany Family*) ....................................... 79
Geraniaceae (*Geranium Family*) ...................................... 80
Oxalidaceae (*Wood-Sorrel Family*) ................................... 81
Linaceae (*Flax Family*) ......................................... 82–83
Rutaceae (*Citrus Family*) ........................................... 84
Malpighiaceae (*Malpighia Family*) ................................... 85
Polygalaceae (*Milkwort Family*) ..................................... 86
Euphorbiaceae (*Spurge Family*) .................................. 87–90
Anacardiaceae (*Sumac Family*) ....................................... 91
Hippocastanaceae (*Buckeye Family*) .............................. 92–93
Sapindaceae (*Soap-Berry Family*) .................................... 94
Rhamnaceae (*Buckthorn Family*) ...................................... 95
Malvaceae (*Mallow Family*) ...................................... 96–100
Sterculiaceae (*Cacao Family*) ...................................... 101

Cistaceae (*Rockrose Family*) .............................................. 102
Cochlospermaceae (*Cochlospermum Family*) ............................... 103
Violaceae (*Violet Family*) ................................................ 104
Passifloraceae (*Passionflower Family*) ................................. 105–106
Loasaceae (*Stick-Leaf Family*) ........................................ 107–108
Cactaceae (*Cactus Family*) ............................................ 109–110
Lythraceae (*Loosestrife Family*) .......................................... 111
Onagraceae (*Evening Primrose Family*) ............................... 112–119
Umbelliferae (*Parsley Family*) ....................................... 120–125
Cornaceae (*Dogwood Family*) ............................................. 126
Ericaceae (*Heath Family*) ............................................... 127
Primulaceae (*Primrose Family*) .......................................... 128
Styracaceae (*Storax Family*) ............................................ 129
Oleaceae (*Olive Family*) ................................................ 130
Gentianaceae (*Gentian Family*) ...................................... 131–133
Apocynaceae (*Dogbane Family*) ........................................... 134
Asclepiadaceae (*Milkweed Family*) ................................... 135–141
Convolvulaceae (*Morning Glory Family*) .............................. 142–146
Polemoniaceae (*Phlox Family*) ....................................... 147–150
Hydrophyllaceae (*Waterleaf Family*) ................................. 151–152
Boraginaceae (*Borage Family*) ....................................... 153–156
Verbenaceae (*Verbena Family*) ....................................... 157–161
Labiatae (*Mint Family*) ............................................. 162–175
Solanaceae (*Nightshade Family*) ..................................... 176–180
Scrophulariaceae (*Figwort Family*) .................................. 181–190
Bignoniaceae (*Catalpa Family*) .......................................... 191
Martyniaceae (*Unicorn-Plant Family*) .................................... 192
Acanthaceae (*Acanthus Family*) ...................................... 193–196
Rubiaceae (*Madder Family*) .......................................... 197–198
Caprifoliaceae (*Honeysuckle Family*) ................................ 199–200
Valerianaceae (*Valerian Family*) ........................................ 201
Cucurbitaceae (*Gourd Family*) ....................................... 202–203
Campanulaceae (*Bluebell Family*) .................................... 204–206
Compositae (*Sunflower Family*) ...................................... 207–254
    Tribe Vernonieae ..................................................... 207
    Tribe Eupatorieae ................................................ 208–209
    Tribe Astereae ................................................... 210–219
    Tribe Inuleae ........................................................ 220
    Tribe Heliantheae ................................................ 221–234
    Tribe Helenieae .................................................. 235–242
    Tribe Anthemideae .................................................... 243
    Tribe Senecioneae ................................................ 244–245
    Tribe Cynareae ................................................... 246–248
    Tribe Mutisieae .................................................. 249–250
    Tribe Cichorieae ................................................. 251–254

Bibliography ........................................................... 255–256
Illustrated Glossary ................................................... 257–258
Glossary ............................................................... 259–263
Index .................................................................. 264–275

# Introduction

A broad band of limestone cuts across the center of Texas, entering from Arkansas and Oklahoma and continuing on into Mexico. To the early settlers, this was the "mountainous region" of Texas. We know it today as the Hill Country.

The immigrants of the early 1800's recognized the beauty and potential of the area and were drawn to its fertile river valleys. Through struggle and sacrifice, they were able to establish their farmsteads and transform the countryside. Today, we can enjoy the beauty of the Hill Country in comfort and tranquility. This book deals with one aspect of that beauty, the colorful wildflowers that grace the landscape from early Spring to late Fall.

The plant life of a region is usually determined by the soil type of the area. In turn, the soil type is determined by the underlying geology. The common denominator of the Hill Country is the presence of Mesozoic (Cretaceous) limestones, which degrade to produce soils ranging from dark calcareous clays to cream-colored caliche. Disregarding variations of plant range caused by differences in mean temperature and rainfall, the landforms and vegetation of the Hill Country are remarkably uniform. A person walking the bluffs overlooking Meridian, in Bosque Co., would find little to distinguish them from the bluffs near Kerrville, in Kerr Co.

*Wildflowers of the Texas Hill Country* covers the mid-section of the limestone belt, as far south and west as San Antonio, Uvalde, and Rocksprings and as far north as Waco, Meridian, and Comanche. This limited area is large enough to give a fairly complete sample of the regional flora.

Squarely in the middle of the Hill Country is the Llano Uplift. Here, the underlying basement rock has pushed to the surface, exposing igneous and metamorphic rocks which are totally unlike those of the surrounding Hill Country. The Llano Uplift is an interesting geological and botanical island in a sea of limestone. Rather than gerrymander the borders of the area covered by this book, it was decided to include the Llano Uplift in the Hill Country area.

This results in an area with three major subdivisions: 1.) the Edwards Plateau, 2.) the Lampasas Cut Plains, and 3.) the Llano Uplift. Each subdivision is distinctive enough to warrant its own brief description.

The Edwards Plateau covers an extensive area south of the Colorado River and west of a line between Austin and San Antonio, extending to the west almost as far as Fort Stockton and Midland. The portion of it covered by this book, the eastern third, is comparatively green and lush, as it receives about 30 inches of rainfall a year, in contrast to the western third, which receives only 10–15 inches per year. It is a land of rugged hills and deeply cut canyons, with clear streams running over beds of solid limestone. In the opinion of the author, it reaches its finest expression in the section bounded by Uvalde, Bandera, Kerr, and Real counties. It is an area rich in endemic species such as Sycamore-Leaf Snow Bell (*Styrax platanifolia*), Texas Barberry (*Berberis Swaseyi*), Canyon Mock-Orange (*Philadelphus Ernestii*), Scarlet Leatherflower (*Clematis texensis*), Bracted Twist-Flower (*Streptanthus bracteatus*), Plateau Milkvine (*Matelea edwardsensis*), and Two-Flower Anemone (*Anemone edwardsiana*).

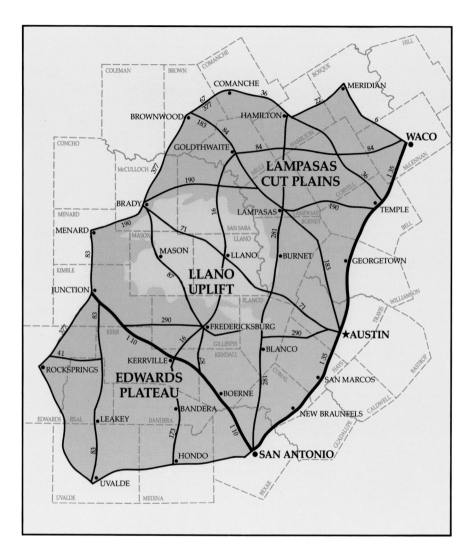

The Lampasas Cut Plains lie north of the Colorado River (and the Llano Uplift) and east of a line drawn between Austin and Waco. Geologically and vegetationally, the area is very similar to the Edwards Plateau, but tends to be more gently rolling. Ranges of limestone hills, usually soft fossiliferous marls capped by a thin layer of hard resistant limestone, tend to be scattered through the area, with intervening stretches of rolling prairie. In general, this area lacks the thick layers of solid limestone that characterize the Edwards Plateau. The underlying limestone is commonly overlain by dark, calcareous prairie soils with a substantial clay content. In this area, we find plants that are more suited to prairie habitats, such as Wild Hyacinth (*Camassia scilloides*), Prairie Phlox (*Phlox pilosa*), and Purple Coneflower (*Echinacea angustifolia*). There are even a few plants that normally have a more northerly distribution, such as Hall's Dalea (*Dalea Hallii*) and White Dog's-Tooth-Violet (*Erythroniium albidum*).

The Llano Uplift centers on Llano Co. and includes large parts of Burnet, Mason, and Gillespie counties. Geologically diverse, it contains all three major rock types: a.) igneous (granite), b.) metamorphic (gneiss and schist), and c.) sedimentary (sandstones and limestones). Where the Uplift has exposed limestones of Paleozoic age, the vegetation is identical to that found on the Mesozoic limestones of the Edwards Plateau and the Lampasas Cut Plains. However, where the underlying rock is granite, gneiss, schist, or sandstone, a niche is provided for those species that love sandy soils. Several species that are normally found only in East Texas or on the Gulf Coast have somehow established themselves in these isolated sands. Rockrose (*Helianthemum georgianum*), Lindheimer's Sida (*Sida Lindheimeri*), and Viperina (*Zornia bracteata*) are examples of this. There is even a sweet dwarf plum (*Prunus texana*) normally found in South Texas which makes a home in this region, at the northernmost limit of its range. The region also shelters its own rare endemic, the Texas Bluebell, *Campanula Reverchonii*.

The Hill Country has a charm and beauty that is all its own. However, we should keep in mind that the Hill Country we see today is not the Hill Country the early settlers saw. They saw the land before it was fenced and subsequently overgrazed by sheep, goats, and cattle. Their accounts describe the unspoiled hills as an endless sea of wildflowers in the Spring. Imagine your favorite patch of roadside flowers multiplied a million times, stretching as far as the eye can see in all directions and you begin to have an idea of what has been lost.

Currently, most of the Hill Country is covered in scrub Oak and Juniper. In the early 1800's, many of the same hills were covered in tall grasses. It is difficult to imagine, but in those days Buffalo and Antelope, both of which are animals of the open plains and prairies, were common in the Hill Country.

A Texas Ranger, James Gillett, recorded his experiences in the fascinating book *Six Years with the Texas Rangers, 1875–1881* (University of Nebraska Press and Yale University Press, 1976). Most of his service with the Rangers was in the Hill Country area, which he recalled as an earthly paradise. "In the Springtime, one could travel for hundreds of miles on a bed of flowers . . . How happy I am now in my old age that I am a native Texan and saw the grand frontier before it was marred by the hand of man."

So something has been lost, but much remains. The Hill Country is still one of the most beautiful and scenic parts of Texas. Go out and see the canyons and the hills. Enjoy the wildflowers and the wildlife. The Hill Country is a natural treasure that will well repay your exploration.

In order to avoid confusion, the
scientific names presented here follow
the *Manual of the Vascular Plants of Texas*,
by Donovan S. Correll and Marshall C.
Johnston (Texas Research Foundation,
1970). In those cases in which a plant
name has been altered since
publication of that work, the new name
is given in parentheses below the old
name.

Each plant illustrated was collected,
pressed, dried, and preserved by the
author. Genus and species
determinations were made by
comparison with herbarium specimens
at the Plant Resource Center of the
University of Texas at Austin.

I would like to thank the faculty, staff, and graduate students of the Botany Department of the University of Texas at Austin. Without their instruction and assistance, this book could not have been produced.

WILDFLOWERS
OF THE
TEXAS
HILL COUNTRY

## Green Dragon
*Arisaema Dracontium*

Green Dragon is an herbaceous plant 1–2' high, usually with one compound leaf on a long, erect petiole. When growing on limestone, it prefers the shade of moist, wooded canyons. On granite, it exposes itself to full sun from crevices in seep areas or alluvial soils near streams.

The compound leaf may reach 1' in width, on a petiole 1–2' long which emerges directly from the ground. Sometimes, the elliptic to oblanceolate leaflets are simply palmate at the end of the petiole, especially on smaller, immature leaves. On the larger leaves, there is a division into 3 parts: at the end of the main petiole is a single leaflet occupying a central position between two symmetrical sub-petioles, each having 2–7 additional leaflets arranged in a scorpioid manner on one side of the sub-petiole's axis.

The flower stalk is usually 4–10" long, topped by a light green spathe 1–2½" long from which emerges a pale, yellow-green, tapering spadix about 6" long. Male flowers are above the female flowers on the spadix and both are partially concealed within the spathe. Clusters of bright red berries ¼–⅜" in diameter top the stalks in late June and July. Perennial.

Bloom Period: March to May.
*Lake Austin, Travis Co.*

## Mormon-Tea, Joint-Fir
*Ephedra antisyphylitica*

On the southeastern edge of our area, Mormon-Tea is a low, spreading bush normally found on limestone cliffs. In Kimble and Menard counties, it can also occur as a rounded shrub on the sandy, rocky soil of desert flats. It rarely grows over 3' tall, but can spread laterally to cover an area 10' across or more.

In the abscence of any obvious leaves (which are reduced to the point of being scale-like), the most obvious feature of the plant is the presence of numerous green, striated stems. Each stem is divided into several short segments, bounded by the leaf nodes. The small opposite leaves are connate, that is, basally joined. In addition, there is a narrow (1–2 mm. wide) pale orange or tan band around the stem at each node. This band is distinctive, and separates this species from all others in Texas.

Bloom Period: March to May.
*San Saba R., Menard, Menard Co.*

## False Day Flower
*Commelinantia anomala*
*(Tinantia anomala)*

False Day Flower can be found growing in colonies on moist, shaded slopes, usually near watercourses. It is an erect plant 1–2' high.

Young plants commonly have a solitary, unbranched stem, but in time branches are added, rising from the nodes through the lower back of the leaf sheath. Low on the stem, the leaves are linear-spatulate and long petiolate. The upper leaves are lanceolate with a cordate or clasping base. They average 2–4" long, though they are sometimes much longer. The uppermost leaf stands erect and acts as a spathe for the scorpioid raceme of flowers.

The petals and stamens are so arranged as to give each flower the appearance of a small face. There are 3 petals; two large lavender-blue petals and one small white petal which is usually hidden under the central stamen. The upper 3 stamens are tufted in yellow and purple hairs. Of the lower 3 stamens, the outer 2 have purple hairs only at the base, while the middle one is essentially glabrous. The pistil mimics the drooping-curled shape of the lower stamens. Annual.

Bloom Period: April to July.
*Brushy Creek, Uvalde Co.*

## Widow's Tears, Day Flower
*Commelina erecta*

A gentle squeeze on the spathe of this plant will produce a tear-like drop of liquid at the tip, hence the common name.

Erect at first (6–18″ high), the growing stems soon bend and trail, often reaching 3′ in length. The linear-lanceolate leaves are up to 6″ long, with a basal sheath ¼–¾″ long wrapping the stem.

The terminal, boat-shaped spathe contains 3–5 buds which open above the spathe. Each flower is composed of 2 large, blue petals and 1 small colorless petal. There are 3 fertile stamens: the lower two are drooping-incurved while the central and largest stamen has a broad cross-shape. The central stamen is surrounded by 3 cross-shaped staminodia. Perennial.

Bloom Period: May to October.
*Kerrville, Kerr Co.*

## Giant Spiderwort
*Tradescantia gigantea*

*Tradescantia gigantea* is an erect plant 1–3′ tall. It is found in limestone soils at the edge of woods and on roadsides.

In contrast to the lower leaves and stems, which are glabrous or nearly so, the upper stems and leaves are densely covered with short hairs. The linear-lanceolate leaves are 4–12″ long.

Flower color may vary from lavender-blue to pink. The bracts, pedicels and sepals are all densely pubescent. Notably ballooned into a sac-like shape at the base, the bract may be 3–6″ long. Beyond the sac-like base, the bract is much reduced in width. Perennial.

Bloom Period: March to April.
*Pedernales R., Travis Co.*

## Granite Spiderwort
*Tradescantia pedicellata*

This xeric species of Spiderwort is found only on granite-derived soils of the Llano Uplift. It has many erect to prostrate stems spreading from the base, making a clump about 6" high.

Short hairs (which may be glandular, non-glandular, or both) cover the plant and are most dense on the upper portions. The linear to linear-lanceolate leaves are 3–8" long.

Slender pedicels ¾–1¼" long support the flowers, which range in color from light blue to pink. There is some speculation that this plant is the result of a cross between *T. humilis* and *T. occidentalis*. Perennial.

Bloom Period: April and May.
*Near Granite Mt., Burnet Co.*

## Western Spiderwort
*Tradescantia occidentalis*

Common throughout the state, *Tradescantia occidentalis* is an erect, few-branched plant 12–18" high.

Its linear-lanceolate leaves are 6–12" long and very narrow, usually ¼–⅜" wide. Glandular hairs are found only on the sepals and the pedicels. All other parts of the plant are hairless and smooth.

Slightly expanded in the first ¼–⅜" of the base, the bracts are linear and may be as long as 7". Flower color ranges from blue to pink and flower width ranges from ⅝–1¼". The pedicels are ½–¾" long. Perennial.

Bloom Period: April to June.
*Comanche, Comanche Co.*

## Death Camas
*Zigadenus Nuttallii*

   Rising from dark brown bulbs, these
poisonous plants dot the prairies and
open hillsides on calcareous soils.
*Zigadenus Nuttallii* has an upright
flowering stalk 1–2′ high and arching-
trailing leaves. It is said to be danger-
ous to grazing livestock.
   Most of its leaves arch up from the
base and then curve over and touch the
ground. These basal leaves are 12–18″
long and tend to be withered or dried
in their last few inches. A few leaves
are scattered on the stout flower stalk
but they are greatly reduced and
bract-like.
   Closely spaced, the white flowers are
carried in dense racemes 3–7″ long. Individual flowers are ⅜–½″ wide on
pedicels ½–1¼″ long. Each perianth
segment has a small yellow dot at its
base. Additional color is provided by
six bright yellow-orange anthers.
Perennial.
   Bloom Period: March to April.
*Bee Cave, Travis Co.*

## Green Lily
*Schoenocaulon texanum*

Until it sends up its scape and
blooms, Green Lily could be dismissed
by the casual observer as a long-bladed
grass. The 1–1½' leaves are only about
⅛" wide. They arch up from the base,
but not very high, before they curve
back to the ground and trail for most of
their length.

Smooth and leafless, the scape
stands erect and is 1–2' long. The
flowers are in a slender, crowded spike
1–3" long. Perianth parts are light
green and the filaments are white to
lavender. Salmon colored before they
open, the anthers turn bright golden-
yellow (due to the exposed pollen) after
they open. Perennial.

Bloom Period: April and May.
*Garner State Park, Uvalde Co.*

## Crow-Poison
*Nothoscordum bivalve*

Crow-Poison is easily distinguished
from *Allium* because it lacks the characteristic onion odor. It is a common
plant of prairies, open slopes and roadsides throughout the state.

In the dry Hill Country environment,
these plants tend to run smaller than
elsewhere, with narrowly linear basal
leaves rarely over ⅛" wide and
4–8" long.

Terminated by an umbel of 6–12
white flowers, the naked scapes stand
4–12" tall. Individual flowers are ⅜–¾"
wide, and have 6 yellow-orange anthers
on colorless filaments. Perennial.

Bloom Period: Spring and fall.
*Twin sisters, Blanco Co.*

## Wild Onion, Canada Onion
*Allium canadense* var. *canadense*

This particular variety of Canada Onion is easily distinguished by its reproductive strategy. The erect scapes, 6–18″ tall, are terminated by umbels in which most flowers have been replaced by bulblets. Nothing more than miniature bulbs, the bulblets soon fall to the ground and reproduce the mother plant.

Narrowly linear, the fleshy leaves are 6–12″ long. They, and all other parts of the plant, have the characteristic onion odor.

White or pink and often lined, the flowers are about ⅝″ wide. Only rarely will they produce capsules or seeds. Perennial.

Bloom Period: April and May.
*Georgetown, Williamson Co.*

## Wild Garlic
*Allium Drummondii*

Wild Garlic is a small plant with scapes 6–10″ high and slender, linear leaves 3–8″ long. It prefers to colonize open grassy areas and is usually abundant where found.

Flower color may range from white to pink to purple-red. Individual flowers are ⅜–½″ wide in an umbel of 12–24 flowers. Each umbel is subtended by a membrane-like spathe, which breaks into 2 or 3 lanceolate bracts before the flowers open. Perennial.

Bloom Period: March to May.
*Fredericksburg, Gillespie Co.*

## White Dog's-Tooth-Violet
*Erythronium albidum*

White Dog's-Tooth-Violet is a low, un-common plant with a single scape and one or two leaves. It is found in shaded areas, usually under brush or small trees, in dry or moist woods.

A plant with only one leaf is imma-ture. Plants with two leaves are mature and will flower. The elliptic-lanceolate leaves are 3–5″ long and are mottled with purple-brown and light green patches.

Nodding from a scape 3–6″ high, the white to pale violet flowers are 1½–2″ in diameter, with petals that are often curved back. The stigma is 3-parted. In our area, *E. albidum* is reported from Bell, McLennan, Coryell, and Bosque counties. Perennial.

Bloom Period: February and March.
*Bluff over Meridian, Bosque Co.*

### Wild Hyacinth
*Camassia scilloides*

### Androstephium, Funnel-Flower
*Androstephium coeruleum*

Androstephium is a low plant of open grassy areas, with basal leaves reaching 10″ in length. It is most common in north-central Texas, but a few patches can be found in Travis, Hays, and Blanco counties.

The flower scapes are 3–10″ high (averaging 4–5″) with an umbel of 1–6 flowers, 1 or 2 of which may bloom at a given moment. The lower half of the flower, the corolla tube, is ⅜–½″ long. At the midpoint are the 6 spreading perianth parts (analogous to petals), which are also ⅜–½″ long. An upright circle of perianth segments ¼–⅜″ high, called the crown, encloses the anthers. The flowers may be white, light blue or pale lavender. Perennial.

Bloom Period: March to April.
*W. of San Marcos, Hays Co.*

Colonies of Wild Hyacinth can be found growing in open grasslands in the northern part of our area. The plants have light green leaves 12–15″ long by ⅜–⅝″ wide, which arch upwards and then trail on the ground.

The erect scapes are 1–2½′ tall, including a terminal raceme 3–8″ long. Light blue to violet-blue, the flowers are ½–¾″ in diameter. A prominent yellow-green ovary (soon to become a 3-parted capsule) is at the center of the flower and is surrounded by six bright yellow anthers on colorless to light blue filaments. Each flower is on a slender pedicel ½–1″ long. The pedicels are subtended by bristle-like bracts which usually are longer than the pedicels. Perennial.

Bloom Period: March to May.
*Sycamore Creek, Hamilton Co.*

## Twist-Leaf Yucca
*Yucca rupicola*

Twist-Leaf Yucca is a common plant of the Hill Country area and is found in brush country, grasslands and rocky open woods.

The twisted, glaucous leaves are 1–2′ long with light brown or yellow margins. Minute, sharp teeth line the margins.

Its scape is 2–5′ long, including the panicle which is 6–18″ long with 8–16 short branchlets up to 5″ in length. Heavily scented, the white flowers are 1½–2″ long. Perennial.

Bloom Period: April to June.

*Near Bee Creek, Travis Co.*

## Rain-Lily
*Cooperia pedunculata*

Two similar species of *Cooperia* grow in the Hill Country area. Fortunately, they are easily differentiated by the length of their floral tubes and the time of year they bloom.

The floral tube is measured from the swelling of the ovary to the point at which the tube divides into the 6 perianth lobes. *C. pedunculata* has a floral tube 1–1½" long. Blooming primarily in the spring, its flowers are 1¼–2" in diameter. *C. Drummondii* has a floral tube 3–7" long and blooms most frequently in September and October, though a few collections have been made as early as June. Perennial.

Bloom Period: April and May.
*Near Packsaddle Mt., Llano Co.*

## American Aloe, Amole Plant
*Polianthes maculosa*
*(Manfreda maculosa)*

Native to the South Texas brush country, *M. maculosa* extends its range to the southern edge of the Edwards Plateau north of Uvalde. It looks much like the Old World genus *Aloe*, but it is not a true Aloe.

Thick and succulent, the leaves are light green with purple-brown spots. Minute teeth line the leaf margins.

The scape is 1–2' tall, in some cases reaching 4'. It carries well-spaced green to purple-brown flowers 1" wide and 1–1¾" long. Red filaments extend the anthers well past the floral tube. Perennial.

Bloom Period: May to July.
*N.W. of Uvalde, Uvalde Co.*

## Blue-Eyed Grass
*Sisyrinchium ensigerum*

Several species of *Sisyrinchium* grow in the Hill Country area. They are difficult to separate, a task made harder by their tendency to hybridize freely between species. This plant, *S. ensigerum*, is an erect to decumbent plant 6–18″ tall that is found in open woods and open grassy areas.

A pair of narrow wings (approx. 1 mm. wide) run the length of each slender, glaucous stem.

The blue flowers are ½–¾″ wide, on pedicels projecting ¼″ beyond the spathe. Sparse, minute hairs cover the ovary. Perennial.

Bloom Period: March to April.
*River Hills Rd., Travis Co.*

## Celestials
*Nemastylis geminiflora*

Attractive and delicate, Celestials are found in grassy areas throughout the Hill Country. They grow 5–10″ tall, and are often found in colonies.

The linear, arching leaves are plicate, that is, folded. In cross section, they have a "w" shape, and are 4–16″ long by ⅛–⅜″ wide.

The flowers may be white or blue, with perianth segments up to 1¼″ long. No matter how blue the perianth segment, there is always a white spot at the base, giving the flower an "eyed" look. The flowers average 1–2¼″ in diameter.

Bloom Period: March to May.
*Medina River, Bandera Co.*

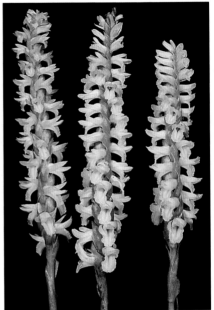

## Chatterbox Orchid, Giant Hellebore
*Epipactis gigantea*

Few people will be fortunate enough to see this rare plant. Giant Hellebore is an erect to decumbent colonial orchid 1–2′ tall. It is usually found in wet areas near streams, seeps, and springs.

Some stems may be as long as 3′, but at that point they become partially prostrate. The narrowly to broadly lanceolate leaves clasp the stem and grow to 6″ in length.

The flowers are ½–1″ across and are green and brown with brownish-red or rust-colored markings. The lower lip of the flower moves freely in the breeze or when touched, jiggling up and down like the jaw of a ventriloquist's dummy, hence the name Chatterbox Orchid. Perennial.

Bloom Period: April to July.
*Westcave Preserve, Travis Co.*

## Ladies' Tresses
*Spiranthes cernua*

Ladies' Tresses is a small, erect orchid 6–14″ high. It prefers a habitat that is wet at least part of the time, and is found on seepage slopes and stream banks. It is occasionally found in low spots in bar ditches along the roadside.

Most of the leaves (ovate to elliptic) are basal, though a few go up the stem, becoming lanceolate and bract-like. The lower part of the stem is glabrous, the upper part slightly pubescent.

Spirally arranged on a 2–4″ spike, the white flowers are ¼″ wide and ⅜″ long. These small beauties should be admired in place, as they are next to impossible to transplant. Perennial.

Bloom Period: September to December.
*Cedar Valley, Travis Co.*

## Texas Mulberry, Littleleaf Mulberry
*Morus microphylla*

Whitetail deer are fond of young Texas Mulberry leaves and stems, and will keep one in the open pruned back to a densely twiggy dwarf. With a little protection, *M. microphylla* becomes a shrub or small tree 4–15′ tall. It is found on bluffs or rocky slopes, often as an understory species.

Ovate in gross outline, the serrate leaves have a pointed tip, and may be simple or 3 to 5-lobed. When mature, they are 1–3″ long, with a surface texture like fine sandpaper.

The greenish-yellow flowers are in ovoid catkins ⅜–¾″ long. These soon become fruits ⅜–¾″ long, turning purple-black when ripe. Sweet and edible, the fruits are a bit less tart than dewberries and are sought after by wildlife.

Bloom Period: March to April.
*Vanderpool, Real Co.*

## Pilostyles
*Pilostyles Thurberi*

There is only one member of the Rafflesia family in Texas. This member, *Pilostyles Thurberi*, has a flower that is only 1/16–1/8″ in diameter. It is interesting to note that this family contains the largest flower in the world, *Rafflesia Arnoldii*, a native of Sumatra which grows as much as 3′ in diameter.

*Pilostyles Thurberi* is a parasitic plant whose vegetative body (filamentous and comparable to a fungal mycelium) is entirely concealed within the tissues of its host plant. Only its flowers are visible. Crowded along the lower stems of the host, the flowers have 4–7 purple-brown bracts and 4–5 perianth segments, with a yellowish central column which hides the stamens or stigma beneath it.

This parasite is uncommon and very specific, growing only on a few members of the Legume family. In the Hill Country area, it lives on *Dalea frutescens*; in West Texas, it lives on *D. frutescens* and *Dalea formosa*. The flowers illustrated bloomed from May 20 to June 12. Seemingly uneffected, the host plant (*D. frutescens*) bloomed normally in mid-September. Perennial.

Bloom Period: May to August.
*Headwaters of Barton Creek, Hays Co.*

## Pink Smartweed
*Persicaria bicornis*
*(Polygonum bicorne)*

Pink Smartweed is found on moist soils near streams or drainages. It is a low, bushy plant 1–3' tall with an erect or decumbent habit.

The older stems are red, while the newer ones are green, often with a scattering of glandular hairs (most dense just above the nodes). The lanceolate leaves are 1–3" long.

Erect to slightly drooping racemes (½–¾" long) of pinkish-white to pink flowers are terminal on the stems. The fruit is a round, black achene, pointed at one end, that is slightly ridged on one side and flattened on the other. It is about ⅛" long. Annual.

Bloom Period: July to October.
*Johnson City, Blanco Co.*

## Wild Buckwheat
*Eriogonum annuum*

One of our weedier-looking species, Wild Buckwheat is an erect plant 1½–6' tall (averaging 2–4'). It is most common on sandy soils in the northern half of our area and in the Llano region.

A woolly white pubescence covers the stems and leaves. The obovate leaves may grow to 2½" long and are densely covered with white hairs on the lower surface of the leaf, but less so on the top surface.

The flowers are in open cymes or umbels, the inflorescence reaching upward in a cup-like shape. Annual to biennial.

Bloom Period: July to October.
*Near Cherokee, San Saba Co.*

### Snake-Cotton
*Froelichia gracilis*

Snake-Cotton is a much-branched plant with ascending or decumbent branches 6–24″ long. It is found on sandy or alluvial soils.

Short white hairs (with a few longer hairs mixed in) densely cover the short-petioled opposite leaves. The linear-lanceolate leaves are 1–3″ long.

The flowers are in spikes ½–1″ long and about ¼″ thick. Long hairs tightly pressed to the perianth tube give the flowering spikes a shiny silvery-white look. As the flowers are fertilized and mature, the tightly pressed hairs loosen into a fibrous mass similar to cotton. Annual.

Bloom Period: April to October.
*Near Katemcy, Mason Co.*

## Four-O'Clock
*Mirabilis linearis*

Although capable of living on lime-stone soils as well as igneous soils, Four-O'Clock is most abundant locally in the dry sands of the Llano region. It is an erect plant 1–3′ tall.

Often very light-colored near the base, the stem is sometimes almost white. The upper stems are pale green. Linear to linear-lanceolate, the opposite leaves are 1–3″ long.

The purple-red to pink flowers are ½–⅝″ wide, and consist of 5 colored perianth lobes, each lobe deeply in-cised. Perennial.

Bloom Period: April to October.
*Miller Creek, Llano Co.*

## Scarlet Musk-Flower
*Nyctaginia capitata*

Adapted to dry sandy soils or caliche, Scarlet Musk-Flower is an attractive plant that would make a nice addition to a rock or cactus garden.

Several erect to decumbent branches 6–18″ long radiate from the taproot. The opposite, gray-green leaves are ovate to deltoid in outline and are 1½–5″ long on petioles 1–3″ long (petiole length increases down-stem).

The reddish-orange flowers are in clusters 1½–3″ across, each consisting of about a dozen blooms. Members of this family do not have true corollas (or petals). The reddish-orange 5-lobed perianth can be thought of as a fused, elongate, colored calyx. Perennial.

Bloom Period: March to November.
*Near Reichenau Gap, Kimble Co.*

## Angel Trumpets
*Acleisanthes longiflora*

Angel Trumpets opens its flowers as the sun goes down, blooming through the night and occasionally lasting until mid-morning. A low plant with prostrate stems, it is found on dry caliche soils on the southern edge of the Hill Country in Bexar, Medina, and Uvalde counties, and also up in Kimble and Menard counties.

Dusty gray-green in color, the opposite leaves are lanceolate to deltoid, with petioles ⅛–⅜" long and blades ½–1" long.

The pale reddish-brown to pale green perianth tube rises 3–7" above the ovary, finally expanding into a white perianth ½–¾" broad. Perennial.

Bloom Period: April to October.
*Montell, Uvalde Co.*

## Scarlet Spiderling
*Boerhaavia coccinea*

An ascending to trailing plant with stems 1–4' long, Scarlet Spiderling prefers disturbed or grassy areas on sandy or alluvial soils.

Small hairs are scattered along the stems, reaching their greatest concentration at the nodes and on the petioles. Oval to deltoid in outline, the opposite leaves are 1–3" long.

The inflorescence is a loose axillary or terminal cyme, with the ultimate flower cluster itself a miniature cyme. The perianth parts are purple-red. Perennial.

Bloom Period: May to October.
*Hwy. 71, Llano Co.*

## Pigeon-Berry
*Rivina humilis*

Pigeon-Berry normally grows in colonies on deep, moist soils in full to partial shade. In some stream valleys, it also grows on boulders of honeycomb limestone.

Its leaves are ovate to lanceolate, with an undulate (wavy) margin, and are 1–3" long. During the dry summer months, the leaves often wither and drop away, but return with the Fall rains.

Short racemes (1–2" long) rise from the axils or are terminal on the stems. Reddish-pink buds open into small flowers ⅛–³⁄₁₆" wide that are usually white with a pink blush. Each flower has 4 sepals and no petals. The fruit is an attractive bright red or orange berry. Perennial.

Bloom Period: May to October.
*Town Lake, Austin, Travis Co.*

## Talinum
*Talinum parviflorum*

This small succulent (3–7″ tall, flower stalk included) grows on shallow soils over granite in the Llano Uplift. It can be found where rainwater collects in stone pools or along minor drainage patterns.

Due to the erosional environment in which the plant lives, its fleshy reddish-brown root is often partly exposed. The linear leaves are round in cross-section and are ½–2″ long, rarely extending more than 3″ above the ground.

Loose cymes of white to pink flowers ⅛–¼″ wide rise above the leaves on peduncles 2–6″ long. Perennial.

Bloom Period: April to September.
*Near Fredonia, Mason Co.*

## Purslane
*Portulaca umbraticola*

Dry, sandy soils are home for this prostrate to partly ascending succulent. It forms clumps or mats 4–8″ high by the roadside or in other open grassy areas.

Its spatulate to rounded leaves are ½–1″ long and fleshy. In periods of drought, the leaves dry and fall off, conserving moisture in the stems.

Opening in the morning and withering away by late afternoon, the flowers cluster at the ends of the stems and may be yellow, orange, or red. This species is easily distinguished by its fruit, which is a capsule ringed by a narrow, translucent membrane ¹⁄₁₆–⅛″ wide. Annual.

Bloom Period: July to November.
*S.E. corner of Llano Co.*

## Flame-Flower
*Talinum auranticum*

Flame-Flower grows 6–12" high, with an erect to reclining habit. It is often semi-woody at the base, growing from a thickened, elliptic taproot 2–7" long. In our area, it lives on dry, poor soils derived from metamorphic or igneous rocks in Llano and Mason counties, and is often abundant there. A few scattered individuals live on limestone soils in Uvalde and Medina counties.

The alternate, fleshy leaves are linear to linear-lanceolate and ¾–1¾" long.

Orange to red-orange flowers ¾–1" wide rise from the axils of the leaves. They have 5 petals and numerous stamens (20 or more) surrounding the red, three-parted stigma. Short-lived, the flowers in the Llano region tend to open in mid-afternoon and close before sunset. Two sepals clasp the slightly elongate ¼" capsule. Perennial.

Bloom Period: May to September.
*S.W. of Katemcy, Mason Co.*

## Chickweed
*Stellaria media*

An introduced Eurasian species that thrives in moist environments, Chickweed is a weakly ascending to trailing plant with a tendency to form loose mats. It is well known to many homeowners as an invader of lawns.

The opposite leaves are ovate to elliptic and are ¾–1¼″ long. The lower leaves are petiolate while the upper leaves are sessile.

Deceptive in appearance, the white flowers are about ¼″ wide and have only 5 petals. There appear to be 10 petals, but this is because each single petal is so deeply cleft that it appears to be two. Each flower has five sepals which are slightly longer than the petals. The ovoid fruits are pendulous. Annual to perennial.

Bloom Period: January to May.
*Meridian Creek, Bosque Co.*

## Whitlow-Wort
*Paronychia virginica*

Whitlow-Wort is an erect to ascending plant 6–12″ high that grows from a woody base. It thrives under xeric conditions and is found on barren rocky soils or caliche.

Its linear, sessile, opposite leaves are ½–1″ long. They tend to be strongly ascendant and often parallel the stem. The leaves rise from well-defined internodes, and have silvery-translucent stipules at their base. Just below the inflorescence, the stem is green, while the lower part of the stem is reddish-brown.

The flowers are arranged in flat-topped cymes 2–4″ across. Each flower is actually composed of 5 yellow sepals (petals are absent). *Paronychia* occurs on the eastern edge of the Hill Country, on a line from Bell county to Bexar county. Perennial.

Bloom Period: July to November.
*Near Bee Cave, Travis Co.*

## Columbine
*Aquilegia canadensis*

Columbine lives in moist, shaded canyons, frequently growing on what appears to be the solid rock of cliff faces and boulders. Most of the year, it exists as a rounded, leafy clump 4–8" high. In the Spring, it sends up flower stalks 1–2' tall, sometimes to 3' in deep shade.

Its leaves are twice to three times ternately divided (divided into 3 parts 2 or 3 successive times). A somewhat glaucous green on the upper surface, the leaflets are pale green on the lower surface and are deeply cleft.

Five-spurred and nodding, the red and yellow flowers are 1–1½" long and about 1" wide. The petal blades are yellow and the petal spurs are red. Between the yellow petal blades, like the points of a star, are the red sepals. Five tightly grouped follicles, each about 1" long, follow the flowers. When the seeds inside are mature, a small open-ing appears in the end of each follicle.

Columbines seem to be distributed along an arc from Bell county to Real county, paralleling the southern and eastern edge of the Hill Country. Perennial.

Bloom Period: March to May.
*Near Hunt, Kerr Co.*

## Large Buttercup
*Ranunculus macranthus*

Take a little time and locate this plant one Spring. For brightness and purity of color, its flowers are hard to beat. It can be found on the moist soils of streams, seeps, and roadside ditches.

Large Buttercup may have erect or reclining stems; the erect stems average 1' tall while the reclining stems reach 3' in length, curling upward at the tip. The stems and petioles are densely covered with coarse hairs. For the most part, the leaves are dissected into 3 leaflets, but sometimes into 5 or 7. Commonly deeply cleft into three lobes, the leaflets are densely hairy on the underside and sparsely hairy on the upper surface.

The bright yellow flowers are 1–1¼" across, with 8–16 petals. They are followed by crowded heads of loose achenes.

A close relative from East Texas, *R. fascicularis*, is found in a couple of isolated outposts in Bandera and McLennan counties. It is easily distinguished since it usually has only 5 petals, though some individuals may have a few more. Perennial.

Bloom Period: March through April.
*Cypress Mill, Blanco Co.*

## Prairie Larkspur
*Delphinium carolinianum* ssp. *penardii*
(white)
*Delphinium carolinianum* ssp. *vimineum*
(blue)

Formerly, a Prairie Larkspur found in
the Hill Country might belong to one
of three different species. White-
flowered forms were *D. virescens*. Blue-
flowered forms were *D. carolinianum* or
*D. vimineum*, depending on whether
there were more or less than 20 flowers
on the raceme. Since species differ-
entiation by color phase and number of
blossoms is somewhat arbitrary, a more
useful approach has been adopted. The
three separate species have now been
combined into one species, *D. carolinianum*, with several variants that are
considered subspecies.

Prairie Larkspur is an erect plant
1–3' tall found in open woods, mead-
ows and fields. Its leaves are from
1¼–4" wide and are deeply palmately
divided.

The flowers, ½–1" wide and ½–1"
long, range in color from white to
bright blue, with a range of hues in between. Like Columbine, these flowers
are a combination of petals and colored
sepals. Four small petals lie in the center of the flower. The upper two are
usually glabrous, while the lower two
are coated with long hairs. The outer 5
flower parts, including the spur, are
sepals.

Though neither subspecies has an
exclusive range, it is possible to gener-
alize and say that ssp. *penardii* tends to
range through the upper two-thirds of
our area, while ssp. *vimineum* tends to
range in the lower one-third.

Bloom Period: April to June.

*Ssp. penardii (white), between Sabinal and
Concan, Uvalde Co.*

*Ssp. vimineum (blue), Twin Sisters, Blanco
Co.*

*Delphinium carolinianum* ssp. *vimineum*

*Delphinium carolinianum* ssp. *penardii*

## Wind-Flower
*Anemone heterophylla*

Early Spring brings a profusion of these variably colored flowers to open hillsides and grassy areas throughout the Hill Country.

Lying close to the ground (and usually obscured by neighboring grasses), the lower leaves are divided into three segments. They are often a dark reddish-purple on the underside.

Wind-Flowers are ¾–1½" wide and may be white, pink, lavender, light blue or deep blue. Colored, petal-like sepals make up the flowers; there are no petals. The flowers are carried on slender, solitary scapes 6–15" tall. Midway up the scape are three deeply cleft involucral bracts arranged in a ring. A distinctive trait of this species is that each scape carries only one flower, never any more.

The cylindric fruiting head is composed of numerous separate achenes and may reach 1½" in length. Perennial.

Bloom Period: February to April.

*Fredericksburg, Gillespie Co.*

## Old Man's Beard
*Clematis Drummondii*

Old Man's Beard is a climbing vine that grows over weeds, shrubs and fences. Its common name comes from the clusters of achenes, which have tails covered in long silky hairs, giving the plant a bearded appearance.

The opposite leaves are composed of 5–7 leaflets, each simple to 3-cleft, and ½–1" long. Peduncles with one to three flowers rise from the axils of the leaves.

Like the other *Clematis* species, the flowers have no petals. They are composed of yellow-green sepals and are ½–1" in diameter. The clusters of achenes become prominent around July and linger into Winter. Perennial.

Bloom Period: April to September.
*New Braunfels, Comal Co.*

## Two-Flower Anemone
*Anemone edwardsiana*

Two-Flower Anemone grows 6–12" tall in shade or in tall grass and is often found on the moist banks of shaded canyons. A casual observer might confuse it with *A. heterophylla*, but a close look will quickly separate the two.

The stems are essentially glabrous but become densely pubescent just below the flowers. Midway or higher up the scape are three involucral bracts. Side-scapes can grow from the axils of these bracts, with each side-scape having a potential of producing three flowers, for a theoretical total of 10 (only 1 flower on the central scape). In reality, a single plant normally carries only 2 or 3 flowers, which are ½–1¼" wide. The flowers are commonly white, but can exhibit the same range of colors as *A. heterophylla*. Perennial.

Bloom Period: February to April.
*River Hills Rd., Travis Co.*

### Scarlet Leatherflower
*Clematis texensis*

A Hill Country endemic, the beautiful Scarlet Leatherflower is found in
Bandera, Kerr, Kendall, Comal, Blanco,
Hays, and Travis counties. It is found
nowhere else. *C. texensis* is an uncommon climbing vine that grows over cliffs
and shrubs, usually near streams.

The long-petiolate leaves have 4–5
pairs of glaucous, rounded leaflets,
each of which may be entire or shallowly cleft. At the end of the compound
leaf is a curling, grasping tendril, which
enables the plant to climb.

Composed of 4 leathery red or pink
sepals that are slightly recurved at the
tips, the flowers are about 1″ long. They
are carried on peduncles 4–8″ long
rising from the axils of the leaves. The
tails of the achenes are covered with
fine hairs ⅛–³⁄₁₆″ long. Perennial.

Bloom Period: April to June.
*Bull Creek, Austin, Travis Co.*

## Purple Leatherflower
*Clematis Pitcheri*

Purple Leatherflower often escapes
the glance of the casual passerby because its dark flowers blend so well
with shadows. The flowers are carried
on axillary peduncles and are about
1″ long, with 4 leathery, dark purple
sepals which are slightly recurved at
the tips. The flowers nod at the end
of the long peduncles. Of the three
*Clematis* species described here, the
achene tails of *C. Pitcheri* are the least
pubescent, having only minute, velvety
hairs.

The bright green glabrous leaves
have 3–4 pairs of leaflets which are
often deeply incised into 2 or 3 lobes,
with blunt to sharply pointed tips.
A climbing vine, it can be found on
shrubs along watercourses or in seep
areas and is most common east of a
line drawn between Bosque and Real
counties. Perennial.

Bloom Period: May to July.
*Lake Georgetown, Williamson Co.*

## Texas Barberry
*Berberis Swaseyi*

An uncommon shrub, Texas Barberry grows 3–4' tall on dry, rocky soils or caliche. Though it commonly lives on dry, open flats, it also occurs as undergrowth around larger trees and along watercourses. Endemic to the Hill Country, it is found primarily in Travis, Hays, Comal, Kerr, Bandera, and Real counties.

The compound leaves have 5–9 leaflets, each of which is a little longer than broad and has 3–6 sharply pointed teeth on a side.

Short racemes of yellow flowers appear in early Spring, intermingling with the new leaves. The flowers are about ¼" wide and are composed of 6 petals and 6 colored sepals. They are followed by fruits that are yellow with a red blush, and are about ¼–⅜" wide.

*Berberis Swaseyi* hybridizes freely with *B. trifoliolata*, producing forms intermediate between the two. The leaves of *B. Swaseyi* turn deep red to purple in the Fall, but the leaves of *B. trifoliolata* do not change color. Where the parentage of a particular plant is in doubt, the degree of color change in the Fall may serve as a rough guide to the genetic purity of that plant.

Bloom Period: March to April.
*Henly, Hays Co.*

## Agarita
*Berberis trifoliolata*

Adapted to xeric conditions, Agarita can be found on dry, rocky flats and slopes throughout the Hill Country. Normally, it is a low, rounded shrub 3–4' tall, though some specimens can reach 7'.

Individual leaves are composed of three stout leaflets, each leaflet having 3–7 sharp points. The leaves are glabrous and glaucous, which some-times gives the plant a light blue-green tinge.

The small, fragrant, yellow flowers are an important early bee browse. Bright red fruits (about ¼" in diameter) follow the flowers. Tart and sweet, they are edible and make a fine jelly.

Bloom Period: February to April.
*Gatesville, Coryell Co.*

## Spicebush
*Lindera Benzoin*

Spicebush is a multi-trunked large shrub to small tree (reaching 15') that grows in rich soil or sandy gravel in shade along streams and near springs.

Obovate to elliptic, the simple leaves are 2–4″ long and are aromatic when crushed. They are green on the upper surface and pale green on the lower surface.

Tiny, yellow-green flowers appear before the leaves, in tight sessile clusters at the leaf nodes. The fruit is a red drupe (sometimes with yellow streaks) about ⅜″ long.

Bloom Period: February and March.
*Krause Springs, Burnet Co.*

## White Prickly Poppy
*Argemone albiflora*

## Mexican Poppy
*Argemone mexicana*

A common plant in South Texas, Mexican Poppy is sparsely distributed in our area in Uvalde and Real counties. It is found in disturbed soils and in fields, where it reaches 3' in height.

Cuts on the leaves or stems will reveal a bright yellow sap. The glaucous leaves have a blue-white blush and long prickles. In comparison to *A. albiflora*, the prickles on the stems are few in number.

The yellow flowers are 1–2½" across with numerous stamens surrounding a purple stigma. Annual.

Bloom Period: March to May.
*N.W. of Sabinal, Uvalde Co.*

Often held in low regard as a noxious weed, *A. albiflora* nevertheless has a delicate beauty to its flower. It is a well defended, erect plant 3–4' high, sometimes reaching 6'. Common throughout the state, White Prickly Poppy is found in waste places, fields, and open grassy areas.

On the stems, the prickles may be moderately to densely crowded. The glaucous leaves have fewer prickles, with most emerging from the margins or the primary and secondary veins.

The white flowers have numerous yellow stamens which are shorter than or equal to the purple stigma. Annual to biennial.

Bloom Period: March to May.
*Loyal Valley, Mason Co.*

## Scrambled Eggs
*Corydalis curvisiliqua*

Common, but rarely abundant, *C. curvisiliqua* is found throughout Texas. One of our earlier bloomers, this erect to ascending plant (8–10″ tall) grows along the roadside and in disturbed soils or open fields.

Its light green to glaucous leaves are deeply divided, the pinnae being twice pinnately divided themselves.

Born on the ends of the stems, the flowers exceed the surrounding foliage. The numerous yellow flowers are ½–¾″ long, and are replaced by curving-ascending capsules ¾–1¼″ long.

This species can be distinguished from other species by the concentric rings of minute bumps on the seed surface, visible under high magnification. Annual.

Bloom Period: February to April. *Harper, Gillespie Co.*

## Bracted Twist-Flower
*Streptanthus bracteatus*

Bracted Twist-Flower was once scattered throughout south-central Texas. It is now a rare plant, possibly due to the combined effect of picking and overgrazing. *S. bracteatus* has an erect stem 2–4' high and is found growing on rocky, wooded slopes.

Near the base of the plant, the leaves are long petiolate and lyrately lobed. Traveling up the stem, the petioles become shorter and the incised lobes become shallower, until the uppermost leaves are sagittate, clasping, and entire.

The vibrantly colored violet-purple flowers form an inflorescence 4–10" high. As the species name indicates, each flower has a small bract at the base of its pedicel. The fruit is a linear, striated silique up to 6" long. Annual.

Bloom Period: April to May.
*Near Medina Lake, Medina Co.*

## Rock-Cress
*Arabis petiolaris*

An erect, wand-like plant 1–3' tall, Rock-Cress can be found in open, rocky areas along roadsides and is especially abundant in Llano and Burnet counties.

Its stems are simple below and branched above. A few simple hairs are scattered on the lower stem, while the upper stems are mostly glabrous.

At the base of the plant, the leaves are long petiolate and lyrate. Farther up the stem, the leaves remain long petiolate but the leaf blades are no longer incised and they become narrowly triangular.

Rock-Cress has pale lavender flowers that are ¼" across. Its fruit is a straight, flattened, erect silique 2–3" long. Annual.

Bloom Period: April to May.
*S. of Marble Falls, Burnet Co.*

## Tansy-Mustard
*Descurainia pinnata*

Common in early Spring, Tansy-Mustard can be seen along roadsides in sandy or calcareous soils. It is 1–2½′ tall and usually branches in its upper half.

On the lower half of the plant, the leaves approach 4″ in length and are twice pinnate. Going up the stem, the leaves decrease in size and become once pinnate. Different plants from the same location may vary from sparsely to densely pubescent.

The small, yellow flowers are in an open, elongate inflorescence. As the flowers go to fruit, the infructescence elongates still more. The fruit is a gently curved silique ½–1″ long which ascends slightly from the end of a 1″ pedicel. Annual.

Bloom Period: February to May.
*Near Packsaddle Mt., Llano Co.*

## Water-Cress
*Rorippa Nasturtium-aquaticum*

Any permanent stream or spring may harbor this species which has been introduced from Europe. It can be found standing at waters edge or floating in the shallows, where it often forms extensive mats.

Dark green and glabrous, the leaves are pinnately divided, with ovate to oval leaflets. The leaflets are somewhat fleshy.

The white flowers are each about ¼″ in width and are carried in loose racemes. The fruit is an elongate silique ½–1″ long. Perennial.

Bloom Period: March to October.
*Hunt, Kerr Co.*

## Whitlow-Grass
*Draba cuneifolia*

An erect plant 3–10″ tall, *D. cuneifolia* can be found on sandy, granitic, or calcareous soils in the early Spring. It usually has only 1 stem, but can have several.

Sessile to short-petiolate, the leaves are mostly basal and rarely extend more than half-way up the stem. The leaves are obovate-cuneate (wedge-shaped) with a few coarse teeth on either margin contributing to the wedge-like appearance.

Densely clustered white flowers ⅛–¼″ in diameter make up the inflorescence. Annual.

Bloom Period: February to April.
*Meridian, Bosque Co.*

## Peppergrass
*Lepidium virginicum*

Peppergrass is distributed throughout Texas and can be found on sandy, calcareous, or disturbed soils. It is an erect plant with multiple branches, growing 6–24″ tall.

Near the base, the leaves are up to 5″ long and are often deeply pinnately incised. The segments or leaflets resulting are normally toothed. At the midstem, the leaves are oblanceolate and serrate, but usually not incised. Proceeding up the stem, the leaves become less divided and smaller, until they become linear and entire. The uppermost leaves may be only ½″ long.

The small, white flowers are 1/16–⅛″ in diameter and are carried in an inflorescence 2–4″ long. Rounded, flattened siliques (on pedicels ¼–½″ long) follow the flowers. Annual or biennial.

Bloom Period: March to May.
*Marble Falls, Burnet Co.*

## Silver Bladderpod
*Lesquerella argyraea*

Silver Bladderpod is easily identified by its sigmoid (doubly curved or S-shaped) pedicels. It is a small plant growing to 1' in height, with several spreading to reclining stems.

A fine pubescence gives the plant a gray-green to silvery-gray appearance. The long-petiolate basal leaves are up to 3" long and sometimes are deeply pinnately incised. On the stems, the leaves are usually ½–¾" long, with 1 or 2 shallow teeth on either margin.

The yellow flowers are ¼–¾" wide. Though it can be found on calcareous soils, *L. argyraea* is most common on the sandy soils of Burnet, Llano, and Gillespie counties. Biennial or perennial.

Bloom Period: March to May.
*Buchanan Dam, Llano Co.*

## Engelmann's Bladderpod
*Lesquerella Engelmannii*

Growing as a low clump of dusty-gray leaves with spreading, ascending flower stalks up to 18" tall, *L. Engelmannii* is easily distinguished by its compact flower and fruit clusters. These clusters are often so tight as to appear to be umbels.

Overall, the stems and leaves are covered with a fine, dense, stellate pubescence, giving the plant a gray-green appearance. The spatulate basal leaves are long petiolate, with an entire or dentate margin. They may be up to 2½" long. On the flower stalk, the leaves are few and are typically narrowly linear (¼–1" long). Perennial.

Bloom Period: March to May.
*E. of Lampasas, Lampasas Co.*

## Fendler's Bladderpod
*Lesquerella Fendleri*

Woody, branching stems give this attractive silvery plant the appearance of a small (10″) shrub. Most of its range is in West Texas. Locally, it can be found in dry, barren environments on caliche or limestone marl outcrops in Edwards, Real, Bandera, Uvalde, and Kendall counties.

Its leaves are covered with a fine, silvery-gray pubescence. In West Texas, the leaves are more rounded and elliptic, with margins that vary from entire to coarsely dentate. Here, at the eastern limit of its range, the leaves are much narrowed, taking a linear shape. The basal leaves are long petiolate and linear, while the linear stem leaves are short petiolate to sessile. The stem leaves are ½–1″ long.

Compact clusters of yellow, 4-petaled flowers ⅜–½″ wide are carried at the ends of the stems. The hollow fruits and their pedicels usually equal but do not exceed the stem leaves. Perennial.
Bloom Period: March to May.
*S.W. of Boerne, Kendall Co.*

## Low Bladderpod
*Lesquerella densiflora*

Colonies of *L. densiflora* create a low carpet of golden-yellow flowers along roadsides in the Spring. Though it may grow to 12″ in height, it normally averages 2–5″.

Low Bladderpod may have one or several erect to decumbent-spreading stems. A fine, dense pubescence of stellate hairs covers the leaves and stems. The basal leaves are long petiolate and deeply lobed, sometimes to the point of being pinnately divided. The light green stem leaves are short petiolate to sessile, and between ½–1″ long. The leaf margins may be entire to shallowly few-dentate (2 or 3 shallow points on either side of the blade).

The yellow flowers are densely crowded (hence the species name) at the ends of the stems, and are ¼–½″ in diameter. Directly below are the spherical fruits, on ½″ pedicels. Annual to biennial.

Bloom Period: March to May.
*Between Brady and Rochelle, McCulloch Co.*

## Cleomella
*Cleomella angustifolia*

In our area, Cleomella is a tall (2–5'), bushy, uncommon plant that can be found on sandy soils along watercourses in southern San Saba Co. Its stems are smooth and glaucous with a whitish blush, causing them to appear white from a distance.

Linear and trifoliolate, the leaves grow to 2½" long. They reduce in size going up the stem towards the flowers, finally becoming 1-foliolate and bractlike.

The yellow, 4-petaled flowers are in loose, terminal racemes. Roughly ¾" long, the flower pedicels grow to 1" long in fruit. Annual.

Bloom Period: August to October.
*S. of Cherokee, San Saba Co.*

## Clammy-Weed
*Polanisia dodecandra*

Appropriately named, Clammy-Weed is covered with glandular hairs which exude a sticky liquid. It is an upright slender or bushy plant 1–3' tall found in open areas along roadsides or in alluvium near streams.

Most of the leaves are trifoliolate, with oblanceolate leaflets. Reducing in size near the racemes, the leaves become unifoliolate and bractlike.

The white flowers have pink to purple stamens which usually much exceed the petals. The fruit is an erect capsule about 3" long, containing small, flattened, circular, reddish-brown seeds. Annual.

Bloom Period: May to July.
*Katemcy, Mason Co.*

## Yellow Stonecrop
*Sedum Nuttallianum*

Yellow Stonecrop can be found in very shallow soil on rock or in crevices between rocks. It is a low succulent (2–4″ high) with minimal water require-ments and can thrive where other plants are unable to live.

The pale green, linear, sessile leaves are roughly ¼″ long.

Arranged in small cymes, the sessile to short-pedicelled yellow flowers are individually only ¼″ in diameter. Each flower has 5 narrow petals.

Yellow Stonecrop occurs throughout the Hill Country area and does equally well on limestone or granitic soils. Where found, it tends to form mats several inches to several feet across. Annual.

Bloom Period: April to June.
*S. of Burnet, Burnet Co.*

## Canyon Mock-Orange
*Philadelphus Ernestii*

Found growing on boulders and bluffs in moist, shaded canyons, Canyon Mock-Orange is a relatively uncommon shrub. It is usually 1–4' tall, with open, diffuse branching in the larger specimens.

Strongly 3-nerved, the ovate to lanceolate leaves are about 1" long. A few well-spaced hairs are found on the upper leaf surface, while the lower leaf surface is much more densely covered in short straight hairs.

The solitary, white blossoms (about ¾" in diameter) have numerous stamens and a pleasant fragrance.

*Philadelphus Ernestii* is found in Travis, Hays, Blanco, and Kendall counties. Its close, almost identical relative, *Philadelphus texensis*, differs chiefly in having its lower leaf surfaces covered with a mix of short straight hairs and long tangled hairs. *P. texensis* is found on the southern edge of the Edwards Plateau, in Edwards, Real, Uvalde, and Bandera counties.

Bloom Period: April and May.
*Curry Creek, near Kendalia, Kendall Co.*

## Witch-Hazel
*Hamamelis virginiana*

Witch-Hazel is a plant ordinarily found in the bogs and mixed pine-hardwood forests of East Texas. It's surprising, then, to find it growing in limestone canyons on the southern edge of the Hill Country. *Hamamelis virginiana* is a rare inhabitant of a few moist, protected canyons in Kerr and Bandera counties.

Occurring in the shade of larger trees, *Hamamelis virginiana* is a large, open, multi-trunked shrub reaching 12'. The oval to obovate leaves are up to 3" long with an undulate margin and an oblique base.

The flowers have 4 yellow petals which are each ½" long, but only ¹⁄₁₆" wide, and tend to be curled and twisted. Seeds can be obtained in late September by collecting the green capsules before they mature (mature capsules are explosively dehiscent and will fling their 2 black seeds several yards).

Let the green capsules dry in a closed paper bag and in a couple of days they will begin going off with a pop and a rattle as the seeds bounce off the sides of the bag.

Bloom Period: October to November. *Lambs Creek, Kerr Co.*

## Blanco Crabapple
*Pyrus ioensis* var. *texana*

Used by early Texas settlers as a tasty preserve for the table, the Blanco Crabapple is little known to modern Texans. It is a small tree (growing to 12′) with a rounded crown and is well suited for landscaping.

Ovate, dentate, and shallowly lobed, the leaves are 1½–2½″ long. They are lightly covered with fine hairs on the upper surface and densely so on the lower surface. Many of the stems are modified into leaf-bearing thorns 2½″ long.

The pink flower buds open into white flowers ¾–1″ in diameter. In October, the small (1¼″ wide), yellow-green, flattened apples mature. They are extremely bitter if eaten raw.

Bloom Period: early to mid-April.
*Crabapple Creek, Blanco Co.*

## Hawthorn
*Crataegus* sp., series *Molles*

These small to medium trees are found in the Leon River bottomlands of Comanche Co., often in association with *Viburnum rufidulum*.

Coarsely dentate, the leaves are glabrous above, but densely covered with fine, white hairs on the lower surface. The very widely ovate leaves average 2–4" in length, with a pair of dentate, scimitar-shaped stipules at the base of the petiole. Thorns may be few or absent.

The white flowers are about ¾" in diameter.

Bloom Period: March to April.
*Near Gustine, Comanche Co.*

## Hawthorn
*Crataegus* sp., series *Virides*

Several very similar "species" of Hawthorn are native to the Hill Country and are here described collectively. They have been found in Comanche, Brown, San Saba, Hamilton, Mills, Travis, Blanco, Llano, Kerr, Gillespie, Edwards, Menard, Bandera, and Uvalde counties.

Hawthorns of this series occur in the wild as large shrubs to small trees 5–16' tall. Normally ¾–1½" long, the leaves are shiny, dark green, and evenly to doubly serrate. The thorns are long and slender, often approaching 3" in length.

In bloom, the trees are covered with corymbs of white flowers, each flower ½–¾" in diameter. Generally, these attractive plants are found in fertile valley bottoms and along intermittent streams.

Bloom Period: mid-April.
*Near Menard, Menard Co.*

## Dewberry
*Rubus trivialis*

The Dewberry is a common plant which graciously provides the raw material for pies and cobblers. It is also utilized by wildlife for both food and shelter.

Well-armed with numerous recurved prickles, the low-arching or trailing canes may be 1–6' long. In our area, the leaves are usually trifoliolate but occasionally are 5-foliolate. The leaflets are coarsely dentate and 1½–3" long.

Each cane carries numerous white flowers 1" in diameter. Black when ripe, the delicious fruits vary from ½ to 1 inch in length. *R. trivialis* is easily found along fencerows and roadsides. Perennial.

Bloom Period: March to April.
*Onion Creek, Blanco Co.*

## White Avens
*Geum canadense*

A small, herbaceous plant, White Avens rarely exceeds 2' in height, and is usually found in moist, shaded canyons. Though scattered in distribution, it is locally most abundant on the extreme eastern and southern edge of the Hill Country.

Leaf shape is variable. Near the base, the leaves are long petiolate, with 3–7 serrate leaflets. The upper leaves are short petiolate to sessile, with 3 leaflets. Directly below the flowers, the leaves are either 3-cleft or simple.

The white flowers are ½–¾" wide, and are followed by spherical fruiting heads crowded with numerous achenes. Perennial.

Bloom Period: April to June.
*Lake Austin, Travis Co.*

## Escarpment Black Cherry
*Prunus serotina* var. *eximia*

The Escarpment Black Cherry is one of the most accessible, easily grown, and desirable trees on the Edwards Plateau. In the Spring, its shiny green leaves and long racemes of flowers are very attractive. In early Summer, its fruits are beneficial to wildlife. Then, in the Fall, its leaves turn a beautiful golden yellow.

Dark green on the upper surface and pale green on the lower surface, the leaf blades are 3–5″ long. They are lanceolate and dentate, on slender petioles ½–1″ long.

Slender racemes of white flowers hang among the foliage in the Spring. The racemes are up to 6″ long and bear numerous flowers ¼–⅜″ in diameter. Round, purple-black fruits ¼–⅜″ in diameter soon follow the flowers. The fruits have only a thin flesh over a large stone and may be either sweet or bitter.

Younger stems and limbs have the silver and gray banded bark typical of all plum species. The older limbs and the trunk are covered in a dark, rough bark.

Bloom Period: March to April.
*Between Vanderpool and Medina, Bandera Co.*

## Texas Almond
*Prunus minutiflora*

Due to its low (1½–3' high), rounded habit, Texas Almond is often overlooked as just another bit of brush. On closer inspection, its silver and gray banded bark reveals it as a member of the plum family. The small leaves rarely exceed ¾", and are usually entire, though sometimes a few small teeth are apparent.

The tightly clustered flowers are small (³⁄₁₆–¼") and easily lose their petals in a light breeze. Their fragrance is sweet and heavy.

About ⅜" in diameter, the fruits have a very thin covering of flesh and a large stone. They remain green when they ripen in May and June.

Bloom Period: February and March.
*Marble Falls, Burnet Co.*

## Peach Bush, Texas Plum
*Prunus texana*

Texas Plum is at the northernmost limit of its range in the deep, sandy soils of Llano and Burnet counties. Only 3' tall when fully grown, it is subject to heavy browsing by deer and usually is 1–1½' tall with a flattened, bonsai-like appearance.

Ovate to elliptic, the leaves are only 1" long and have rounded teeth at the margin plus a rugose surface. *P. texana* has white flowers ¼–½" in diameter.

The yellow, plum-like fruits are ¾–1" long, with a coating of fine, velvety hairs. Sweet and juicy with a tangy flavor, they ripen in April.

Bloom Period: February.
*Inks Lake, Burnet Co.*

## Creek Plum
*Prunus rivularis*

A thicket forming species, Creek Plum can be found in colonies along fencerows, creeks, and the edge of woods. These colonies can be extensive, but the individual plants are rarely taller than 6'.

Emerging at about the same time the flowers bloom, the lanceolate leaves are smooth, shiny, and serrate. The white flowers are ⅜–½" in diameter and are grouped in clusters of 2–4 blossoms along the length of the stem.

For all its abundance of flowers, *P. rivularis* produces very little fruit. The translucent plums may be either yellow or red when they mature in mid to late summer.

Bloom Period: February to March.
*Ingram, Kerr Co.*

## Mexican Plum
*Prunus mexicana*

Mexican Plum is a solitary tree 7–15' tall which tends to have a rounded crown. It is usually found in ravines and creek bottoms, but is also occasional in fields and on hillsides.

Its leaves are ovate to slightly obovate and evenly to doubly serrate. About 4" long, they are dark green above and light green below with a rugose (bumpy or wrinkled-looking) surface texture.

Appearing well before or just as the leaves emerge, the white flowers are ½–¾" in diameter. Trees in full bloom have a strong, sweet fragrance detectable from many yards away. The fruit is a purple-red plum ¾–1" long with a whitish blush. Jellies and preserves can be made from the fruits, although they are usually bitter if eaten raw.

By late April, seeds from the previous year's crop will have germinated and can be found under the parent tree. These seedlings, usually only 2–4" high, are easily dug up and transplanted.

Bloom Period: February to April.
*Near Albert, Gillespie Co.*

## Catclaw Acacia
*Acacia Roemeriana*

Catclaw Acacia is an open shrub averaging 6' in height, with some specimens reaching 9'. It is usually found on the rocky ground of canyons, hillsides and prairies in the southern half of our area. A few are scattered in Brown and McCulloch counties.

Recurved, claw-like prickles protect the stems from browsing animals. Each leaf has 1–3 pairs of pinnae and each pinna has 4–7 pairs of leaflets ¼–⅜" long.

Numerous small flowers are compacted into fragrant, creamy-white globes ⅜" in diameter, on purple-red peduncles 1" long. The fruit is a flat pod 2–4" long and 1" broad. *A. Greggii* and *A. Wrightii* are similar to *A. Roemeriana*, but their flowers are in long spikes, not globes.

Bloom Period: April to May.
*Near Medina Lake, Medina Co.*

## Huisache
*Acacia Farnesiana*

Even at a distance, the fine, feathery foliage of Huisache is hard to mistake. In the Hill Country, it is a shrub or small, rounded tree (up to 15' tall) with multiple trunks.

The twice pinnately compound leaves are 1–3" long, with 2–6 pairs of pinnae. Each pinna has 10–18 pairs of leaflets ⅛–¼" long. Pairs of short (⅛") stipular spines are found at the leaf nodes.

The flowers are bright yellow globes ¼–⅜" in diameter, and have a strong, pleasant fragrance.

Bloom Period: March and April.
*Austin, Travis Co.*

## Golden-Ball Lead-Tree
*Leucana retusa*

Very much at home in the dry Trans-Pecos region, *Leucana retusa* ranges east on the Edwards Plateau to Kimble, Edwards, Real, and Uvalde counties. A few scattered individuals are found as far east as Blanco Co. It is an open shrub or spindly tree, 6–15' tall, found on rocky slopes in caliche or marl.

The leaves are 4–6" long, with 2–4 pairs of pinnae, each pinna having 3–6 pairs of leaflets. The obovate to elliptic leaflets are about ½–¾" long.

Each bright yellow, globe-like flower cluster (¾–1" in diameter) is composed of numerous small individual flowers. Careful pruning would probably help correct the spindly shape of this plant and maximize its considerable ornamental qualities.

Bloom Period: April and May.
*Garner State Park, Uvalde Co.*

## Pink Mimosa
*Mimosa borealis*

Pink Mimosa is an erect, tortured-looking shrub 3–6′ tall found on brushy flats and hillsides.

Straight or recurved prickles protect the striate stems. The leaves are ¾–1¼″ long, with 2 or 3 pairs of pinnae. Each pinna has 3 to 6 pairs of leaflets (each leaflet is about ⅛″ long).

The flowers are white to pink globes roughly ½″ in diameter. *M. biuncifera* is very similar but usually has 4–8 pairs of pinnae with 5–12 pairs of leaflets per pinna. *Mimosa borealis* is found throughout our area, but is most common south of a line drawn between Menard and Austin.

Bloom Period: March to May.
*Volkmann Draw, Menard, Menard Co.*

## Illinois Bundleflower
*Desmanthus illinoensis*

A small semi-woody plant 1–3′ tall, Illinois Bundleflower is found on clay or caliche soils in open areas, often near water.

Almost fern-like in appearance, the leaves are 1½–3½″ long, with 6 to 14 pairs of pinnae, each pinna having 20 to 30 pairs of leaflets. Each leaflet is about ¹⁄₃₂″ long.

The flowers are creamy-white globes about ⅜″ wide. Dense heads of flat pods ¾–1¼″ long follow the flowers. Green at first, the pods turn brown or black with age. In addition to its normal bloom period, *D. illinoensis* flowers opportunistically in Summer and Fall following sufficient rainfall. It is considered a nutritious browse for livestock. Perennial.

Bloom Period: May to June.
*Blanket, Brown Co.*

## Yellow-Puff
*Neptunia lutea*

Low and prostrate, the stems of Yellow-Puff are 1–5′ long, radiating outwards from a woody taproot. This plant can be found on dry sand or on calcareous clays.

Like *Schrankia*, the leaves of *Neptunia* are sensitive and will fold up after being touched. The leaves are 1–3″ long with 3 to 5 pairs of pinnae, each pinna having 10–16 pairs of leaflets. Each leaflet is roughly ⅛″ long.

The flower clusters are slightly elliptic yellow globes ¾″ long on peduncles up to 3½″ long. Perennial.

Bloom Period: May to June.
*Near Cranfills Gap, Bosque Co.*

## Sensitive Briar
*Schrankia* sp.

Children are easily fascinated by this pretty little plant. They enjoy touching the leaves and seeing them immediately fold up.

Sensitive Briar has sprawling, prostrate stems 1–6′ long which are armed with recurved prickles. It can be found on granite or limestone soils throughout our area.

The leaves have 2–5 pairs of pinnae, each pinna with 6–13 pairs of leaflets.

The flower clusters are round or slightly elongate pink globes on peduncles ¾–2½″ long. The slender pod is 1¼–3″ long and is covered with stout prickles. Perennial.

Bloom Period: April to July.
*Pedernales R., Travis Co.*

## Anacacho Orchid Tree
*Bauhinia congesta*
*(Bauhinia lunarioides)*

Although this plant does not grow wild within the area this book covers, it does grow on the Edwards Plateau a county or two over to the west. It is becoming more readily available through the nursery trade and is mentioned here simply to acquaint a wider audience with its existence.

An interesting and attractive rare plant, Anacacho Orchid Tree is a shrub or small tree 6–12′ tall inhabiting a few limestone canyons in the Anacacho Mountains of Kinney Co. It has also been found in Val Verde Co.

The alternate leaves have short petioles ¼–½″ long. Each leaf consists of two symmetrical leaflets ½–1″ long.

The 5-petaled white flowers are ½–¾″ wide and occur in clusters. Each flower has 9 or 10 stamens, only one of which is functional.

Bloom Period: April and May.
*Cultivated specimen, University of Texas campus, Austin, Travis Co.*

## Texas Redbud
*Cercis canadensis* var. *texensis*

Texas Redbud is a xeric variety of the Eastern Redbud. Locally, it is more appropriate for ornamental plantings because it is better able to withstand the scorching Texas sun and requires less water.

The alternate, simple leaves are cordate to reniform, and are up to 5″ wide. The leaves of var. *texensis* are dark green and waxy-shiny in contrast to the lighter green matte-finish leaves of the common horticultural variety, var. *canadensis*.

Clusters of reddish-pink flowers precede or emerge with the leaves. Individual flowers are ¼–⅜″ wide on pedicels ¼–½″ long. Each flower has 5 petals and 10 stamens.

Bloom Period: March to April.
*Twin Sisters, Blanco Co.*

## Two-Leaved Senna
*Cassia Roemeriana*
*(Senna Roemeriana)*

Dry, open flats and hillsides are the home of Two-Leaved Senna. It may have 1 or several erect stems averaging 1–2′ high.

The leaves grow to 3″ long with petioles up to 1″ long. Each leaf has a pair of leaflets 1–2″ long and ¼″ wide. Peduncles 1–2″ long rise from the axils, each with 2–5 yellow flowers ¾–1″ across.

Two-Leaved Senna has a dwarf cousin, *C. pumilio*, that is only 3–4″ tall. It has linear paired leaflets 1¼″ long, with the flowers standing above the foliage on 1½″ peduncles, and is found in Edwards, Real, Brown, and Mills counties. Perennial.

Bloom Period: April to October.
*Near Doss, Gillespie Co.*

## Partridge Pea
*Cassia fasciculata*
*(Chamaecrista fasciculata)*

Found mainly in the northern half of our area, Partridge Pea is an erect plant with one to several stems. It varies in height from 1–3' and shows a preference for sandy or alluvial soils.

The leaves are up to 1½" long, with 5–10 pairs of leaflets, each ¼–⅝" long.

The yellow flowers have 5 obovate petals, each with a small red spot at its base. One petal is incurved. Annual.

Bloom Period: May to October.
*Lake Waco, McLennan Co.*

## Lindheimer's Senna
*Cassia Lindheimeri*
*(Senna Lindheimeri)*

This Fall-blooming plant has 1 to several ascending/erect stems rising from a woody root. It grows 1½–3' tall and is found on open rocky ground.

Both the stems and the leaves are covered with soft, velvety hairs. The leaves are 3–6" long, usually with 5–6 pairs of oblong leaflets which are asymmetric at the base.

Lindheimer's Senna has yellow-orange flowers that are carried on racemes 3–6" long. Each flower is about 1" wide, with red veins permeating the 5 elliptic to obovate petals. Perennial.

Bloom Period: September to November.
*Near Packsaddle Mt., Llano Co.*

## Eve's Necklace
*Sophora affinis*

In competition with larger trees, *S. affinis* becomes very spindly and unattractive as it struggles to reach the light. Alone in the open (as along fencerows), it develops a very pleasing shape and may be a shrub or small tree 6–18' tall with an evenly rounded crown. Unlike *S. secundiflora*, it is deciduous. It can be found in sandy or calcareous soils throughout our area.

The leaves are up to 8" long with 13–17 leaflets, which are elliptic to obovate.

Delicately colored, the flowers are light pink with pale yellow-green centers, in racemes 3–5" long. The fruit is a black pod (1–6" long) which is strongly constricted between the seeds, giving the appearance of a bead necklace.

Bloom Period: March to May.
*N. of Goldthwaite, Mills Co.*

## Retama, Paloverde
*Parkinsonia aculeata*

Retama is a small, open tree or shrub with green bark. It is more of a South Texas plant, in its northern limit ranging up to Williamson Co. along the eastern edge of the Hill Country.

The leaves are alternate and pinnately twice-compound, and are protected by three sharp spines at the base. Each leaf has 1 or 2 pairs of pinnae, each pinna with a slender, green, flattened rachis 10–16" long. Along each pinna are 20–30 pairs of small leaflets ⅛–³⁄₁₆" long.

The yellow, 5-petaled flowers are ⅜" in diameter and occur in short racemes. As the petals wither, they turn orange.

Bloom Period: April to September.
*Pease Park, Austin, Travis Co.*

## Texas Mountain Laurel
*Sophora secundiflora*

Glossy, evergreen foliage and showy racemes of fragrant flowers make Texas Mountain Laurel a very desirable ornamental for the landscape. It is a xeric species with low watering requirements, well adapted to the extremes of Texas weather.

*S. secundiflora* is a shrub to small tree (3–12' tall) that can be found on dry rocky slopes or open plains.

The pinnately compound leaves are up to 7" long with 5 to 11 leaflets. Elliptic to obovate in outline, the leaflets may have a rounded or notched tip and are somewhat tough and leathery.

Thick racemes (2–6" long) of purple-blue flowers appear in early Spring. The individual flowers are ½–¾" long. The fruit is a tough semi-woody pod 1–4" long, slightly constricted between the bright red seeds.

Bloom Period: February to April.

*E. of Leakey, Real Co.*

## Texas Bluebonnet
*Lupinus texensis*

No other plant enjoys such strong identification with the state of Texas. Our state flower, Texas Bluebonnet is an annual herb 8–16" tall. Most of its stems are upright, though the outer ones are sometimes partially decumbent. It can be found along roadsides and in fields throughout the Hill Country area.

*Lupinus texensis* has palmately compound leaves with 5 oblanceolate leaflets, each up to 1¼" long. The mature leaves have petioles twice as long as the leaflets, if not longer. A soft pubescence covers the entire plant.

The flowers are blue and white in racemes 1½–4" long. Each flower has a white center that turns reddish-purple with age.

Bluebonnets are winter annuals. In order to grow them, rake the seeds into the ground in the last week of August or the first week of September. The first Fall rains will germinate the seeds (usually by mid to late September), which will then form low rosettes of leaves about the size of a silver dollar and build a strong root system over the winter months. In early Spring, rain and warming soil will stimulate leaf and stem production, culminating in some of the finest floral displays in the country. Annual.

Bloom Period: March to May.
*Cypress Mill, Blanco Co.*

## White Sweet Clover
*Melilotus albus*

White Sweet Clover can be found along roadsides and in fields throughout our area. It grows 1–4' tall, with several upright, glabrous stems and an open appearance.

Its leaves are trifoliolate, with serrate, oblanceolate leaflets ½–1" long.

Axillary racemes up to 6" long bear the numerous small white flowers, which are only ¹⁄₁₆" wide. Annual or biennial.

Bloom Period: May to September.
*E. of Harper, Gillespie Co.*

## Sour Clover
*Melilotus indicus*

Sour Clover is an erect plant 6–24" tall, with several stems. It is distributed throughout our area.

The leaves are trifoliolate. Each serrate leaflet is roughly ½–¾" long. The yellow flowers are ¹⁄₁₆" wide or less, on axillary peduncles ½–2" long.

Sour Clover has a nearly identical cousin, *M. officinalis*, from which it differs by having smaller flowers and a rounded seed pod (versus the oblong pod of *M. officinalis*). Otherwise, these plants are very much alike. *M. officinalis* seems to be found mainly in the far northern part of our area, in Hamilton, Bosque, and McLennan counties. Annual.

Bloom Period: April to June.
*Buchanan Dam, Llano Co.*

## Scarlet Pea
*Indigofera miniata*

## White Clover
*Trifolium repens*

Most often seen in this area as a mat-forming lawn weed, White Clover is a low plant averaging 3–4″ tall, though it can reach 6–8″ in height.

Its creeping stems root at the nodes, gradually increasing the size of the mat as it invades the grass. The leaves are trifoliolate with elliptic or obovate leaflets ½–1″ long.

The white flowers, sometimes suffused with pink, stand above the leaves and stems in slightly racemose globose heads. Perennial.

Bloom Period: March to September. *Austin, Travis Co.*

Scarlet Pea grows to 8″ in height, with several decumbent, herbaceous stems radiating from a woody taproot. It is found in open areas of roadsides and fields.

The pinnately compound leaves are 1½″ long with 5–9 leaflets. The leaflets are ¼–½″ long.

The pinkish-red flowers are on axillary racemes 2–4″ long. Var. *texana*, found in the Llano region, is a more stiffly upright and xeric version that is less herbaceous and more woody. Its racemes are more numerous but the flowers are smaller. Perennial.

Bloom Period: April to October. *Bulverde, Comal Co.*

## Wand Psoralea
*Psoralea cyphocalyx*

One of the more graceful members of the *Psoralea* genus, Wand Psoralea is 1–3' tall with erect, slender, wand-like stems. It can be found on open rocky ground or in shade.

Its leaves are palmately 3–5 foliolate, each leaflet narrowly lanceolate or linear (for example, 3" long by ⅜" wide). Small glands dot the surface of the leaflets. A pair of narrow, threadlike stipules (¼" long) flank the base of the petiole.

The pale purple-blue flowers are in short, dense racemes. *P. cyphocalyx* is found on the south-eastern edge of the Edwards Plateau, and in Hamilton, Coryell, and Lampasas counties to the north. Perennial.

Bloom Period: May
*Red Bluff Creek, Bandera Co.*

## Scurf-Pea
*Psoralea latestipulata*

Scurf-Pea grows 6–14" tall, with an herbaceous few-branched habit, and is found on dry rocky slopes. It is almost always erect, rarely lying stem to the ground as is the habit with *P. cuspidata*.

The leaves are palmately 5–7 foliolate, with narrowly elliptic or obovate leaflets. The stipules are ovate to broadly lanceolate, mostly 2 or 3 times as long as wide.

The purple-blue flowers are in globose to ellipsoid racemes, and are similar to those of *P. cuspidata*. Perennial.

Bloom Period: March to April.
*Bee Cave Rd., Travis Co.*

## Indian-Turnip
*Psoralea cuspidata*

*Psoralea cuspidata* is an erect to decumbent plant 1–1½' tall, found on roadsides and in fields.

The decumbent semi-woody stems are up to 2½' long, trailing on the ground and rising at the tips. The leaves are 3–5 foliolate, with obovate leaflets. The uppermost stipules are linear to linear-lanceolate and very narrow (for example, ⅜" long by ⅟₃₂" wide).

The flowers are purple-blue, in racemes up to 3" long. The bracts and calyx are conspicuously gland-dotted. Perennial.

Bloom Period: April to May.
*Lake Eanes, Comanche Co.*

## Brown-Flowered Psoralea
*Psoralea rhombifolia*

This low plant likes to hide in the grass, camouflaging its true identity. It grows to 6" high, with several trailing stems from a woody rootstock.

The leaves are pinnately trifoliolate, with ovoid to rhomboid leaflets averaging ⅜–¾" long. The stipules are short (⅛") and linear to lanceolate.

Of the *Psoralea* species mentioned here, this is the easiest to identify due to its red-brown to brick-red flowers. The flowers are few on short spikes (¼–⅝"). Individual flowers are ¼" long. Perennial.

Bloom Period: May to June.
*Blanco State Park, Blanco Co.*

## False Indigo
*Amorpha fruticosa*

When in bloom, False Indigo is a real eye-catcher. The long spikes of deep purple flowers, set off by golden-yellow anthers, wave gently on slender stems in a streamside habitat. It is an open shrub (4–8′ tall) with several small trunks, and is best enjoyed in its natural environment.

The once pinnately compound leaves are 2½–8″ long with 9–30 oblong-elliptic leaflets. Each leaflet is about 1″ long. The flowers of the 4–6″ spikes are followed by numerous small pods ¼″ long, which are slightly curved and dotted with raised glands.

Bloom Period: mid-April.
*Barton Creek, Austin, Travis Co.*

## Kidney Wood, Bee-Brush
*Eysenhardtia texana*

Kidney Wood is a broad, open, multi-trunked shrub 4–10′ tall, found on dry, rocky soils.

Its leaves are 1½–3½″ long, with numerous leaflets (13–47) only ¼″ long. Small, linear stipules grow at the base of each leaf.

The fragrant white flowers are in axillary or terminal spikelike racemes about 1¼″ long. Individual flowers are small, about ¼″ long. Kidney Wood blooms through the summer, providing a good sustaining bee forage.

Bloom Period: May to September.
*Twin Sisters, Blanco Co.*

## Black Dalea
*Dalea frutescens*

Found in dry, rocky situations in fields and along roadsides, Black Dalea is an open, rounded shrub 1–3' tall. In full bloom, it is a mass of purple and white flowers lasting 1–1½ weeks. The individual flowers are ⅜–½" long, in compressed terminal spikes.

*D. frutescens* has pinnately compound leaves ¼–1" long, with 9–17 leaflets, each leaflet about ⅛" long. Minute glands dot the undersides of the apically rounded to retuse (shallowly notched) leaflets. The light gray to straw-colored stems are striate.

Bloom Period: July to October.
*S.W. of Brady, McCulloch Co.*

## Purple Dalea
*Dalea lasiathera*

Healthy specimens of *D. lasiathera* form low rosettes (1½–3' wide) of decumbent stems which curl upwards at the tips. A few short flowering stems may rise erect from the center, but the majority of the 1–3" spikes are on the perimeter of the rosette. This plant is usually only 4–10" high and can be found on flat, open ground along roadsides and in fields.

The stems and leaves are essentially glabrous. The leaves are about 1" long with 7–13 oblanceolate, gland-dotted leaflets.

The bright orange to yellow anthers contrast nicely with the dark purple flowers. Individual flowers are ¼–⅜" long. Perennial.

Bloom Period: April to June.
*Near Hackberry Creek, Uvalde Co.*

## Golden Dalea
*Dalea aurea*

Golden Dalea grows 1–2½' high, with 1 to several erect stems rising from a woody taproot. It is found on barren, dry ground, usually in caliche or marl.

A fine silvery pubescence covers the stems and leaves. The leaves are ½–1¼" long, and are pinnately 5–7 foliolate. Each leaflet is roughly ³⁄₁₆–¼" long. A minute pair of subulate (pointed) stipules lie at the base of each leaf.

The bright yellow flowers are on rounded, compact terminal spikes. Individual flowers are ⅜–½" long. Another common name, Pussy-Foot Dalea, refers to the effect given by the crowded, densely silky bracts. Perennial.

Bloom Period: June and July.
*Indian Gap, Hamilton Co.*

## Hall's Dalea
*Dalea Hallii*

This North Texas plant ranges down into the Hill Country, where it is an uncommon member of the flora of Brown, Mills, and Hays counties. *D. Hallii* grows 6″ high, with several erect and decumbent stems rising from a woody taproot. Ascending at the tips, the decumbent stems may reach 1′ in length. It is found on dry, barren ground, often on caliche or clay banks. 1–1½″ long. Individual leaflets are up to ¾″ long.

The flowers are in loose, terminal spikes. They are yellow (fading with age to an orange tint) and are ⅜–½″ long. The distinctive red-lined, red-tipped calyx is covered in long silky hairs. Perennial.

Bloom Period: May to September.
*Near Blanket, Brown Co.*

## Dwarf Dalea
*Dalea nana*

Small and inconspicuous, Dwarf Dalea is a low plant 2–8″ tall (commonly 2–4″), with numerous decumbent stems branching from the base.

Short, silky hairs cover both the leaves and the stems. The leaves are ½–1″ long, with 5–9 leaflets, each leaflet ¼–⅜″ long.

The yellow flowers are in dense terminal spikes (½–1″ long) which become looser with maturity. The ovate bracts have a single short point at the tip and are densely covered with a silky pubescence. Perennial.

Bloom Period: April to July.
*Enchanted Rock, Llano Co.*

## White Prairie Clover
*Petalostemum multiflorum*
*(Dalea multiflora)*

White Prairie Clover grows 1–3' tall with several erect stems rising from a woody base. It is found on rocky, dry soils.

The striate (grooved) stems carry leaves ½–1" long which consist of 3–9 leaflets. Linear to linear-oblong, the leaflets are ¼–½" long, with gland-dotted undersides.

The white flowers are in nearly globose spikes ⅜–½" across, each flower ³⁄₁₆–¼" long. Perennial.

Bloom Period: June and July.

*S. of Johnson City, Blanco Co.*

## Purple Prairie Clover
*Petalostemum pulcherrimum*
*(Dalea compacta)*

A number of similar species come under the common name Purple Prairie Clover, and are differentiated by calyx pubescence, thickness of the flower spike, and leaflet number. This species, *P. pulcherrimum*, has several stems 1–2' tall and is found in open grassy areas.

The leaves are ¾–2" long with 3–7 leaflets, each leaflet linear and ⅜–⅝" long.

The light purple to rose-purple flowers are in dense terminal spikes ¾–1½" long by ½" wide. Perennial.

Bloom Period: May to July.

*Wimberly, Hays Co.*

## Hoary Pea
*Tephrosia Lindheimeri*

Hoary Pea is a ground-hugging plant with prostrate stems up to 3' long, which ascend at the tips to about 10" in height. Locally, it is found on the sandy soils of the Llano Uplift region and of Bexar and Medina counties.

The pinnately compound leaves are 6–8" long with 7–15 leaflets, which may be obovate to oval. The apex of the densely pubescent leaflets may be broadly rounded with a short point or retuse (notched). A conspicuous white line traces the margin of each leaflet.

*Tephrosia Lindheimeri* has vibrantly purple-red flowers in loose racemes 3–10" long. The individual flowers are about ½" long. Perennial.

Bloom Period: April to June.

*N. of Mason, Mason Co.*

## Low Milk-Vetch
*Astragulus lotiflorus*

Low Milk-Vetch is found throughout the central plains of the United States, ranging north into Canada and southwest into Mexico. It also occurs in the northern third of our area, with a few locations as far south as Travis Co.

*A. lotiflorus* is a low silvery-pubescent plant 6–10″ high that grows on barren caliche soils. It develops a short (½–1″) semi-woody stem from which the leaves and flowers rise. The pinnately compound leaves are up to 5″ long, with 7–15 elliptic leaflets.

Erect peduncles carry the lavender flowers in short racemes ½–¾″ long. Individual flowers are ¼–½″ long. In fruit, the peduncles bend from the weight of the pods until they touch the ground. The pods are ¾–1″ long and are almost equilaterally triangular in cross section. Perennial.

Bloom Period: March and April.
*N.E. of Cranfills Gap, Bosque Co.*

## Nuttall's Milk-Vetch
*Astragulus Nuttallianus*

Milk-Vetch is a highly variable plant with 6 recognized varieties, 5 of which can be found in our area. On average, it is 6–12″ tall, with a sprawling-erect to decumbent habit. It is often found in colonies on roadsides and in grassy areas.

Pinnately compound, the leaves are 1½–3″ long, with 7–19 leaflets. The linear-elliptic leaflets may have a rounded or notched tip. Stem pubescence ranges from nearly glabrous to densely pubescent.

The flowers may be white, pink, lavender, or light blue and are ¼–½″ long. The slender, gently curved pod is about 1″ long. Annual.

Bloom Period: February to May.
*Near Honey Creek, Llano Co.*

## Lindheimer's Astragulus
*Astragulus Lindheimeri*

Lindheimer's Astragulus is similar to *A. Nuttallianus*, but it is slightly larger and coarser. It is an upright to sprawling plant 6–12″ high that grows in colonies on open flats and hillsides in San Saba, Mills, Brown, and Comanche counties.

The leaves are 1–3″ long, with 13–21 leaflets. The oblong, cuneate (wedge-shape) leaflets are ³⁄₁₆–³⁄₈″ long and are usually notched at the tip.

The deep amethystine purple and white petals of the flowers make a very showy display. Individual flowers are ½–⅝″ long. The fruit is a thick, curved pod 1–1½″ long and about ¼″ broad. Annual.

Bloom Period: March to May.
*Near Bend, San Saba Co.*

## Milkpea
*Galactia heterophylla*

## Ground Plum
*Astragulus crassicarpus*

Ground Plum takes its name from its fruit, an inflated globose or ellipsoid pod (¾–1½" long) with a depressed line down its center giving it the appearance of a somewhat flattened and elongate plum. These large pods lie directly on the ground and turn brownish-red when mature. *A. crassicarpus* is found on dry caliche soils, mostly in the southern part of our area.

A low plant, Ground Plum has prostrate, trailing stems with leaves up to 5" long, each having 13–25 elliptic leaflets.

Flower color varies from white to lilac-purple. Perennial.

Bloom Period: March and April.
*Twin Sisters, Blanco Co.*

This South Texas plant is occasionally found on the sandy soils of the Llano Uplift. It has numerous prostrate stems 6–24" long.

Palmately compound, the leaves are 1–2" long and have 5 leaflets, each about ½–¾" long. The leaflet arrangement is very distinctive, with 4 leaflets attached to the rachis at the same point, and the fifth and terminal leaflet on a rachis stalk ⅛–¼" long.

Short peduncles rise from the axils of the leaves, carrying loose, few-flowered racemes of lavender to pink flowers. The individual flowers are about ⅜" long. Perennial.

Bloom Period: April to September.
*Near Art, Mason Co.*

## Viperina
*Zornia bracteata*

Viperina is one of our little known, rarely seen flowers that will probably always remain obscure since it does not form massive, showy displays. It has only a few sprawling to semi-erect stems 3–6″ high growing from a woody taproot. In the Hill Country area, it is mainly found on dry, sandy soils of the Llano Uplift region.

Dark green and glossy, the leaves are composed of 4 leaflets, which are linear-lanceolate to broadly lanceolate. The individual leaflets are ¼–¾″ long.

The bright yellow-orange pea-like flowers are lined with red markings and are about ⅜″ long. Viperina's fruit is a flat, spiny legume which appears jointed due to the sharp constrictions between the seeds. Perennial.

Bloom Period: April to June.
*Near Babyhead Mountain, Llano Co.*

## Deer Pea Vetch
*Vicia ludoviciana*

Deer Pea Vetch is valuable both as a nutritious browse for wildlife and as a soil builder through nitrogen fixation. It has decumbent or climbing stems 6–36″ long, and is found in both sandy and calcareous soils throughout our area.

The pinnately compound leaves grow to 3″ long, with 6–12 leaflets. Leaflet shape may vary from linear-oblong to linear-elliptic, with either a rounded or notched apex. The leaf rachis ends in a forking tendril.

Short peduncles carry the open racemes of small (³⁄₁₆–¼″) lavender-blue flowers. The fruit is a flat pod, ¾–1″ long and ³⁄₁₆–¼″ wide. Annual.

Bloom Period: March to May.
*Inks Lake State Park, Burnet Co.*

## Tall Bush-Clover
*Lespedeza Stuevei*

Tall Bush Clover is a slender, erect plant 1–3′ tall, with a few stems growing from a woody base. It is found in the Llano Uplift region on sandy soils or granite.

The stems are densely leafy, with dark, threadlike, pointed stipules ³⁄₁₆″ long at the base of the trifoliolate leaves. The elliptic leaflets are ½–1″ long.

Arranged in short axillary racemes intermingled with the foliage, the small purple flowers (³⁄₁₆–¼″ long) usually extend only slightly beyond the leaves. Perennial.

Bloom Period: May to September.
*Enchanted Rock State Park, Llano Co.*

## Ratany
*Krameria lanceolata*

The family Krameriaceae contains only a single genus, *Krameria*, with 15–25 species in North and South America. Texas has 4 of these species, only one of which grows in our area.

Ratany has sprawling, prostrate stems 1–5' long growing from a woody base. Its silky-pubescent leaves are ⅜–¾" long and are linear or sometimes oblong.

The flowers have 5 large red to reddish-purple sepals which surround the 5 true petals. The upper three petals are ¹⁄₁₆–⅛" long and are united at their base. The lower 2 petals have been highly modified and look like red-rimmed green glands flanking either side of the flower's center. Perennial.

Bloom Period: April to June.
*Near Democrat, Mills Co.*

## Wild Geranium
*Geranium carolinianum*

Wild Geranium is low, sprawling plant 6–10″ tall of open, grassy areas. Its leaves are orbicular to kidney-shaped in gross outline, and are deeply incised into numerous lobes. The white to pink flowers are usually less than ¼″ wide, with petals shorter than the underlying sepals. Annual to biennial.
Bloom Period: March to May.
*Sunset Valley, Travis Co.*

## Pin Clover
*Erodium cicutarium*

Pin Clover grows 6–18″ tall, with finely divided, fernlike leaves that are once to twice pinnately compound. The basal leaves reach 7½″ in length while the upper leaves are only 1–1½″ long. The flowers are small (³⁄₁₆–¼″ wide) and lavender, with 5 petals. The style columns grow to 2″ long. Annual to biennial.
Bloom Period: February to May.
*Leakey, Real Co.*

## Stork's Bill
*Erodium texanum*

Stork's Bill grows 6–18″ tall, with a semi-erect to prostrate habit. Its leaf blades are ¾–1½″ long on petioles up to 3½″ long. The blades are dissected into numerous shallow lobes with crenate margins. About 1″ across, the flowers are reddish-purple. The seed is ⅓″ long, with a tail up to 3″ long. Annual to biennial.
Bloom Period: February to April.
*Stonewall, Gillespie Co.*

## Yellow Wood-Sorrel
*Oxalis Dillenii*

This low plant is extremely common and can be found almost anywhere after a brief search. It tends to grow in a compact mass up to 6" high, with several erect to decumbent stems.

The stems are usually densely pubescent. The trifoliolate leaves are slightly less pubescent and range from ⅜–1¼" wide. They tend to fold in the heat of the day.

Axillary peduncles carry the yellow flowers in an umbel-like arrangement. The flowers average ¼–⅜" wide. Perennial.

Bloom Period: March to October.
*Hollywood Park, Bexar Co.*

## Wood-Sorrel
*Oxalis Drummondii*

Several pink-flowered *Oxalis* species have the common name Wood-Sorrel. *O. Drummondii* is the common native of the Hill Country area. The individual plants grow 4–12" tall from small bulbs. They are found in open grassy areas, open woodlands, and brushlands of either calcareous or sandy soils.

The leaves stand 2–5" tall and are composed of 3 broad, shallowly V-shaped leaflets, each 1¼–2" across.

Cymes of 4–8 pink flowers crown the slender scapes, which stand about twice as high as the leaves. The pink flowers are ⅜–¾" across and bell-shaped, on pedicels ½–1¼" long. Perennial.

Bloom Period: September to November.
*S.E. corner of Llano Co.*

## Rock Flax
*Linum rupestre*

Rock Flax usually grows 1–2' tall with few to many erect stems. It is found on dry, rocky ground, often on sun-baked caliche.

Scattered sparsely along the stem, the alternate leaves (sometimes opposite at the base) are linear and ⅜–¾" long.

The inflorescence is panicle-like, with 5-petaled yellow flowers ¼–½" wide. Tiny gland-tipped teeth line the margins of the lanceolate-ovate sepals. The fruit splits into 10 segments. Perennial.

Bloom Period: April to August.

*Bee Cave Rd., Travis Co.*

## Meadow Flax
*Linum pratense*

A delicate plant with slender stems and fragile flowers, Meadow Flax grows in extensive, diffuse colonies along the northwestern edge of our area with a few out-lying populations extending east to Bell Co. It grows 6–15" tall, with several sprawling stems branching from the base. It can be found in open grassy areas on calcareous soils.

The numerous linear to linear-lanceolate leaves are ¼–½" long.

Dark blue veins line the petals of the light to deep blue flowers, which are ½–¾" wide. Those plants with dark blue flowers deserve widespread propagation. Annual.

Bloom Period: March to April.

*Near Menard, Menard Co.*

## Yellow Flax
*Linum rigidum* var. *Berlandieri*

Yellow Flax is an erect plant 6–12″ high, usually with several branching stems in its upper half. Of the 4 varieties found in Texas, var. *Berlandieri* is the most common in our area, and is easily found in grassy places on limestone soils.

Glabrous and linear, the alternate leaves are ½–1″ long.

A large, dull-red spot lined with red veins extends ½–⅔ up the length of the yellow to yellow-orange petals. The flowers average ¾–1″ across. Glandular-toothed sepals surround the fruit, which splits into 5 parts. Annual.

Bloom Period: April and May.
*Blanco, Blanco Co.*

## Yellow Flax, Hudson Flax
*Linum hudsonioides*

Found mainly on the granite-derived soils of the Llano Uplift, Hudson Flax averages 6–8″ tall, and has an ascending to erect habit.

Opposite at the base, but becoming alternate above, the linear leaves are about ¼″ long, and tend to hug (or parallel) the stem.

The pale yellow flowers are approximately ¾″ across, usually with a brick-red spot on the lower ⅓ of each petal. The sepals are ⅛–³⁄₁₆″ long, persisting around the broadly ovoid fruit which splits into 5 segments. Annual.

Bloom Period: April and May.
*W. of Burnet, Burnet Co.*

## Wafer-Ash
*Ptelea trifoliata*

Wafer-Ash is an aromatic shrub to small tree, reaching 12' in height. It prefers some shade and is usually an understory species.

The leaves are trifoliolate, with lanceolate to ovate leaflets 1–2" long. Crushed leaflets release a citrus odor typical of members of the Citrus family.

Grouped in terminal clusters, the yellow-green flowers have 4–5 sepals, 4–5 petals, and 4–5 stamens. The wafer-like fruit is an indehiscent samara, with a translucent wing all around.

Bloom Period: April.
*Wild Basin, Austin, Travis Co.*

## Dutchman's Breeches
*Thamnosma texana*

Dutchman's Breeches is not obviously a member of the Rutaceae (Citrus family), but when the leaves and stems are crushed, the characteristic lemon-citrus odor becomes evident. *Thamnosma texana* is a loose, sprawling plant 6–12" tall, found on rocky slopes and in open grassy areas.

The alternate, linear leaves are ¼–⅜" long and gland-dotted.

The small, yellow, urn-shaped flowers have 4 sepals and 4 petals. The common name comes from the resemblance of the inflated 2-lobed capsule to a pair of pantaloons. Form *purpurea*, found in Kimble and Menard counties, has rose-red flowers and purple-red capsules. Perennial.

Bloom Period: March to May.
*Helotes, Bexar Co.*

## Thryallis
*Thryallis angustifolia*

Thryallis can be found mingled with the grasses on dry, rocky ground and also in a man-made ecological niche—crevices on the sides of low road cuts through limestone. It is usually 6–18" high, consisting mainly of a rounded, bushy clump of leaves sending up several flower stalks 3–6" above the foliage.

Its opposite, linear-lanceolate leaves are 1–2" long and are somewhat glaucous. A pair of small glands can often be found near the base of the leaf blade.

The interestingly shaped flowers are ¼–⅜" in diameter and may be yellow, orange, or red. The distinctive petals, narrowed greatly at the base, are typical of the Malpighia family. Perennial.

Bloom Period: May to October.
*New Braunfels, Comal Co.*

## Purple Milkwort
*Polygala Lindheimeri*

Purple Milkwort is a straggling, sub-erect, semi-woody plant 4–10″ tall. It is found on open limestone slopes, bluffs, and bare caliche.

Its stems are covered with very fine, straight, soft hairs. The elliptic to ovate leaves are ¼–¾″ long and mucronate (having a short projection at the tip), becoming shorter and oblanceolate just below the flower stalks.

The reddish-purple flowers are in short, loose racemes. The two large wing-like "petals" are actually modified, colored sepals. Perennial.

Bloom Period: July to November.
*Volente, Travis Co.*

## White Milkwort
*Polygala alba*

The most common of our local Milkworts, *P. alba* grows 8–12″ high with many erect stems ascending from a woody base.

While numerous near the base, the alternate leaves are scattered fairly thinly on the upper part of the stem. Linear and up to ½″ long above, they are obovate and smaller near the base.

The white flowers have yellow-green centers and are in dense, slender racemes 1–3″ long. Membranaceous wings line the sepals. Perennial.

Bloom Period: April to June.
*Tarpley, Bandera Co.*

## Three-Seeded Mercury
*Acalypha Lindheimeri*

Three-Seeded Mercury can be found in weedy habitats of every description. It is usually erect, though sometimes decumbent, and is 6–18″ tall.

The leaves are broadly lanceolate to rhombic with coarse teeth on the margins and scattered hairs on the leaf surface. They are ¾–1″ long in most cases, but can grow to 2″.

Some *Acalypha* species have the male and female flowers on different plants, others have them on the same plant. This species has male and female flowers on the same spike: male flowers on the upper portion of the spike and female flowers on the lower portion. Perennial.

Bloom Period: April to November.
*Hye, Blanco Co.*

## Cardinal Feather
*Acalypha radians*

Two similar species of *Acalypha* overlap ranges in the southern portion of the Hill Country. Both have orbicular to kidney-shaped leaves, and are differentiated by their margins. *A. hederacea* (now *A. monostachya*) has a crenate or wavy margin. *A. radians* has an incised or lobed margin. Soft, spreading hairs sparsely cover the leaves of both. They form low, thick clumps on dry, rocky ground.

This species has male and female flowers on different plants. The male flowers are in long dull-red spikes. The female flowers are in short, thick spikes (with crowded green bracts) from which many threadlike red styles extend. Perennial.

Bloom Period: April to November.
*Little Sandy Creek, Llano Co.*

## Queen's Delight
*Stillingia texana*

This plant grows 8–16″ tall, with multiple erect stems from a thickened, woody taproot. It is found on dry, calcareous soils of fields and hillsides.

Much longer than broad (1–2½″ by ⅛–³⁄₁₆″), the leaves are linear to linear-lanceolate, with serrate to crenate margins. Examination with a hand lens reveals a small dark tip on each tooth.

The yellowish-green male and female flowers are both found on the same spike; male above, female below. The fruit is a smooth pod with 3 lobes. Perennial.

Bloom Period: April to September.
*North Mesquite Creek, Burnet Co.*

## Leather Stem, Rubber Plant
*Jatropha dioica*

Leather Stem is an odd-looking little plant with several erect stems 1–2′ tall. It apparently prefers a harsh, dry, desert-like environment and is found in our area in a few rocky locations in Bandera, Bexar, Medina, and Uvalde counties.

Highly flexible, the stems are fleshy-succulent with a clear sap. The young stems are lined with bundles of spatulate leaves ½–2″ long which fall away as the stems grow older. Ultimately, the stems dessicate, leaving a thin, brittle core loosely covered in papery bark.

Male and female flowers are on separate plants in few-flowered cymes. The white, urn-shaped flowers are about ¼″ long. Perennial.

Bloom Period: April to June.
*Hackberry Creek, Uvalde Co.*

## Bull Nettle
*Cnidoscolus texanus*

A well-defended plant, Bull Nettle is covered on all parts except the flowers with clear, needle-like, stinging hairs. Merely brushing against this plant will produce an intense burning rash. It grows 1–2' high, with an erect, bushy habit, and is common in all soil types throughout our area.

The alternate leaves are usually palmately 3-5 lobed, and are 2–6" wide.

Male and female flowers are found on the same cyme, the female flowers terminal. Male flowers have 5 fused perianth lobes surrounding 10 stamens. Female flowers have 5 perianth lobes which are not fused, except at the very base, surrounding 3 styles. The 5 white perianth lobes are modified sepals; no petals are present. Perennial.

Bloom Period: April to September.
*Near Moody, McLennan Co.*

## Roemer's Spurge
*Euphorbia Roemeriana*
*(Tithymalus Roemerianus)*

Roemer's Spurge is one of 6 very similar species found in the Hill Country area. They are differentiated by branching pattern, longevity, and such arcane matters as the dimension and arrangement of pits on the seed surface. *T. Roemerianus* has erect to decumbent stems 4–12" high and is found in rich soils of moist, shaded canyons.

Cuneate to obovate, the stem leaves are alternate and up to ½" long. Three ovate leaves are whorled at the base of the pleiochasium, which is a multiple-branched cyme. Opposite, semicircular, fused leaves lie at the base of each further pair of pleiochasial branches.

About 10 small yellow to yellow-green flowers lie in each cup-like involucre, which is called a cyathium. Annual.

Bloom Period: March to May.
*Barton Creek, Austin, Travis Co.*

## Poinsettia
*Euphorbia cyathophora*
*(Poinsettia cyathophora)*

Our native Poinsettia grows 6–18"
high, usually with a few branches on a
single erect stem.

Leaves of the same plant may vary
widely, with the lowermost leaves linear
(2½" by ¼"), while leaves near the inflorescence may become broad and
bractlike, often somewhat fiddle-
shaped with bright red spots near the
base. On other plants, all leaves (including the red-spotted bracts) may be
narrowly linear.

Numerous involucral cups (cyathia)
compose the inflorescence, each cup
containing several male flowers and one
female flower. When the female flower
is fertilized and matures, it extends a
3-lobed capsule from the cyathium.
Annual.

Bloom Period: June to October.
*New Braunfels, Comal Co.*

## Snow-On-The-Mountain
*Euphorbia marginata*
*(Agaloma marginata)*

This erect plant has 1 or several
stems 1–3' tall. On the lower stem, the
alternate, sessile leaves are broadly lanceolate to ovate (1–3" long) with entire
margins. A slightly staggered whorl of
3 leaves lies at the base of the first
pleiochasial branches, which branch
in sets of 3. Near the inflorescence,
the leaves narrow and display white
margins.

At the top of the plant are what
appear to be several 5-petaled white
flowers. Each of these is not a flower,
but a cyathium, an involucral cup (with
5 white appendages) which contains
the very small true flowers. One
cyathium will contain as many as 35
male flowers and 1 female flower.
Annual.

Bloom Period: July to October.
*Willow City, Gillespie Co.*

## Smoke-Tree
*Cotinus obovatus*

Smoke-Tree is uncommon in Texas and is found here at only a few locations in Blanco, Kerr, Kendall, Bandera and Uvalde counties. It is a small tree 6–15′ tall found on rocky hillsides and bluffs.

The alternate leaves have short petioles ⅛–⅜″ long and obovate to elliptic blades 1–3″ long. Mature leaves are dark-green above and pale below.

The greenish-yellow, star-shaped flowers are on terminal panicles 1–4″ long. Seen from a distance, the numerous sterile pedicels of the 9″ long mature panicles give *Cotinus* the appearance of being wreathed in smoke.

Bloom Period: April to May.
*W. of Tarpley, Bandera Co.*

## Desert Sumac
*Rhus microphylla*

Desert Sumac is a shrub to small tree 3–10′ tall of upland fields or dry, desert flats.

The deciduous pinnately compound leaves are ½–1¼″ long, with a winged rachis and 5–9 leaflets, each about ¼–⅜″ long.

Usually appearing before the leaves, the flowers are in crowded terminal or axillary inflorescences, with individual flowers varying from ⅛–¼″ long. Desert Sumac apparently attracts pollinator insects with a carrion odor, since its blooms seem to be visited mainly by flies, and only a few bees.

Bloom Period: early April.
*Menard, Menard Co.*

## Texas Buckeye, White Buckeye
*Aesculus arguta*
*(Aesculus glabra* var. *arguta)*

Texas Buckeye is scattered across the Hill Country area with locations in Comanche, Bell, Williamson, Gillespie, Kerr, and Kimble counties. It adapts well to a variety of conditions and can be found on the granite-derived soils of Enchanted Rock State Park or the limestone soils near Junction. Though usually a small single-trunked tree 10–20' tall, it can take the form of a multi-trunked shrub.

The palmately compound leaves have 7 or 9 (sometimes 11) leaflets, each of which is lanceolate to elliptic-lanceolate and finely serrate.

Carried in terminal panicles, the flowers are yellow to greenish-yellow with red-orange markings and are about ½" long. In a suitable habitat,

such as stream bottomlands, Texas Buckeye grows to be a beautiful tree and deserves to be more widely planted.

Bloom Period: March to April.
*East Fork, James River, Kimble Co.*

## Red Buckeye
*Aesculus Pavia*

Two varieties of *Aesculus Pavia* grow in the Hill Country. They can be differentiated according to flower color and range. Both produce large multi-trunked shrubs or small trees 5–10' high (occasionally to 15') that are usually found in canyons or near drainages.

Both varieties have palmately compound leaves, with 5 leaflets. The lanceolate to oblanceolate leaflets are 3–8" long and are serrate.

The flowers of *Aesculus Pavia* var. *Pavia* are dull to bright red and are about 1½" long. This variety grows along the far eastern edge of the Hill Country between McLennan and Bexar counties, and north of a line drawn through the middle of Blanco Co.

The flowers of *Aesculus Pavia* var. *flavescens* are greenish-yellow to bright yellow and are also 1½" long. This variety is common in Kerr, Kendall, Bandera, Uvalde, Real, southern Blanco, and western Comal counties. Where the ranges of the two varieties meet, forms intermediate between the two are often found.

Bloom Period: March to May.
*Var. Pavia- Lake Austin, Travis Co. Var. flavescens- Crabapple Creek Rd., Blanco Co.*

*Aesculus Pavia* var. *Pavia*

*Aesculus Pavia* var. *flavescens*

## Mexican Buckeye
*Ungnadia speciosa*

Mexican Buckeye is not a true Buckeye, but is a member of the Sapindaceae (not the Hippocastanaceae). It is a multi-trunked large shrub up to 15' tall, found on rocky ground in canyons, on hillsides, and along fencerows.

The alternate leaves are pinnately compound with 5–7 serrate lanceolate leaflets, each leaflet 2–3" long.

Fascicles of pink flowers rise from the axils of the previous season's leaves, appearing before or just as the new leaves emerge. Roughly 6–10 drooping stamens extend from the flowers, with anthers that are bright red before they open and release their pollen. The style of the ovary is white to colorless, becoming red after fertilization. The fertilized ovary becomes a 3-lobed pod which carries 3 dark-brown seeds (each ½" in diameter) when mature.

Bloom Period: March to May.
*Bluff over Meridian, Bosque Co.*

## Redroot
*Ceanothus herbaceus*

*Ceanothus* is a New World genus with over 50 species in North America and Central America. Two of these species grow in the Hill Country area. This one, *C. herbaceus*, is a low, sprawling shrub 1–2½' high that can be found on open prairie or in crevices on bluffs.

It has glabrous (or nearly so) alternate leaves that are elliptic to elliptic-lanceolate and ¾–1¼" long. The leaf margins are serrate with reddish-brown tips on the teeth.

The white flowers are in umbel-like inflorescences mainly at the ends of the stems, producing numerous 3-celled capsules which turn black at maturity.

Our other local species, *C. americanus*, differs by having ovate to broadly elliptic leaves, short hairs on the upper leaf surfaces, and mainly axillary inflorescences.

Bloom Period: March to May.
*Hwy. 281, Blanco Co.*

## Turk's Cap
*Malvaviscus arboreus* var. *Drummondii*
*(Malvaviscus Drummondii)*

The margins of woods near rivers and streams sometimes shade colonies of this bushy plant. Turk's Cap is a loose herbaceous shrub 2–4' high. Its palmately veined leaves are 2–4" long and about as wide, usually very shallowly 3- to 5-lobed.

Rising from the center of the flower, the staminate column exserts itself above the petals. The petals of the bright red flowers (1–2" long) stand erect and are folded into one another. Turk's Cap is a good ornamental for shady situations, but is aggressive and must be controlled to keep it from taking over. Perennial.

Bloom Period: June to October.
*River Hills Rd., Travis Co.*

## Rose Mallow, Rose Pavonia
*Pavonia lasiopetala*

Rose Mallow can be obtained at most native plant nurseries. It requires little care beyond watering and occasional pruning. In return, it will bloom daily all Summer and Fall. In its natural environment, it is a low semi-woody shrub 1–3' tall found in open woods or on bluffs.

The velvety, alternate leaves are covered in short, white hairs. Coarsely serrate, the leaf blades are ovate to subcordate and 1–2½" long, on petioles ½–1" long.

The rose-pink flowers are solitary on axillary peduncles and are 1–1¼" wide. They open in early morning and are gone by mid-afternoon.

Bloom Period: March to November.
*New Braunfels, Comal Co.*

## Winecup
*Callirhoe involucrata*

This species of Winecup is a decumbent, sprawling plant 6–12″ tall, with
trailing stems up to 18″ long. It is found
in open grassy areas.

A little wider than long, the leaves
are shallowly or deeply incised into
5–7 lobes. Two rounded ⅛–¼″ stipules
lie at the base of each leaf.

The goblet-shaped flowers of *C. involucrata* var. *involucrata* consist of 5
reddish-purple petals 1″ long. Below
the petals are 5 bracts, and below the
bracts are 3 bract-like structures collectively known as the involucel. *C. involucrata* is the only Winecup in our
area with an involucel. Var. *lineariloba*
(found in Williamson, Menard, and
Kimble counties) has petals that are
pure white or white with a reddish-
purple streak down the center.
Perennial.

*Var. involucrata—Llano Co.*
*Var. lineariloba—Williamson Co.*

*Callirhoe involucrata* var. *lineariloba*

## Standing Winecup
*Callirhoe digitata*
*(Callirhoe pedata)*

Two similar species of Standing Winecup grow in the Hill Country area. Both are erect plants 1–3' tall. Their leaves are deeply incised into 5–7 lobes and have long petioles. The flower petals are about 1" long and may be reddish-purple, dark purple, or white. They are easily distinguished from *C. involucrata* because neither of these two species has an involucel.

The easiest way to differentiate these 2 species is by root type. *C. digitata* is a perennial and has a thickened, carrot-like taproot. Its near cousin, *C. leiocarpa* is an annual species with a diffuse (fibrous) root system.

Bloom Period: March to May.
*Near Bee Cave, Travis Co.*

## Velvet-Leaf Mallow
*Wissadula holosericea*

Velvet-Leaf Mallow is a bushy, semi-woody plant 2–6' tall, found on dry, rocky soils in the southern half of our area.

A pleasure to touch, the leaves are thickly covered in a soft, velvety pubescence of stellate hairs. The triangular-ovate leaves are heart-shaped at the base and up to 7" long. They may be coarsely crenate or dentate, and are often shallowly 3-lobed.

The 5-petaled yellow-orange flowers are ¾–1½" in diameter, in short panicles. The compound fruit consists of 5 carpels, each with 2 cells. Perennial.

Bloom Period: June to October.
*Medina Lake, Medina Co.*

## Indian Mallow
*Abutilon incanum*

Growing from a woody taproot, Indian Mallow raises several erect stems 1–2' high. Like *Wissadula*, it prefers dry, rocky ground, but has a greater range, being found throughout our area.

To the naked eye, the leaf surfaces look essentially glabrous, but under magnification very minute stellate hairs are found. The ovate-cordate leaves, acute at the tip and irregularly serrate, can reach 4" in length, but average 1–2".

Solitary and axillary, the yellow-orange flowers are about ⅜" wide. Perennial.

Bloom Period: May to October.
*Miller Creek, Llano Co.*

## Globe Mallow
*Sphaeralcea angustifolia*

Globe Mallow is more at home in West Texas, but does extend east on the Edwards Plateau into this region. It is an erect plant 1–3' tall.

Lanceolate to oblong-lanceolate, the gray-green leaves are cuneate at the base, on short petioles less than ¼ the length of the blade. They are finely crenate to crenate-dentate and average 1½–3½" long.

The flowers may be orange or pink and are ⅜–⅝" wide, arranged in short, cyme-like clusters in the axils of the leaves. The lanceolate to oblanceolate calyx lobes are 3/16–¼" long. A pink-flowered form is found near Concan. Perennial.

Bloom Period: Spring to Fall.
*Calf Creek School, McCulloch Co.*

## Sida
*Sida filicaulis*
*(Sida procumbens)*

This species of *Sida* is common
throughout our area. It is a ground-
hugging, spreading plant with stems as
long as 18″, and is found in open,
grassy areas or on bare caliche.

Broadly lanceolate, the leaves are cordate to truncate at the base, with blades
¼–¾″ long. They are rounded at the
apex and are crenate-dentate.

Solitary in the axils of the leaves, the
yellow-orange flowers are ¼–½″ wide.
The pedicels are ½–¾″ long. Perennial.

Bloom Period: March to October.
*Round Mountain, Blanco Co.*

## Lindheimer's Sida
*Sida Lindheimeri*

Lindheimer's Sida is 6–18″ tall with
erect to decumbent stems. It is a plant
of South Texas and the Gulf Coast, with
an outlying population in the sandy
soils of the Llano Uplift region.

Its linear to linear-lanceolate leaves
are 1–2″ long. They are truncate at the
base and have serrate margins, with
the margin often traced in a purple-
black line.

Pedicels 1–2″ long rise from the
upper axils. The pale yellow-orange
flowers (1–1½″ in diameter) have
strongly asymmetric petals. The ovate
calyx lobes are about ¼″ long. Perennial.

Bloom Period: May to August.
*Valley Spring, Llano Co.*

## Broom-Wood, Pyramid Flower
*Melochia pyramidata*

Bushy and erect, Broom-Wood is a semi-woody plant growing 1–2' tall in our area. It is found on dry, rocky ground at the extreme southern edge of the Hill Country in Comal, Bexar, Medina, and Uvalde counties.

The leaves are ovate to lanceolate, with serrate blades up to 1½" long on petioles up to 1" long.

Pink and 5-merous, the flowers are ¼–½" wide, in axillary cymes. The lanceolate sepals have dark red veins and pointed tips. Perennial.

Bloom Period: May to October.
*Hackberry Creek, Uvalde Co.*

## Mexican Mallow
*Hermannia texana*

Mexican Mallow is not a Mallow at all, but is a member of the Chocolate family. It has orange-red, urn-shaped flowers ¼–⅜" long, nodding on elongate cymes. The 5 petals curl into one another, forming a hollow tube. Soft, spine-like projections cover the fruit, which is 5-parted capsule.

Erect to decumbent (6–18" tall), the entire plant is densely covered in stellate hairs. The leaf blades are orbicular to ovate-elliptic, on petioles ¼–⅝" long. Coarsely dentate, the leaves are 1–2½" long, and are rounded to truncate at the base. *H. texana* is found on the southern edge of the Hill Country, and north to Kerr Co. Perennial.

Bloom Period: April to October.
*N. of Hondo, Medina Co.*

## Rockrose
*Helianthemum georgianum*

Rockrose ranges through the sandy-lands of East Texas, with an outlying population on the sandy soils of the Llano Uplift. It grows as a small, bushy clump of erect to decumbent stems 6–10″ high, and is often mulched by its own fallen leaves.

A fine, white, woolly pubescence covers the stems. The lanceolate to oblanceolate leaves are ⅝–1″ long, with the midvein elevated on the underside of the leaf. The leaf blades are dark green on the upper surface and light green on the lower surface.

The pale yellow flowers are ½–¾″ wide, with 5 triangular petals and numerous stamens (10–50). As a group, the stamens tend to favor one side or the other of the flower. Opening in the morning, the flowers last a few hours, the petals falling away by mid-afternoon, if not sooner. Rockrose can be found in Mason, Llano, and Burnet counties. Perennial.

Bloom Period: April and May.

*Inks Lake State Park, Burnet Co.*

## Yellow-Show
*Amoreuxia Wrightii*

A plant of the Rio Grande Plains, Yellow-Show ranges up into the western Edwards Plateau and is found within our area in Uvalde Co. It is erect (6–12″ high), with 1 or a few stems and is found in rocky soil.

Deeply parted into 5 lobes, the leaf blades are up to 2″ long, on petioles 1–2½″ long. The serrate leaves are usually slightly wider than long.

The large, eye-catching flowers are 2–2½″ wide, with 5 orange petals. Dark red blotches of color lie at the base of the 4 lower petals. If we assume the fifth (unpaired) petal to be the "top" petal, then we find that the flower almost always opens in a position rotated 90 degrees from vertical. There are two sets of stamens, which tend to cluster at opposite sides of the flower. The fruit is an inflated, oblong-ovoid capsule, about 1¼″ long. Perennial.

Bloom Period: May to July.
*Uvalde Co.*

## Missouri Violet
*Viola missouriensis*

A low plant of creek and river bottoms, Missouri Violet grows in a clump 3–6″ high.

Numerous leaves spread from a single crown. Ovate to orbicular, the leaves have a cordate base and a rounded or triangular apex. The petioles are up to 4″ long and the blades are 1–3″ long.

The flowers are pale to dark blue, on peduncles 2–4″ long. The lanceolate sepals each have a small ear-shaped appendage at the base. *V. missouriensis* has a close relative, *V. Langloisii*, with which it intergrades in this area. *V. missouriensis* will have 0–6 teeth on one margin of the upper third of the leaf blade. *V. Langloisii* will have 10–14 teeth on one margin of the upper third of the leaf blade. Perennial.

Bloom Period: February to April.
*River Hills Rd., Travis Co.*

## Slender-Lobe Passionflower
*Passiflora tenuiloba*

Slender-Lobe Passionflower is a vine 1–4' long, growing over boulders, shrubs, and grass on dry, caliche soils. Its leaves are highly variable, but in general have 2 common types, each with 3 main lobes.

In the case of the first leaf type, like the illustration, the 2 side lobes are each lobed again. The lower (central) lobe is also lobed again. This form of leaf has side lobes 1–2" long and a central lobe ½–¾" long. The second leaf type, often found in more xeric situations, has two undivided side lobes, each up to 3" long and ¼–⅜" wide. The central lobe is very short, only ⅛–¼" long. Such leaves tend to be tough and leathery, with an attractive silver streak along the main veins.

Both leaf types have 2 small cup-like glands at the junction of the leaf blade and the petiole. The green flowers are about ¾" wide. Perennial.

Bloom Period: May to October.
*San Antonio Botanical Garden, Bexar Co.*

## Yellow Passionflower
*Passiflora lutea*

Yellow Passionflower is a vine which climbs over shrubs and into small trees. Its broadly 3-lobed leaves are 1–4½" wide. Unlike *P. tenuiloba*, there are no glands at the leaf blade-petiole junction.

Intricately structured but otherwise unremarkable, the flower is yellow-green and about ¾" in diameter. The fruit is an ovoid capsule-like berry ⅜" in diameter, turning purple-black when ripe. *P. lutea* has a similar cousin, *P. affinis*, which can be distinguished by the prescence of a few minute (1–2 mm.) stipule-like appendages along the length of the peduncle. *P. affinis* is found in a variety of environments, from moist creek bottoms near San Marcos to dry crevices among granite boulders on Enchanted Rock. Perennial.

Bloom Period: May to September.
*Wimberly, Hays Co.*

## Corona de Cristo
*Passiflora foetida* var. *gossypifolia*

An attractive climbing vine of South Texas, Corona de Cristo can occasionally be found farther north, usually around older homes.

Its leaves are 3-lobed and longer than wide, from 2–2½" long. Both the leaves and the stems are covered in long soft white hairs, to the point that the leaves are velvety to the touch. The stipules at the base of the leaves are finely divided, much like the bracts of the flowers, with small glands at the tips of the segments.

The flowers open in early morning and close within a few hours. They are white to pale lavender and are 1–2" wide. Each flower is underlain by filiform bracts ¾–1¼" long that are 2 or 3 times pinnately divided. These bracts persist from the flowering stage through the fruiting stage, until the 1" fruits are bright red, at which point they fall away. As the fruits age and decay, they turn pink. *P. foetida* produces numerous fruits and has some value as an ornamental. Perennial.

Bloom Period: May to October.

*Near Travis County Courthouse, Austin, Travis Co.*

## Stinging Cevallia
*Cevallia sinuata*

Sprawling-decumbent to semi-erect, *Cevallia* grows to 18″ tall, and is found on open rocky ground or alluvial soils on the extreme southern edge of the Hill Country.

Averaging 1–2½″ in length, the leaves are sinuate to pinnatifid and may be sessile or short-petiolate. Intermingled with the fine hairs of the stems and leaves are many long stinging hairs.

The flowers are ⅜–⅝″ wide in dense heads on peduncles up to 4″ long. The peduncles rise on the side of the stem opposite from the leaf axil. Each flower has 5 yellow sepals fringed with soft white hairs and 5 yellow petals. Perennial.

Bloom Period: April to October.
*Sabinal R., Uvalde Co.*

## Stick-Leaf
*Mentzelia oligosperma*

Stick-Leaf is a semi-woody, bushy plant with several stems that grows 1–2' tall. It does well on either calcareous or granite soils.

The leaves may be lanceolate, ovate, or 3-lobed, all with coarsely toothed margins. They are sessile to short petiolate and are ½–2" long. The common name comes from the fact that the leaves will cling to clothing so tenaciously that only slow decay will remove them. Under high magnification, barbed hairs that look like miniature Christmas trees become visible. Once these hairs penetrate fabric, they will not come out.

Opening in the morning and the evening, the orange to yellow-orange flowers are ¾" in diameter. The fruit is a sessile, cylindrical, slightly curved capsule ¼–½" long. Perennial.

Bloom Period: April to October.
*Lake Georgetown, Williamson Co.*

## Reverchon's Stick-Leaf
*Mentzelia Reverchonii*

Usually having a single white stem, *M. Reverchonii* grows 2–4' tall on granite-derived or calcareous soils.

Sessile to virtually clasping, the leaves are lanceolate in overall outline, with a shallowly pinnately-lobed margin. They may be up to 5" long.

The pale yellow flowers have spatulate petals and numerous stamens. Opening in the late afternoon or evening, the flowers are ¾–1½" wide. The cylindrical capsules are ½–1¼" long. Perennial.

Bloom Period: May to September.
*Marble Falls, Burnet Co.*

## Prickly Pear
*Opuntia macrorhiza*
*(Opuntia compressa* var. *macrorhiza)*

This variety of Prickly Pear has a prostrate to semi-erect habit (6–12″ tall) and small pads 2–5″ long. Spines are present only on the upper portion or the perimeter of the pad. The flowers are yellow-orange with red markings in the center and are 2–3″ wide.
Bloom Period: Spring.
*Near Granite Mt., Burnet Co.*

## Tasajillo
*Opuntia leptocaulis*

Tasajillo is an upright, bushy cactus growing to 5′ tall. Its stem joints are ¾–1″ long and cylindrical. Tubercles are almost lacking. There is only one spine ¼–1¾″ long per areole. The pale yellow-green flowers are ½–1″ in diameter. This cactus is a prolific pest and will take over large areas.
Bloom Period: May and June.
*Brady, McCulloch Co.*

## Lace Cactus
*Echinocereus Reichenbachii*
*(Echinocereus caespitosas)*

One of our most common and beautiful cacti, Lace Cactus has a cylindrical solitary or branching stem 3–8″ high. It may be erect or reclining and can be found on either limestone or granite. The rose-pink or purple-pink flowers are 2–4″ in diameter with green stigma lobes. Long, soft, woolly hairs cover the flower tube.
Bloom Period: May.
*Merrell Creek, Mills Co.*

## Claret Cup, Strawberry Cactus
*Echinocereus triglochidiatus*

Claret Cup is a colonizing cactus found in clumps 5–8″ high and 1 to several feet broad, with numerous stems 3–12″ long. Each cylindrical stem has 5–9 ribs. The areoles have up to 9 radial spines and sometimes 1 spine perpendicular to the stem. The red-orange flower is 1–1½″ wide, with stiff, waxy tepals and light-green stigma lobes.
Bloom Period: March to May.
*Telegraph, Kimble Co.*

## Hedgehog Cactus
*Ferocactus setispinus*
*(Echinocactus setispinus)*

In the Hill Country area, *E. setispinus* grows to about 6″ tall and 3–5″ in diameter, with 13 spiral ribs. Each areole has numerous radial spines and 1 perpendicular spine that is slightly hooked at the end. The flowers are pale yellow, with red or orange markings in the center.
Bloom Period: Spring and Summer.
*Near Granite Mt., Burnet Co.*

## Nipple Cactus
*Coryphantha sulcata*
*(Mammillaria sulcata)*

Nipple Cactus is a colonizing species, often found in large clusters. Individual stems are 1–3″ tall and about as wide. The cylindrical tubercles are ¾″ long with up to 15 radial spines and 0–3 central spines. Its flowers are 2–3″ wide, with pale yellow tepals and numerous stamens with red filaments whorled around the yellow stigma lobes.
Bloom Period: Spring.
*S.E. corner of Llano Co.*

## Stream Loosestrife
*Lythrum ovalifolium*

Relatively uncommon, *L. ovalifolium* is an erect to decumbent plant 3–12" tall found growing in mud or gravel, in or along streams of the Edwards Plateau.

The stems are much branched and carry elliptic to obovate leaves up to 1" long. Leaves near the inflorescence are smaller, usually ¼–½" long.

Born in the leaf axils, the light purple flowers are about ¼" long and ¼–⅜" wide. Bright yellow anthers cluster at the throat of the flower. Perennial.

Bloom Period: May to October.
*Bee Creek, Travis Co.*

## California Loosestrife
*Lythrum californicum*

California Loosestrife is an upright, much branched plant, 1–2' tall, found in ditches, moist grassy areas, and near seep slopes.

Narrowly linear to linear-oblong, the leaves are ½–1" long. They are alternate, mostly sessile, and somewhat rounded at the base of the blade. Near the inflorescence, the leaves are linear and smaller, commonly ¼–½" long.

The purple flowers (about ⅜" wide overall) have obovate petals ³⁄₁₆" long. The stamens extend slightly beyond the throat of the flower, past the round stigma. Perennial.

Bloom Period: May to August.
*Near Fredonia, Mason Co.*

## Western Primrose
*Calylophus Hartweggii*

Plants of the genus *Calylophus* are distinguished by their peltate (rounded) stigmas, as opposed to plants of the genus *Oenothera*, which have cross-shaped stigmas. *Calylophus Hartweggii* grows 6–12″ tall, with several erect to decumbent stems from a woody tap-root. It can be found on caliche soils of the western and northwestern edges of our area.

Linear to lanceolate, the leaves are ½–1½″ long and may be glabrous or pubescent. The leaf margins may vary from entire to sparsely dentate. The uppermost leaves are rounded at the base while the basal leaves are narrowly cuneate at the base of the blade.

Opening in the morning and evening, the yellow flowers sometimes stay open all day long. They are 1½–2″ long and about 2–3″ wide. Unopened flowers are 1¾–2½″ long and ⅜–½″ wide. Perennial.

Bloom Period: April and May.
*S. of Leakey, Real Co.*

## Square-Bud Primrose
*Calylophus Drummondianus*
*(Calylophus Berlandieri)*

Square-Bud Primrose is an erect, bushy, semiwoody plant 6–24″ tall. In various forms, it is found throughout the Hill Country area.

Its shallowly dentate leaves are linear to narrowly oblanceolate and are 1–3″ long.

The yellow flowers are about 2″ wide, with a black throat and a black stigma which extends well past the stamens. Some varieties have a yellow throat and yellow stigma, or a combination in which one of these two features is black and the other yellow. A close relative, *C. serrulatus*, is distinguished by a stigma which does not extend past the stamens. Perennial.

Bloom Period: March to August.
*Near Anhalt, Comal Co.*

## Limestone Gaura
*Gaura calcicola*

The species name *calcicola* means "limestone dweller". True to its name, this plant is found on xeric limestone soils. It is an erect plant 1–3′ tall, with several branches in its upper half.

The semi-woody stems carry linear to oblanceolate leaves ¾–1½″ long, with sinuate-dentate leaf margins. At maturity, the entire plant takes on a rusty-red color.

Often branched at its base, the inflorescence is 4–12″ long. The uncrowded flowers are up to ½″ wide, with petals that are white to pink on the inside and red on the outside. A slender stipe ⅛–¼″ long bears the 4-sided capsule. Perennial.

Bloom Period: May and June.
*S.W. of Brady, McCulloch Co.*

## Scarlet Gaura
*Gaura coccinea*

Scarlet Gaura grows 6–15" tall with many short branches from a woody base. It can be found on sandy or calcareous soils throughout the Hill Country area.

A handy identifying characteristic of this species is the fact that the unopened flower buds tend to be crowded together at the top of the inflorescence, giving it a somewhat flat-topped appearance. The inflorescence tends to be short, usually 1–3" long. Individual flowers are about ½" wide, with petals that are white on the inner surface and pink to red on the outer surface. Long white filaments carry the red anthers. The capsule is essentially sessile or is constricted at the base into a short stipe less than ¹⁄₁₆" long.

The leaves average ½–1½" long, and are linear to linear-oblanceolate with entire or sparsely dentate margins. Perennial.

Bloom Period: April to July.
*W. of Waco, McLennan Co.*

## Wild Honeysuckle
*Gaura suffulta*

A common, sweet-smelling plant, Wild Honeysuckle has erect stems 1–2½' tall. It prefers moister, richer soils than other *Gaura* species and is often found in bar ditches along roads.

Usually narrowly lanceolate, the leaves are 1–3" long with subentire to sinuate-dentate margins. Both the stems and the leaves are sparsely covered with long hairs.

As they age, the white flowers fade to pink. They are about ½" wide, with purple-red anthers. The buds at the top of the inflorescence are usually tightly crowded. The sessile capsules are well distributed over the stalk. Annual.

Bloom Period: late March to June.
*San Antonio, Bexar Co.*

## River Primrose
*Oenothera Jamesii*

River Primrose is said to bloom around sunset, but the plants seen and collected by the author have bloomed about 2 hours after sunset. Its erect, semi-woody stems may reach 6' in height, sometimes with 2–5 branches. *O. Jamesii* grows on the banks of creeks and rivers, near the water. Its elliptic to lanceolate leaves grow to 4", but are 1–2" long near the flowers.

The yellow flowers are 2–2½" wide, with a floral tube up to 4½" long. The pistil equals the petals in length. Cylindric capsules 1–1½" long are staggered along the stem. Biennial.

Bloom Period: July to October.
*Pedernales R., Gillespie Co.*

## Pink Evening Primrose
*Oenothera speciosa*

Pink Evening Primrose is a lax, sprawling plant 6–24″ tall, sometimes with a few erect stems but more often with long reclining stems rising at the tips. It prefers rich, moist soils.

Lanceolate to oblanceolate in overall outline, the 1½–3″ leaves have subentire to sinuate-pinnatifid margins.

Flower color varies from white to rose-pink. White-flowered forms are common in Kimble, Edwards, and Real counties. The flowers are 2–3½″ wide with a floral tube ½–¾″ long. *O. speciosa* spreads by rhizomes and, given a little care, will provide massive, dense banks of beautiful pink flowers. Perennial.

Bloom Period: March to July.
*Turnersville, Coryell Co.*

## Fluttermill, Missouri Primrose
*Oenothera missouriensis*
*(Oenothera macrocarpa)*

Fluttermill may have several reclining stems from a woody base or sometimes may have no apparent stem at all, the leaves and flowers emerging directly from the base. This plant is found on dry caliche and averages 4–18″ tall.

Narrowly lanceolate, the leaves are 2–4″ long with entire or sparsely fine-toothed margins.

The yellow flowers are up to 3½″ wide, with a floral tube 2–4″ long. Lying directly below the 4 petals, the sepals are ¾–1¼″ long. Mature capsules are 1–2½″ long, with 4 broad wings. Perennial.

Bloom Period: April to August.
*Near Bee Cave, Travis Co.*

## Four-Point Evening Primrose
*Oenothera rhombipetala*

An inhabitant of sandy or sandy-calcareous soils, Four-Point Evening Primrose is uncommon in our area and is found infrequently in Mason, Lampasas, Brown, and Comanche counties. It stands 1–3' tall, usually with a single erect stem, but sometimes with multiple ascending branches.

The leaves are densely arranged around the stem and become progressively smaller going towards the inflorescence. Narrowly lanceolate, they are 2–3" long with sparingly dentate to mildly sinuate-pinnatifid margins.

Numerous unopened erect-ascending buds are crowded at the top of the long, slender inflorescence, with several open flowers lying just below. Unopened flower buds may be obscurely or vividly covered in red spots. Opening just before sunset, the yellow flowers are 1–1½" in diameter with a floral tube 1–1¼" long. The mature capsules curve upwards and are ⅜–¾" long. Winter annual or biennial.

Bloom Period: May and June.
*Near Pontotoc, Mason Co.*

## Stemless Evening Primrose
*Oenothera triloba*

A common lawn invader, *O. triloba* can also be found in open grassy areas and rocky fields. It is a very low plant that consists mainly of a ground-hugging rosette of leaves.

Oblanceolate in gross outline, the leaves are deeply incised and irregularly pinnatifid. They average 3–7″ long.

Opening in the evening near dark, the pale yellow flowers rise from the center of the leaf rosette. They are about 2″ wide on a floral tube 1–3″ long. Winter annual or biennial.

Bloom Period: March to May.
*Near Payton Colony, Blanco Co.*

## Cut-Leaf Evening Primrose
*Oenothera laciniata*

Cut-Leaf Evening Primrose is an erect to reclining-ascending plant 2–10″ tall. It prefers sandy or alluvial soils, but occasionally is found on limestone.

True to the common name, its elliptic to oblanceolate leaves (1–2½″) have shallowly sinuate to deeply lobed margins.

Small for a Primrose, the yellow flowers are only ¼–1″ wide, with a floral tube ½–1½″ long. The fruit is a cylindrical, curved capsule ¾″ long. A distinctive variety of this species, var. *grandis*, is found in the same range and is easily recognized by its large flowers which are up to 3″ wide. Annual.

Bloom Period: March to October.
*Pedernales R., Gillespie Co.*

## Water-Primrose
*Ludwigia octovalvis*

Water-Primrose is an erect, much branched plant 1–5′ tall, found at streamsides and in wet ditches.

Narrowly lanceolate, the leaves are up to 4″ long and may be sessile or short petiolate. The stems are striate.

Rising from the axils of the leaves, the light yellow flowers are about 1″ wide, with 4 sepals about ⅜″ long. The slender reddish-brown capsules are roughly ⅛″ wide and 2″ long, with the four sepals persisting at the tip.

Bloom Period: July to October.
*Bull Creek, Austin, Travis Co.*

## False Gaura
*Stenosiphon linifolius*

This large but very open plant grows 3–8′ tall with only a few slender branches. False Gaura is found in fields and on gentle slopes in limestone soils.

The stems are semi-woody and red-brown in the lower part of the plant, but stiffly herbaceous and light green in the upper part. The alternate leaves are narrowly lanceolate and are 1¼–2¼″ long. They are sessile with entire margins, becoming smaller as they near the inflorescence.

Crowded on a long, slender inflorescence, the flowers open in a rounded or elongate cluster. Individual flowers are ¼–⅜″ wide, and are 4-merous. Perennial.

Bloom Period: July to October.
*Henly, Hays Co.*

## Water-Hemlock, Beaver Poison
*Cicuta maculata*

Water-Hemlock is an extremely poisonous native species found at the water's edge on lakes, rivers, and creeks. It is an erect, open plant 2–6' tall.

The broad leaves are once to three times pinnately divided, with lanceolate, serrate leaflets. An individual leaf may be 1–3' long.

Composed of numerous compound umbels, the white inflorescence may be 3–7" across. The peduncles are both terminal and axillary. *C. maculata* has a close cousin, *C. mexicana*, which can be distinguished by minor characteristics of the seeds, but for all practical purposes they are essentially identical. Perennial.

Bloom Period: June to October.
*Town Lake, Austin, Travis Co.*

## Poison Hemlock
*Conium maculatum*

An introduced Eurasian species, Poison Hemlock has now become a common and prolific weed of creek and river bottoms in Travis, Blanco, Gillespie, Kerr, and Kendall counties. It is an erect, branching plant 3–8' tall, and is extremely poisonous.

Purple-red spots dot the green stems. Three times pinnately divided, the leaves are 3–12" long, with the ultimate divisions pinnately incised, giving the leaves a fern-like appearance.

The white inflorescence is a compound umbel 2–6" across, and may be terminal or axillary. Biennial.

Bloom Period: March to June.
*Pedernales Falls State Park, Blanco Co.*

## Prairie Bishop's-Weed
*Bifora americana*

*Bifora* is exceedingly common along roadsides and in fields in the Spring. It is a slender, erect, branching plant 6–24″ tall.

Its stems are striate. The glabrous leaves are up to 2″ long and are three times pinnately divided into slender, threadlike filaments.

A few entire to pinnately divided linear bracts lie at the base of the compound inflorescence, which is composed of several small umbels. Each ultimate umbel is itself subtended by small bractlets. Individual flowers are ¹⁄₁₆–⅛″ wide. The rounded fruits are joined in pairs, turning tan to straw-colored at maturity. Annual.

Bloom Period: April to June.
*I-35 between Jarrell and Corn Hill, Williamson Co.*

## Daucosma
*Daucosma laciniatum*

Growing 1–3½′ tall, *Daucosma* is an erect, branching plant usually found in colonies on dry soils. It can be found in the southern half of our area.

The leaves are two or three times pinnately divided and are about 4″ long.

Linear to pinnately divided bracts lie at the base of the compound inflorescence, which may be 1½–3″ across. Roughly 10–20 peduncles bear the ultimate, individual umbels, each subtended by linear to pinnately divided bractlets. The individual flowers are about ⅛″ in diameter. Annual.

Bloom Period: June and July.
*Near Welfare, Kendall Co.*

## Thoroughwax
*Bupleurum rotundifolium*

Introduced from the Mediterranean area, *Bupleurum* has become established on open ground in or near ditches and wet areas. Erect and single stemmed to few-branching, it grows 6–18″ tall.

On the lower stem, the oval to obovate leaves clasp the stem, but they become perfoliate (pierced by the stem) near the inflorescence. The leaves are ½–2½″ long.

An involucel of 5 or 6 obovate, pointed bractlets lies at the base of the flower cluster. There are 6–10 small (½₂–⅟₁₆″) yellow flowers in each cluster. Annual.

Bloom Period: April and May.
*W. of Waco, McLennan Co.*

## Venus'-Comb, Crow-Needles
*Scandix Pecten-Veneris*

With some stems erect and others reclining, *Scandix* is a weak herbaceous plant rarely growing over 6–12″ high. It is found in wet, moist soils or in ditches along the roadside.

The highly dissected leaves are about 6″ long and are 2 or 3 times pinnately divided, with the ultimate divisions deeply incised.

Always in pairs, the flower clusters are ¼–¾″ wide, with individual flowers ⅟₁₆–⅛″ wide. The linear fruit is about ³⁄₁₆″ long, with an elongate linear beak 1–3″ long. *Scandix* is an introduced Eurasian species. Annual.

Bloom Period: March and April.
*West Lake Hills, Travis Co.*

## Water-Pennywort
*Hydrocotyle umbellata*

Water-Pennywort is a low plant 3–10″ tall found growing in the mud in or near streams. Its slender, creeping stems root at the nodes.

Rising from the nodes of the mud-hugging stems are the erect petioles which may be up to 10″ long. The round leaf blades have crenate margins and are up to 2½″ in diameter, with the long petiole attached to the center of the blade.

The inflorescence is a simple umbel with numerous white flowers, and is ¼–1″ wide. Individual flowers are about ¹⁄₁₆″ wide. Perennial.

Bloom Period: April to October.
*Salado, Bell Co.*

## Big-Root Cymopterus
*Cymopterus macrorhizus*

Big-Root Cymopterus consists of a low rosette of glaucous leaves and an erect flower stalk 3–10″ high. It can be found in dry, open, grassy areas in the eastern half of the Hill Country.

A pair of sheathing leaves grow from the top of the large root, around a short stem ½–1½″ long. A whorl of pinnately divided leaves up to 3½″ long grows from the top of this stem. From the center of the leaf whorl comes a peduncle or flower stalk ½–6″ long.

The inflorescence is a compound umbel ½–1¼″ wide. Flower color may vary from white to pink to light purple. *Cymopterus* is an inconspicuous early bloomer that is easily missed. Perennial.

Bloom Period: March.
*Twin Sisters, Blanco Co.*

### Rattlesnake-Weed, Wild Carrot
*Daucus pusillus*

Wild Carrot is an erect plant 1–3' tall with a single stem that sometimes has a few branches in its upper half. Its pinnately divided leaves are up to 7" long. The white infloresence is a compound umbel (with pedicels that are unequal in length) and is on a peduncle 4–12" long. The roots have the characteristic carrot odor. Annual.
Bloom Period: April to June.
*Little Llano R., Llano Co.*

### Texas-Parsley
*Polytaenia texana*

Found on rocky soils throughout the Hill Country, *P. texana* is an erect, stout, branching plant 1–2½' tall. Once or twice pinnately divided and then incised, the leaves are up to 9" long. The fruit is ¼–⅜" long (longer than broad), with lateral wings that are longer and thinner than the body. Perennial.
Bloom Period: April and May.
*Near Bee Cave, Travis Co.*

### Knotted Hedge-Parsley
*Torilis nodosa*

Knotted Hedge-Parsley grows 3–10" tall, with ascending or reclining stems. It is found in moist, grassy areas, and disturbed soils, often invading lawns. The leaves are 1 or 2 times pinnately compound, with the ultimate divisions deeply incised. The white-flowered umbels form tight heads opposite the leaf axils. Annual.
Bloom Period: April to June.
*Buchanan Dam, Llano Co.*

## Hedge-Parsley, Beggar's Ticks
*Torilis arvensis*

Coarse bristles with hooks at the tips cover the seeds of Hedge-Parsley and cause them to stick to socks and pants legs. *T. arvensis* grows 6–18" tall, with an open, much-branched habit, and is found on moist soils throughout our area.

Short, stiff, bristly hairs cover the stems and leaves. The leaves are 2–5" long and are once to twice pinnately divided with the ultimate divisions deeply incised.

The white-flowered inflorescence is a compound umbel ½–1¼" across, on a peduncle ½–4" long. Individual flowers are only about ¹⁄₁₆" wide. Annual.

Bloom Period: April to July.
*Gatesville, Coryell Co.*

## Eryngo
*Eryngium Leavenworthii*

This striking plant attracts the eye with vibrantly colored flower heads. It grows 1–4' tall with either a single stem or several branches and can be found in fields and prairies.

Averaging 1–2" long, the leaves are deeply palmately incised into 3–5 lobes. The lobes end in, and are lined with, flexible prickles or spines.

The inflorescence may consist of one flowering head or several in a cyme-like configuration. Each reddish-purple head is ½–1¼" long and is composed of numerous small flowers which exsert small, pale blue anthers. Annual.

Bloom Period: July to October.
*N.W. of Lampasas, Lampasas Co.*

### Rough-Leaf Dogwood
*Cornus Drummondii*

A large shrub or small tree up to 15′ tall, Rough-Leaf Dogwood is a rugged native found in areas that are moist at least part of the year, often on stream-banks or in bottomlands.

The opposite, deciduous leaves have petioles up to ½″ long and ovate to elliptic-lanceolate blades that are 1–4″ long. Prominent veins (which are slightly raised on the underside of the leaf) assist in leaf identification. The upper leaf surface is slightly rough to the touch.

Numerous white to creamy-white flowers ³⁄₁₆–¼″ wide make a rounded cyme-like or corymb-like inflorescence 2–4″ across. The mature fruits are waxy-white drupes about ¼″ in diameter.

Bloom Period: April and May.
*Block Creek, Kendall Co.*

## Texas Madrone
*Arbutus xalapensis*

Texas Madrone is a beautiful small tree reaching 20' in height, with a rounded, open crown. Its evergreen leaves and smooth, peeling, pink to reddish-brown bark make it a handsome and desirable ornamental.

The ovate to oblong-elliptic leaves are rounded at the base and rounded or pointed at the tip. They have entire to finely serrate margins and are 2–5" long. The petioles and young stems are usually red.

Madrone flowers have an urn-shaped corolla made of 5 fused petals and are about ¼" long. They occur in large panicles up to 6" wide. The fruit is an attractive red berry with a granular surface.

Bloom Period: March.
*W. of Tarpley, Bandera Co.*

## Scarlet Pimpernel
*Anagallis arvensis*

Scarlet Pimpernel is 4–10″ tall, with reclining, mat-forming stems. It requires plenty of moisture and is found in seep areas or near streams.

The opposite leaves are sessile to clasping and are ¼–½″ long. They are ovate with a pointed tip and have entire margins. The stems are 4-sided.

A pedicel ½–1″ long rises from the axil of each opposite leaf. Each pedicel carries a single salmon-colored flower. The 5-petaled flowers are ⅜″ wide, with 5 yellow anthers on red filaments and red markings (tinged with blue or purple) at the petal bases. Across the state, the flowers are variable in color and may be salmon, red, white, or blue. In our area, they seem to all be salmon-colored. The globe-shaped capsules are about ³⁄₁₆″ in diameter. Annual.

Bloom Period: March to May.
*Marble Falls, Burnet Co.*

## Sycamore-Leaf Snow Bell
*Styrax platanifolia*

Sycamore-Leaf Snow Bell is another of our exceptionally beautiful (but neglected) natives. Its entire range is restricted to the Edwards Plateau where it is found on or under bluffs near streams and on creek banks. It is an uncommon multi-trunked shrub to small tree up to 12' tall.

The leaves (1–4" long) are broadly ovate to widely elliptic and often have angular projections like a Sycamore leaf. In some areas, such as Bandera Co., the leaves tend to be densely pubescent. In other areas, such as Blanco Co., the plants have glabrous leaves and are more suitable for ornamental purposes.

*S. platanifolia* has white, bell-shaped flowers ½–¾" long and about ⅝" wide, which usually hang almost straight down. They are arranged in corymb-like racemes at the ends of that year's new growth. A compact, central column of stamens (with bright yellow anthers ³⁄₁₆" long) emerges from the throat of the flower. A close cousin, *S. texana*, is found in Edwards and Real counties and has rounded, elliptic leaves which are very pale green to nearly white on the underside of the leaf.

Bloom Period: April and May.
*Twin Sisters, Blanco Co.*

## Redbud
*Menodora heterophylla*

A small herbaceous plant, Redbud has numerous reclining to semi-erect stems that grow 2–10″ tall. It is very adaptable and can be found on dry flats on granite-derived soils, alluvial deposits, or dry limestone soils.

Usually deeply incised, the opposite leaves are entire to 3–7 lobed. They are crowded on the stem and are about 1″ long.

Prior to opening, the flower petals are folded into a bright red bud. Open flowers (½–¾″ wide) are pale yellow on the inside of the 5 petals and yellow with red streaks on the outside of the petals. The flowers are surrounded by 10–14 calyx lobes, each ¼–⅜″ long. Perennial.

Bloom Period: March to June.
*Chapman Draw, Menard Co.*

## Showy Menodora, Twin-Pod
*Menodora longiflora*

Showy Menodora has numerous erect, semi-woody stems 1–2′ tall growing from a woody base. It prefers dry, rocky, caliche soils in almost desert-like conditions.

The opposite leaves are sessile to short-petiolate with linear to elliptic-lanceolate blades and are ½–1¼″ long.

Several yellow flowers occur in corymb-like cymes at the ends of the stems. They are ¾–1¼″ wide, with 5 corolla lobes, and a floral tube up to 1¾″ long. The flowers are subtended by 8 or more calyx lobes about ½″ long. Perennial.

Bloom Period: June to September.
*N.E. of Junction, Kimble Co.*

## Rose-Gentian
*Sabatia campestris*

Rose-Gentian is an attractive plant
5–16″ high, with one to several
branches. It is found in full sun on
moist soils or in areas that collect
rainwater.

Clasping the stem, the opposite
leaves are lanceolate to ovate-elliptic
and ¾–1½″ long.

The bright rose-pink flowers are
½–1″ wide and have 5 petals, each with
yellow markings at the base that merge
into a star-shaped configuration. Five
stamens rise from the center of the
flower, with yellow anthers that tend to
curl at one end. At the top of the style
are 2 yellow-green stigmatic branches
that are twisted together. The flowers
are carried on axillary pedicels ¾–2″
long. For diagnostic purposes, it is important to note that the calyx tube
(there is no floral tube) is ³⁄₁₆″ long by
⅛–³⁄₁₆″ wide, with spreading calyx
lobes that are equal to or longer than
the petals. Annual.

Bloom Period: April to June.

*Inks Lake, Llano Co. side.*

## Rosita
*Centaurium calycosum*

At first glance, Rosita may look like a small *Sabatia*, but there are important differences. Its pedicels, for instance, are only ¼–⅝" long. In addition, the flower has a floral tube ¼–⅜" long by ¹⁄₁₆" wide and calyx lobes that clasp the tube (they do not spread). Note that the calyx lobes equal or are just slightly shorter than the floral tube. The rose-pink flowers are ½–¾" wide, with 5 stamens and spirally curled yellow anthers.

Rosita is an erect plant 8–18" tall, with numerous branches. It lives in moist soils along streams and intermittent drainages.

The lower leaves are oblong-elliptic to narrowly lanceolate and up to 2" long and ⁵⁄₁₆" wide. On the uppermost stems, the leaves become smaller and linear. Annual.

Bloom Period: May to July.
*Near Katemcy, Mason Co.*

## Mountain Pink
*Centaurium Beyrichii*

Mountain Pink usually grows in the shape of an inverted cone, giving it the appearance of a small pink bouquet. *C. Beyrichii* is an erect, multiple-branched plant 4–12" high. It prefers dry, barren, open areas on caliche or marl outcrops.

All of its leaves are linear, with the lower leaves as long as 1¼" and the upper leaves shorter and virtually filiform (threadlike).

The pink flowers are ½–¾" wide, with a floral tube ⅜–⅝" long that greatly exceeds the clasping calyx lobes. In general, the majority of pedicels are equal to or shorter than the calyx lobes (although exceptions are not hard to find). Annual.

Bloom Period: May to July.
*Horse Thief Mt., Bell Co.*

## Lady Bird's Centaury
*Centaurium texense*

The common name of this plant is an affectionate reference to Mrs. Lyndon Baines Johnson, our former First Lady, who has done so much to advance the cause of natural beauty in Texas and the nation. *Centaurium texense* is a delicate plant 3–7″ high with an erect, diffusely branched habit. It is found in dry, open, grassy areas.

Linear to linear-lanceolate, the lower leaves are about ¾″ long and ³⁄₁₆″ wide. The upper leaves are smaller and linear to threadlike.

Smaller than the other *Centaurium* species, *C. texense* has light pink flowers only ¼″ in diameter and petals barely over ¹⁄₁₆″ wide. The floral tube exceeds the calyx lobes by ¹⁄₁₆–⅛″. Annual.

Bloom Period: May to July.
*White Bluff, Lake Buchanan, Burnet Co.*

## Bluebell Gentian
*Eustoma grandiflorum*

One of our showier wildflowers, Bluebell Gentian grows 1–2′ tall, with one or several erect stems. It favors the moist soils of drainages, prairies, and fields.

Ovate to elliptic-oblong, the opposite, glaucous leaves are up to 3″ long and 1¼″ wide. The leaf blades are conspicuously 3-veined.

Large, showy flowers 2–2½″ wide are carried on pedicels up to 4″ long. A yellow 2-lobed stigma is prominently displayed in the center of the flower. Most flowers are blue-purple but occasionally a white, pink, or yellow specimen will be found. These variants are finding their way into the nursery trade. Annual to short-lived perennial.

Bloom Period: June to October.
*Austin, Travis Co.*

## Blue-Star
*Amsonia ciliata*

Blue-Star can be found throughout the Hill Country on open slopes and prairies on calcareous soils. It grows 6–18″ tall, with several erect to reclining semi-woody stems rising from the woody rhizomes.

Linear to oblong-lanceolate, the alternate leaves are 1½–2½″ long by ⅛–¼″ wide at midstem. Nearing the inflorescence, the leaves become a little shorter and threadlike. At the base of the stem, the leaves become much shorter but retain their width.

The inflorescence barely exceeds the foliage and is composed of a few or numerous pale blue flowers ⅜–½″ wide. Perennial.

Bloom Period: March and April.
*Near Hamilton, Hamilton Co.*

## Indian Hemp, Dogbane
*Apocynum cannabinum*

This erect, weedy-looking plant grows 2–3′ tall with several ascending branches. Dogbane is usually found in wet soils near streams or ditches.

Petioles up to ¼″ long carry the elliptic-lanceolate to oblanceolate leaf blades which are 2–3″ long. Young stems are usually bright red, turning reddish-brown with maturity. The broken stems and leaves exude a white sap.

Dogbane flowers have 5 white petals partially fused into a cylindric to urn-shaped corolla ⅛–¼″ long. The lanceolate calyx lobes are about ⅛″ long. Perennial.

Bloom Period: April and May.
*Llano R., Llano, Llano Co.*

### Antelope-Horns
*Asclepias asperula*

Antelope-Horns is a milkweed 8–24″ tall, with several ascending or reclining unbranched stems rising from a woody rootstock. Healthy specimens form low clumps 1–2′ across in open grassy areas.

The lanceolate to linear-lanceolate leaves are 2½–6″ long by ¼–⅜″ wide on short petioles. They are often conduplicate, that is, folded lengthwise along the midrib.

Each stem has a solitary, rounded, terminal inflorescence composed of numerous pale yellowish-green flowers. The inflorescence is in a cyme-like arrangement, with pedicels ½–1″ long. Individual flowers are ⅜–⅝″ wide and are 5-merous. Perennial.

Bloom Period: March to May.
*Near Blanket, Brown Co.*

### Hierba de Zizotes
*Asclepias oenotheroides*

*Asclepias oenotheroides* is one of the more weedy-looking milkweeds. It grows 8–16″ tall, with a few ascending to reclining stems which may be simple or branched at the base. It lives in open grassy areas on dry soils or caliche.

The dull green leaves have a sort of matte finish and are covered with minute hairs. The leaf blades are ovate to elliptic-lanceolate (1½–3″ long) on petioles ⅜–¾″ long.

A single rounded inflorescence may grow at each of the uppermost nodes. The individual flowers are about ⅝″ long, with the pale green petals curled back parallel to the pedicel. Perennial.

Bloom Period: March to October.
*Near Temple, Bell Co.*

### Green Milkweed
*Asclepias viridis*

Green Milkweed has stout, erect to reclining stems 1–2′ tall. Like many other milkweeds, it prefers the full sun of open grassy areas.

Tough and somewhat leathery, the broadly ovate leaves are 1½–3″ long on petioles ⅛–¼″ long. They are glabrous and sometimes notched at the tip.

The inflorescence is terminal (occasionally lateral) and solitary, with pale green flowers in a rounded head similar to that of *A. asperula*. The individual flowers are ½–¾″ wide and have ascending petal tips. Perennial.

Bloom Period: April to September.
*Sycamore Creek, Hamilton Co.*

## Orange Milkweed, Butterfly-Weed
*Asclepias tuberosa*

Bright orange flowers make this our most striking milkweed. It grows 10–20″ tall, with several ascending to reclining simple stems rising from a woody root. Butterfly-Weed is common in East Texas, but uncommon in the Hill Country, appearing at only a few scattered locations.

Coarse hairs cover both the stems and the leaves. Crowded around the stem, the narrowly lanceolate leaves are 1–3″ long and short petiolate.

The inflorescence is composed of 1 to several umbel-like cymes at the end of several short terminal branches. The individual flowers are ⅜–½″ long. Perennial.

Bloom Period: May to September.
*N.W. Bandera Co.*

## Wand Milkweed
*Asclepias viridiflora*

The common name of this plant derives from its erect, zig-zag, unbranched stem which may be 1–3′ tall. Wand Milkweed can be found in open grassy or rocky areas, often under xeric conditions.

In most of our area, the tough leaves (1–1½″ long) are broadly elliptic to suborbicular, with a notch at the apex. However, the leaves of this species can be highly variable. Some plants from the Lampasas area have narrowly lanceolate leaves (similar to *A. asperula*) up to 4″ long.

A single, hemispherical inflorescence may grow from each of the uppermost nodes. Note that the pale yellow-green petals are drawn back parallel to the pedicels. Perennial.

Bloom Period: June to August.
*Near Mt. Sharp, Hays Co.*

## Texas Milkweed, White Milkweed
*Asclepias texana*

Texas Milkweed is such a pretty plant that you might mistake it for an ornamental that has escaped from cultivation. Its slender, branched, semi-erect stems often curve upward from the base, reaching 6–18″ in height. Well adapted to the Edwards Plateau, it can be found on caliche outcrops, hillsides, and in dry fields.

The herbaceous leaves are broadly to narrowly elliptic (1–2½″ long) with petioles ⅛–½″ long.

Each umbel-like cluster of flowers is solitary from one of the upper nodes, but they come close to coalescing into one large inflorescence. The white flowers are about ¼″ long with reflexed (partially curled back) corollas. Perennial.

Bloom Period: May to July.
*Garner State Park, Uvalde Co.*

## Swamp-Milkweed, Pink Milkweed
*Asclepias incarnata*

Impressively large, Swamp-Milkweed has several stout, erect stems 1½–5' tall. It grows in wet soils at the edge of (or in) streams and rivers.

The linear-lanceolate ascending leaves are 2–6" long by ³⁄₁₆–½" wide, on short petioles up to ³⁄₈" long.

One flower cluster ¾–1½" across rises from each of the uppermost nodes. As with *A. texana*, the separate clusters almost coalesce into one massive inflorescence. The individual flowers are about ³⁄₈" long and are pink to light purple. Perennial.

Bloom Period: August and September.
*South Llano R., Kimble Co.*

## Purple Milkweed Vine
*Matelea biflora*

Radiating from a woody rootstock, the stems of *Matelea biflora* trail along the ground or sometimes arch shallowly upwards. They grow to 2' long. Purple Milkweed Vine inhabits grassy areas and, even though it is relatively common, is often passed over and missed.

All parts of the plant are covered in long, spreading hairs. The opposite leaves (½–1½" long) are triangular-ovate, with a rounded to pointed tip and a heart-shaped base, on petioles ⅛–½" long.

Pairs of star-shaped, dark purple flowers ³⁄₈–½" wide rise from the leaf nodes. The pedicels are about ¼" long. Perennial.

Bloom Period: April to June.
*Honey Creek, Llano Co.*

## Plateau Milkvine
*Matelea edwardsensis*

Without a close look at the flowers, it would be easy to mistake Plateau Milkvine for *M. reticulata*. The leaves and twining habit of the two are very similar.

The flowers of *M. edwardsensis* are not flat, but bell-shaped. They do not have a silver dot in the center. Finally, its flowers are not solely reticulate-patterned. The petals have parallel veins on their lower half and center, with reticulate veins only on the petal margins. Plateau Milkvine is relatively uncommon and is found only on the Edwards Plateau. Perennial.

Bloom Period: April and May.
*Lake Austin, Travis Co.*

## Green Milkweed Vine, Pearl Milkweed
*Matelea reticulata*

*Matelea reticulata* is a robust twining vine that climbs fences and brush, and has been known to rise 12′ into small trees.

Its stems and leaves are covered with soft, spreading hairs. The heart-shaped leaves are 2–4″ long, on 1–2″ petioles. Often, the basal lobes curve back in toward the petiole.

Conspicuous reticulate veins pattern the flat surface of the green flowers, which are ½–¾″ across. There is a small silver or pearl-like dot at the top of the stamen column in the center of each flower. Perennial.

Bloom Period: April to July.
*Fischer Hall, Fischer, Comal Co.*

### Wavy-Leaf Milkweed Vine
*Sarcostemma crispum*

*Sarcostemma crispum* grows up to 6′ long, on granite or limestone soils. Paired along the stem, the narrowly lanceolate to linear leaves are up to 4″ long and ⅜″ wide, with wavy or undulate margins. The flowers (⅜–½″ wide) normally hang straight down and are easily overlooked. Perennial.
Bloom Period: April to June.
*Near Burnet, Burnet Co.*

### Climbing Milkweed, Twine-Vine
*Sarcostemma cynanchoides*

Climbing Milkweed trails on the ground or climbs over bushes and small trees on sandy soils. Its narrowly lanceolate to triangular-lanceolate leaves are 1–2¼″ long. Umbel-like clusters of white to greenish-white flowers (⅜–½″ wide) with pink or light purple markings rise from the nodes. Perennial.
Bloom Period: May to September.
*Coal Creek, Gillespie Co.*

### Cynanchum
*Cynanchum barbigerum*

Cynanchum is a climbing, twining vine growing to 6′ on boulders, shrubs, and small trees. The linear to elliptic-lanceolate leaves are ½–1½″ long and are dark green on the upper surface and light green on the lower surface. White to creamy-white, the ⅛″ flowers are arranged in sessile to short peduncled axillary corymbs. Perennial.
Bloom Period: May to August.
*Balanced Rock, Gillespie Co.*

## White Evolvulus
*Evolvulus sericeus*

White Evolvulus has erect to pros-trate stems 3–9″ long, and is found in dry, grassy areas. It can grow on all soil types but is most common on sandy soils of the Llano region.

The stems and leaves are thinly cov-ered in appressed (flattened against the surface) hairs, giving the plant a gray-green appearance. Narrowly elliptic to linear, the leaf blades are ½–1″ long with entire margins. The top surface of the leaf is sparsely hairy to almost glabrous.

The shallowly cup-shaped white flowers are ⅜–⅝″ wide. They have 5 lobes and are on short pedicels rising from the leaf axils. Perennial.

Bloom Period: April to July.
*Buchanan Dam, Llano Co. side.*

## Silky Evolvulus, Shaggy Evolvulus
*Evolvulus Nuttallianus*

Silky Evolvulus may have few or nu-merous stems, with an erect to ascend-ing habit. It is usually 3–9″ tall and is most common on dry caliche soils.

Densely covered in long appressed hairs, the plants take on a strong silvery-silky look. The lanceolate to nar-rowly oblong-elliptic leaf blades are ¼–¾″ long.

The pale lavender flowers are on short pedicels in the axils of the leaves. They are ⅜–½″ wide. As with most members of the Morning Glory Family, the corolla is twisted in the bud. Perennial.

Bloom Period: April to June.
*Chapman Draw, Menard Co.*

## Texas Bindweed
*Convolvulus equitans*

Common throughout the Hill Country, Texas Bindweed is a prostrate to ascending vine. Not an ambitious climber, it usually confines itself to twining around weeds and low shrubs.

The leaves are 1–3″ long and are highly variable in shape. In gross outline, they are triangular-lanceolate, with 1–5 projecting lobes on either side of the base. Minute hairs cover the entire plant.

Axillary peduncles, equal to or longer than the leaves, carry 1–3 funnel-shaped white flowers. The flowers are ¾–1½″ wide with a purple-red throat. Perennial.

Bloom Period: April to October.
*Energy, Comanche Co.*

## Wild Potato
*Ipomoea pandurata*

*Ipomoea pandurata* is a robust twining vine which easily reaches the tops of 25′ trees. This East Texas plant is at the western limit of its range on the eastern edge of the Hill Country, where it is usually confined to the rich soils of stream and river valleys.

The heart-shaped leaves are 1½–5″ long (sometimes longer), with petioles 1–3″ long. Soft, fine hairs cover the underside of the leaf, while the upper surface is essentially glabrous or sparsely covered with very minute hairs.

Wild Potato has showy white flowers 3″ long and 3½″ wide with purple-red throats. Each peduncle carries 1 or several flowers. Perennial.

Bloom Period: June and July.
*Twin Sisters, Blanco Co.*

## Lindheimer's Morning Glory
*Ipomoea Lindheimeri*

Lindheimer's Morning Glory is a hardy twining vine that does well in full sun under dry conditions. It may sprawl prostrate in the grass, climb to 6′ in low brush, or clamber over the fractured rock of roadcuts. Found in the southern half of our area, it is usually scattered and infrequent, but it is common along Hwy. 281 from the Hwy. 71 intersection to Burnet.

The deeply 3–7 lobed leaves are 1–3½″ long, and are often wider than long. Both the upper and lower leaf surfaces are covered with short, straight hairs.

Opening in the morning and closing before noon, the light blue to lavender flowers are 2–3″ long by 2–3″ wide with white centers. They are apparently solitary on peduncles 1–3½″ long rising from the leaf axils. Five lanceolate to narrowly lanceolate sepals up to 1¼″ long clasp the base of the flowers. Perennial.

Bloom Period: April to October.
*Marble Falls, Burnet Co.*

## Purple Bindweed
*Ipomoea trichocarpa*

Besides its natural habitat, Purple Bindweed shows a partiality for such disturbed soils as flower beds and gardens, and in those situations is widely perceived as an undesirable weedy pest. This low-climbing, twining vine is found throughout the Hill Country.

Its leaves are variable in shape and may be heart-shaped or deeply 3-lobed. They average 1½–2½" long.

Each peduncle may carry one or several flowers. The flowers have pink or rose corollas with a dark purple-red throat, and average 1–1½" long by about 2" wide. Perennial.

Bloom Period: April to October.
*Kyle, Hays Co.*

## Alamo Vine
*Ipomoea sinuata*
*(Merremia dissecta)*

Unlike most members of the Morning Glory Family, Alamo Vine does not open its flowers in the early morning. They open an hour or two before or after noon, blooming in the heat of the day and closing before sunset. *I. sinuata* is a trailing or low climbing vine that is found in the southern half of our area in stream valleys, dry fields, and disturbed soils.

Ovate-orbicular in gross outline, the glabrous leaves are 1½–2½" long, with 5–7 palmate lobes. Each lobe may have a sinuate margin or be deeply incised. The petioles are ¾–1¼" long.

The white flowers have a purple-red center and are about 1½–2" wide. They are normally solitary on a peduncle up to 2" long. Perennial.

Bloom Period: May to October.
*Guadalupe R., Gruene, Comal Co.*

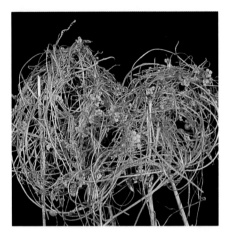

### Dodder, Angel Hair
*Cuscuta* sp.

Dodder is a parasitic twining vine with no roots or leaves. It depends on the juices of other plants for its nourishment. There are 24 species found in Texas, many of which are specific to certain types of host.

The plant in the illustration has yellow-orange to orange stems and cymes of small white flowers about ⅛" long. It was found growing on a patch of Texas Bluebonnets (*Lupinus texensis*), apparently with a strongly detrimental effect. The host Bluebonnets had either no flowers or sickly looking ones.

Bloom Period: Spring.
*Hwy. 71, Llano Co.*

### Cut-Leaf Gilia
*Gilia incisa*

Erect and much branched in the upper half, Cut-Leaf Gilia stands 10–18" tall, and is found on dry sandy or limestone soils.

The basal leaves are long petioled for ½ to ⅔ of their length, with the blade deeply (and asymmetrically) incised to near the midrib. On the upper stem, the leaves are incised to the point of appearing jaggedly toothed, but then become linear near the flowers. They are ⅜–1½" long.

The light purple-blue flowers (¼–⅜" wide) are usually solitary on peduncles 1–1½" long. Each flower has 5 linear sepals (with wide membranaceous wings) which are united for ¼ of their length.

Bloom Period: April to June.
*Near Camp Stanley, Bexar Co.*

### Standing Cypress, Texas Plume
*Ipomopsis rubra*

In its first year, *Ipomopsis rubra* forms a low rosette of divided, threadlike leaves. The second year, it puts up a simple, unbranched stem 2–5' tall and blooms. This attractive plant is found on rocky or sandy ground in the northern two-thirds of our area.

The leaves are 1–2" long, and are divided into numerous long, threadlike segments.

Standing Cypress has orange-red to red tubular flowers up to about 1¼" long, opening ½–⅝" wide. Its linear sepals are ¼–⅜" long, united by a thin membrane ⅓ to ½ the way up from the base. Biennial.

Bloom Period: May and June.
*Wimberly, Hays Co.*

## Blue Gilia
*Gilia rigidula* var. *rigidula*

The deep blue flowers of *G. rigidula*,
with their bright yellow throats, contrast strongly with the cream-colored
caliche they prefer to live on. Under
harsh conditions, the plant may be only
3″ tall, erect with several branches and
a few flowers. In a favorable environment, Blue Gilia can become a low,
spreading, bushy plant 4–10″ high
with dozens of flowers scattered across
the top.

Incised to the midrib, the leaves are
divided into 3–7 linear or threadlike
segments and are up to 1¼″ long. Both
the stems and the leaves are covered in
fine glandular hairs, causing some
plants to be sticky to the touch.

The flowers (⅜–¾″ in diameter) are
solitary on peduncles ¼–1″ long, and
have 5 sepals united by a translucent
membrane for ½ to ⅔ of their length.

Bloom Period: March to July.
*Scalp Creek, Menard Co.*

### Drummond Phlox
*Phlox Drummondii* var. *McAllisteri*

Drummond Phlox is usually thought of as a plant of the sandy soils of East Texas. However, there are 6 varieties of *Phlox Drummondii*, one of which, var. *McAllisteri*, is common in the Hill Country area. Somewhat variable in its growth habit, it may have several stems shortly radiating straight out from the base and then strongly ascending, or may have essentially prostrate stems rising only at the tips. Growing 6–18″ tall, it is most common on the sandy soils of the Llano region, but also does well on calcareous soils.

Opposite to nearly opposite on the lower part of the stem, the sessile to clasping leaves become alternate on the upper stem. They are lanceolate to oblanceolate (often abruptly contracted at the base of the blade), averaging 3–5 times longer than wide. All plants are covered in long hairs which are more or less glandular, resulting in some plants that are soft to the touch and others that are distinctly sticky.

The deep rose to pink flowers are ⅝–⅞″ wide, usually with a pale eye in the center, set off by a slender-rayed star that is slightly darker than the petal color. United for about ⅓ their length, the narrow sepals are ¼–⅜″ long. Annual.

Bloom Period: March to June.
*Near Bend, Lampasas Co.*

## Golden-Eye Phlox
*Phlox Roemeriana*

Growing throughout the Hill Country on dry limestone soils, Golden-Eye Phlox is usually a low plant 3–5″ tall with one or a few branches and one or a few flowers. In parts of Uvalde and Medina counties, it grows to 12″ tall, with several or numerous branches and many flowers.

Oblanceolate and opposite on the lower stem, the leaves become lanceolate and alternate above, with ciliate margins (fringed with hairs).

The flowers are similar to those of Drummond Phlox, having in addition a bright yellow eye. The sepals are up to ⅝″ long and are united for ⅓–½ their length. Annual.

Bloom Period: February to May.
*Mother Neff State Park, Coryell Co.*

## Prairie Phlox
*Phlox pilosa* ssp. *pilosa*

Prairie Phlox grows in clumps with several erect, unbranched stems rising 6–18″ from a semi-woody base. Scattered throughout the Hill Country, but common nowhere, it can be found in open grasslands and by the roadside.

All of the leaves are opposite, except for a few directly below the inflorescence. Linear to narrowly lanceolate, the leaves are up to 2½″ long by ³⁄₁₆″ wide. The leaf surfaces vary from pubescent to almost glabrous.

The inflorescence is a panicle composed of small cymes. Individual flowers are about 1″ wide and may be rose, pink, lavender, or white. The sepals average ⅜″ long, united for ½ their length or less. Perennial.

Bloom Period: March to May.
*Meridian State Park, Bosque Co.*

## Blue Phacelia
*Phacelia patuliflora*

## Baby Blue-Eyes
*Nemophila phacelioides*

Baby Blue-Eyes has erect or lax and reclining stems 6–18″ high, and is found in the moist, shady woodlands of canyons and river valleys.

Its stems and leaves are covered with long white hairs. The oblong leaves reach 3″ in length and are pinnately divided into 5–11 segments, some of which are 3–5 lobed.

Light blue to light purple, with a large white eye, the flowers (½–¾″ wide) may be solitary on long axillary peduncles or in few-flowered terminal cymes. Five earlike appendages separate the 5 sepals. Annual.

Bloom Period: March to May.
*Barton Creek, Austin, Travis Co.*

Given a wet Spring, Blue Phacelia will form massive displays at the partially shaded edge of woods and smaller displays in full sun. Scattered throughout the Hill Country in widely separated populations, *P. patuliflora* is most common in Llano and Burnet counties. It has erect to reclining stems 4–12″ tall and can be found on sandy or calcareous soils.

Oblong to broadly oval, the pubescent, pinnately lobed leaves are 1–2½″ long. The lower leaves are long petiolate, while the upper leaves are sessile.

The light blue to lavender flowers (⅜–¾″ across) have a white center and are broadly campanulate. They are numerous on scorpioid cymes (which straighten when carrying the alternately arranged, globose capsules). The linear-lanceolate sepals are up to ½″ long. Annual.

Bloom Period: March to April.
*W. of Burnet, Burnet Co.*

## Blue-Curls
*Phacelia congesta*

Blue Curls is an erect, branching plant 1–3' tall found on all soil types throughout the Hill Country.

Ovate in gross outline, the leaves are once to twice pinnate, or once pinnate with the segments pinnately lobed. They may be 1½–4" long.

The flowers are carried in a cluster of scorpioid cymes which are reminiscent of the suckered underside of an octopus. The individual flowers are about ¼" long, blue, and bell-shaped. Long filaments exsert the bright yellow stamens well past the throat of the flower. The curled cymes straighten when carrying the fruit, which is an ovoid capsule. Annual or biennial.

Bloom Period: March to May.
*Stillhouse Hollow Reservoir, Bell Co.*

## Sand Bells
*Nama hispidum*

Widely distributed across the Hill Country, Sand Bells can be found on both sandy or limestone-derived soils. It is an erect, broadly branching plant with one or several stems rising from the base and reaching 3–12" in height.

The stems and leaves are covered in strigose hairs. The alternate leaves are linear-oblong and are ½–1¼" long.

The pink to light purple flowers have yellow throats and are solitary or in few-flowered terminal groups. Individual flowers are up to ⅜" long by ½" wide (but on average are smaller) with funnel or bell-shaped corollas. Annual.

Bloom Period: April to July.
*Cibolo Creek, Bexar Co.*

## White Cordia
*Cordia podocephala*

A South Texas species, White Cordia can be found on dry, rocky sites in the extreme southern portion of our area in Bexar, Medina, and Uvalde counties. It is a low, herbaceous to semi-woody plant with several erect stems 1–2′ tall rising from a woody rootstock.

Strigose, antrorse hairs cover the stems and leaves. The lanceolate to oblanceolate leaves are up to 2″ long and have coarsely serrate margins.

The inflorescence is a dense globose head, ¼–⅜″ thick, on a peduncle up to 6″ long. The individual flowers have delicate, funnel-shaped, white corollas about ½″ wide. Perennial.

Bloom Period: April to June.
*Near Concan, Uvalde Co.*

## Anacua, Knock-Away
*Ehretia Anacua*

In our area, Anacua is a large shrub or a tree growing as tall as 30′. It is a South Texas plant that is susceptible to freeze damage in the Hill Country and is largely confined to protected river valleys and canyons. It reaches the northernmost limit of its range along the Colorado River in Travis Co.

Partially deciduous to evergreen, the leaves are 1½–3″ long. They are elliptic-ovate to broadly lanceolate and may be entire or dentate. Mineralized disks surround rough, antrorse hairs on the upper leaf surface, giving it the texture of a medium sandpaper.

The fragrant, terminal inflorescence is composed of white, star-shaped flowers about ⅜″ wide.

Bloom Period: April.
*Landa Park, New Braunfels, Comal Co.*

## Oreja de Perro, Dog's Ear
*Coldenia canescens*
*(Tiquilia canescens)*

Dog's Ear is a low growing, spreading, semi-shrubby plant 1–4″ high found on dry caliche soils. It is a West Texas plant that ranges east into Kimble and Uvalde counties.

A dense covering of long, soft white hairs gives the leaves an overall gray appearance. The elliptic leaves are ⅜–⅝″ long and are pointed at the ends. They tend to be slightly curled.

The flowers are small (³⁄₁₆–¼″ wide) and may be white, pale pink, or rose-colored. Perennial.

Bloom Period: April and May.
*Teacup Mt., Kimble Co.*

## Turnsole
*Heliotropium indicum*

Turnsole is an erect, loosely branched plant 1–2½′ tall. It is mainly an East Texas plant, but does occur along watercourses in various locations throughout our area.

The distinctive ovate to elliptic leaves have a rugose surface and an undulate margin. They are 1–5″ long, on petioles ½–1½″ long. Long white hairs sparsely cover the stem and confine themselves to the petiole and main veins on the underside of the leaf but are randomly and thinly scattered on the upper surface.

Two ranks of flowers line an elongate scorpioid cyme 3–10″ long (which straightens as the fruits mature). The pale blue to violet flowers are ⅛–³⁄₁₆″ long by about ⅛″ wide. Annual.

Bloom Period: July to October.
*Lambs Creek, Kerr Co.*

## White Heliotrope
*Heliotropium tenellum*

White Heliotrope is an erect, bushy, much-branched plant 6–18″ tall found on dry hillsides and along roadsides in rocky soils.

Minute antrorse, strigose hairs cover the stems and leaves, giving them a mildly gray-green appearance. The linear leaves are up to 2″ long by ⅛″ wide.

The white, funnel-shaped flowers have yellow throats and are arranged in elongate, loose, racemose cymes. Individual flowers are ³⁄₁₆–¼″ long and ⅛–³⁄₁₆″ wide. Annual.

Bloom Period: May to October.
*Near Kendalia, Kendall Co.*

## Puccoon
*Lithospermum incisum*

Puccoon has several erect stems 6–12″ tall rising from a woody root. It can be found throughout our area, in all soil types.

The stems and leaves are covered in closely appressed, strigose, antrorse hairs. The linear to linear-lanceolate stem leaves are 1–2″ long.

Puccoon produces two sets of flowers. The showy Spring flowers, illustrated above, are bright yellow and trumpet-shaped. They are about 1″ long by ⅜–½″ wide and are mostly sterile (produce no seed). In late Spring and Summer, small fertile cleistogamous flowers (less than ⅛″ long) are produced. They escape notice since they are hidden within the bracts. These self-fertilizing flowers never open, but are responsible for seed production. Perennial.

Bloom Period: March to May.
*Four Points, Travis Co.*

## Marble-Seed
*Onosmodium Helleri*

*Onosmodium Helleri* is an erect to partially reclining plant 1–1½' tall that is usually protected in the shade of moist woodlands, stream valleys, or other drainages. It is uncommon, almost to the point of being rare, and has been collected in Travis and Kendall counties.

Elliptic to oblong-elliptic, the short-petiolate, bright green leaves are up to 4½" long by 2½" broad. The lower leaves are often spatulate.

The white to greenish-white flowers are short, about ¼–⅜" long, with linear sepals ³⁄₁₆–¼" long. Perennial.

Bloom Period: March and April.
*River Hills Rd., Travis Co.*

## False Gromwell
*Onosmodium bejariense*
*(Onosmodium molle* var. *bejariense)*

False Gromwell has erect stems 1–3' tall that are usually simple but sometimes branch in the upper third. It is found on the southeastern edge of the Hill Country along a line between Medina and Travis counties, exposed to the sun in colonies in open woodlands or by the roadside.

Short, strigose, antrorse hairs cover the stems and dull green leaves. The sessile, lanceolate leaves are up to 4" long by ¾" wide and are strongly nerved.

Greenish-white to cream-colored, the corolla is about ½–⅝" long. The linear sepals are ¼–⅜" long. Perennial.

Bloom Period: April to May.
*Near Spring Branch, Comal Co.*

## Texas Vervain
*Verbena Halei*

Texas Vervain grows 6–18″ tall, with 1 or several erect stems rising from a woody base. It tends to be divided into multiple ascending branches in its upper half (where it is essentially glabrous) and is common throughout the state in open grassy areas.

In gross outline, the 1–3″ midstem leaves may be lanceolate, oblong, or ovate, and are 1–2 times pinnatifid. The leaves of the upper stem are entire to sparsely dentate, becoming narrowly linear on the flowering branches.

The numerous purple-blue flowers are in panicle-like spikes 2–7″ long. They are about ⅛″ across, with a floral tube that exceeds the calyx by ¹⁄₁₆″. Perennial.

Bloom Period: March to June.
*Buchanan Dam, Llano Co. side.*

## Gray Vervain
*Verbena canescens*

Gray Vervain's common name derives from its dense covering of short spreading hairs, which gives it a dusty, gray-green appearance. It has several erect to reclining stems 3–15″ tall and is found on dry soils.

The leaves (⅜–1½″) are lanceolate to oblanceolate in outline, and are shallowly incised-dentate to almost pinnatifid. Raised veins are found on the underside of the leaf, while the upper surface is somewhat rugose.

Small lavender or purple flowers (⅛″ wide) are arranged in spikes 3–6″ long. The sessile or short-stalked flowers each have a calyx about ⅛″ long, and are subtended by a lanceolate bract. Perennial.

Bloom Period: April to October.
*Twin Sisters, Blanco Co.*

## Dakota Vervain, Prairie Verbena
*Verbena bipinnatifida*
*(Glandularia bipinnatifida)*

This species is probably the most attractive Vervain that we have in the Hill
Country. Reclining stems up to 2' long,
with ascending tips, radiate from the
base. Dakota Vervain is usually 4–12"
high and is found in open grassy
places throughout our area.

The petiolate leaves (1–2½" long)
may be simple and twice pinnatifid, or
3-parted with each part twice pinnatifid. In either case, the lobes are linear to oblong.

Individual flowers are ¼" wide, with
a floral tube half again as long as the
calyx. The inflorescence is a peduncu-
late, compressed spike which elongates
in fruit. Perennial.

Bloom Period: March to October.
*Grapetown, Gillespie Co.*

## Pink Vervain, Low Verbena
*Verbena pumila*
*(Glandularia pumila)*

Pink Vervain develops several reclining-ascending stems from its base, reaching a height of 6–12". It is found in open grasslands throughout our area.

Its leaves are ¾–1¼" long (occasionally to 2") and are 3-parted, each part lobed and incised. The base of the leaf is wedge-shaped, creating a short, margined petiole.

The inflorescence is a compressed spike which elongates to about 1¾" in fruit. The pink to lavender flowers are ⅛–¼" across, with a floral tube that is barely longer than the calyx. Annual.

Bloom Period: February to April.
*Marble Falls, Burnet Co.*

## Bee-Brush, White-Brush
*Aloysia gratissima*

Bee-Brush is a slender, diffuse shrub 3–9' tall. It is found on dry limestone or granitic soils virtually throughout our area, except for a few counties in the northeastern portion.

The gray stems are usually sparsely covered with leaves ¼–1" long. The leaf blades are elliptic to oblanceolate, with entire margins, on short petioles about ⅛" long. There are often bundles of smaller leaves in the axils of the main leaves.

Numerous erect to ascending flower spikes ¾–2½" long rise from the axils of the leaves. The individual flowers are ⅛–³⁄₁₆" long and slightly less wide.

Bloom Period: March to October.
*Enchanted Rock State Park, Llano Co.*

## Texas Lantana, Calico Bush
*Lantana horrida*

Texas Lantana is an adaptable, much-branched shrub 2–6' tall that can be found in almost any habitat the Hill Country offers.

Square in cross-section, the young stems soon become rounded with age, and may be smooth or armed with re-curved prickles. The opposite, ovate to subtriangular leaves are 1–3" long with petioles ⅛–½" long. The leaf blades are truncate to subtruncate at the base and have coarsely toothed margins.

The inflorescence is 1–3" across and is composed of yellow and red-orange flowers ¼–⅜" long and ⅛–¼" wide. The 1–3" peduncles slightly surpass the leaves.

Bloom Period: Spring to Fall.
*Sattler, Comal Co.*

## American Beautyberry
*Callicarpa americana*

Found on the eastern edge of our area, American Beautyberry is an open, much-branched shrub growing to 7' in height. It prefers the moist soils of canyons and bottomlands.

The ovate to elliptic leaves are 3–8" long, on cuneately narrowed petioles. The leaf margins are coarsely serrate to crenate-dentate.

Many-flowered cymes cluster at the nodes, with numerous small flowers that may be white, pink, red, or blue. These soon become a showy cluster of pink to reddish-purple fruits.

Bloom Period: May to July.
*Krause Springs, Spicewood, Burnet Co.*

## Frog-Fruit
*Phyla incisa*
*(Phyla nodiflora var. incisa)*

Frog-Fruit is a low plant 3–5" high, with creeping, prostrate stems. Commonly an invader of lawns, it can also be found in the moister soils of roadsides, fields, and bottomlands throughout our area.

Rooting at the nodes, the ground-hugging stems are up to 3' long. The leaf-blades are spatulate to oblanceolate with a cuneate base. They average ½–1¾" long, and are serrate above the middle of the blade.

Globe-like at first, the flower heads expand and become cylindric, sometimes approaching 1" in length. They are carried on axillary peduncles up to 4" long. The individual flowers are usually white. Perennial.

Bloom Period: May to October.
*Zilker Park, Austin, Travis Co.*

## American Germander, Wood Sage
*Teucrium canadense*

American Germander can be found on the moist soils of rivers, streams, and ditches throughout our area. It may have 1 or several erect stems 1–3' tall.

Narrowly elliptic to ovate, the opposite leaves are 2–4" long by 1–1¾" wide, with toothed margins.

The flowers are in dense spikes up to 8" long. Each flower has a short peduncle about ⅛" long and is subtended by a small bract slightly longer than the calyx. Individual flowers are ½–¾" long and may be white, light pink, or pale lavender, with purple-red lines. Perennial.

Bloom Period: May to July.
*Town Lake, Austin, Travis Co.*

## Cut-Leaf Germander
*Teucrium laciniatum*

Ranging through West Texas and the Plains Country, Cut-Leaf Germander extends to the Edwards Plateau and the northwestern edge of our area, where it is found on dry calcareous soils. It normally has several erect stems 2–7" tall.

The ½–1¼" leaves are pinnately incised nearly to the midrib, forming numerous narrow or linear lobes (which are often branched). This plant is sometimes confused with *T. cubense*, a species of the Gulf Coast, whose broadly lobed leaves are incised no more than halfway to the midrib.

Crowded toward the tip of the stem, the ½" long flowers are white to cream-colored with purple-red lines in the throat. Perennial.

Bloom Period: April to June.
*Hwy. 29 at FM 1311, Menard Co.*

## Bushy Skullcap
*Scutellaria Wrightii*
*(Scutellaria resinosa)*

Driving through the hills, you may see small (6–12" high), rounded, bushy masses of purple and white flowers on roadcuts and caliche banks. Bushy Skullcap has numerous erect and curved-erect woody branches combining into a compact, rounded shape. It is found on rocky slopes in xeric conditions.

The oval leaves reach ⅜" in length and are covered with minute hairs.

Violet-blue, the flowers are approximately ⅜" long, with the stamens attached about ³⁄₁₆" above the base of the floral tube. Perennial.

Bloom Period: March to June.
*Near Cranfills Gap, Bosque Co.*

## Drummond's Skullcap
*Scutellaria Drummondii*

Drummond's Skullcap develops several erect to reclining herbaceous stems 6–12" tall, which rise from the base in a loose, open configuration. It is very common and can be found on moist or dry calcareous soils throughout our area.

Soft, spreading hairs are found on the stems, especially in the upper sections. The ovate leaves are ¼–¾" long, with short petioles on the lower part of the stem, but becoming sessile on the upper part of the stem.

The violet to purple flowers are ¼–½" long. Long hairs are found growing on the calyx. Annual.

Bloom Period: March to April.
*E. of Leakey, Real Co.*

## Heart-Leaf Skullcap
*Scutellaria ovata* var. *bracteata*

Small colonies of Heart-Leaf Skullcap can be found around granite boulders on the Llano Uplift. It has several erect stems 1–2′ tall (usually unbranched) which are covered with spreading, glandular hairs.

Softly pubescent on the upper and lower surfaces, the ovate to heart-shaped leaves are 1½–2½″ long with coarsely crenate-dentate margins. They are on petioles ⅛–1″ long.

The light to deep purple flowers are ¾–1″ long. They are carried in racemes 2–5″ long, each flower rising from the axil of an ovate bract ¼–⅜″ long. Annual.

Bloom Period: April to June.
*Inks Lake State Park, Burnet Co.*

## Prairie Brazoria
*Brazoria scutellarioides*

Prairie Brazoria often forms extensive colonies along roadsides on calcareous soils. Branched in the upper third or half, it is a small, erect plant 6–12″ tall, though it may grow to 18″.

All parts are essentially glabrous, except for the inflorescence, which is covered in a very minute pubescence. Sessile above to clasping at the base, the ¾–1½″ leaves are oblanceolate to oblong-spatulate, with several teeth above the middle of the blade.

The pink flowers are ⅜–⅝″ long, in panicles up to 6″ long. Ovate or lanceolate bracts ⅛–¼″ long underlie each flower. The calyx is strongly two-lipped. Annual.

Bloom Period: April to June.
*Concan, Uvalde Co.*

## Obedient-Plant
*Physostegia intermedia*

Obedient-Plant has erect, simple stems 1–3' tall. Though common in South and East Texas, it is uncommon in the Hill Country and is found only on the extreme eastern edge of our area along a line between McLennan and Travis counties. It prefers the alluvial soils of creeks and rivers.

The opposite, linear-lanceolate to linear-oblanceolate leaves are petiolate near the base of the plant and sessile in the upper sections. They are ¾–2½" long, with a slightly sinuate or dentate margin.

Pale lavender-pink or white flowers ½–¾" long are carried on slender spikes 2–6" long. The calyx of each flower is ⅛–³⁄₁₆" long. For all practical purposes, *P. intermedia* is essentially identical to *P. angustifolia* in every respect except its size, in which regard it is consistently smaller. Perennial.

Bloom Period: May and June.
*Salado Creek, Salado, Bell Co.*

## False Dragon-Head
*Physostegia angustifolia*

False Dragon-Head is the largest and most common plant of this genus found growing in the Hill Country area. It has one or a few erect stems up to 4' tall and is found on moist soils in or near creeks and rivers, on limestone or granite.

Near the base of the plant, the leaves sometimes have petioles about ¾" long. Going up the stem, the narrowly lanceolate to oblanceolate leaves become sessile, and may be as long as 5".

Marked with purple lines and spots, the flowers may be pale purple, pink, or whitish, on spikes 3–9" long. Individual flowers are 1–1¼" long, with a calyx ¼–⅜" long. Perennial.

Bloom Period: June and July.
*Slaughter Creek, Travis Co.*

## Beautiful False Dragon-Head
*Physostegia pulchella*

This East Texas species reaches our area only in McLennan county, but deserves recognition and widespread cultivation. Beautiful False Dragon-Head (the most colorful of our local *Physostegia* species) spreads by rhizomes to form colonies of plants 1–3' tall along streams or in wet depressions.

The basal leaves have slender petioles up to 3" long, while the topmost leaves are sessile. They reach 5" in length and are oblanceolate to oblong-elliptic, with subentire to dentate margins.

The ¾–1¼" flowers may be lavender-pink or deep reddish-purple. A minute pubescence covers the stem and the calyces of the inflorescence. Perennial.

Bloom Period: May and June.
*Waco, McLennan Co.*

## Henbit
*Lamium amplexicaule*

Native to Europe, Henbit has become naturalized throughout North America. It grows 6–16″ tall, with erect to reclining-ascending stems which branch from the base. It is found in lawns, disturbed soils, and grassy areas.

Near the base of the stem, the leaves have slender petioles. The upper leaves are clasping. They are broadly ovate to reniform, with coarsely crenate margins.

The reddish-purple flowers stand erect in axillary and terminal clusters, averaging ½–⅝″ long. Annual to biennial.

Bloom Period: February to May.
*Cedar Park, Williamson Co.*

## Lyre-Leaf Sage
*Salvia lyrata*

The greater part of this plant's range is in East Texas, but it is occasionally found in the Hill Country. Lyre-Leaf Sage grows 1–2′ tall from a basal rosette of leaves, in moist, open, grassy areas.

The oblanceolate leaves of the basal rosette are up to 10″ in overall length, with long petioles. The blade of the leaf is sinuately to lyrately pinnatifid, often with purple veins and a purple tinge. Only one or two pairs of much reduced leaves are carried on the stem itself.

Up to 10″ long, the inflorescence is composed of widely separated whorls of pale-blue flowers. Each flower is about 1″ long, in a calyx ¼–⅜″ long. Perennial.

Bloom Period: March to May.
*Near Henley, Hays Co.*

## Blue Sage
*Salvia texana*

Blue Sage usually has only a few spreading-ascending stems, forming a loosely open plant 6–15″ tall. It is found on dry, rocky soils throughout the Hill Country area.

Beneath the long, spreading stem hairs are minute, retrorse hairs on all 4 sides of the stem. There tend to be only 4–6 nodes below the inflorescence. The oblanceolate leaves are up to 2″ long, with a few teeth on the upper two-thirds of the blade.

The inflorescence is a raceme of purple to dark blue flowers ¾–1″ long. Dense white hairs close the throat of the ⅜″ calyx. Perennial.

Bloom Period: March to May.
*Near Valley Mills, Bosque Co.*

## Engelmann's Salvia
*Salvia Engelmannii*

Forming dense, bushy clumps, Engelmann's Salvia grows 6–16″ tall with numerous erect stems. Like its close relative, *S. texana*, it is found throughout the Hill Country on dry, rocky, limestone soils.

Beneath the long, spreading hairs of the stems are minute retrorse hairs. These very small hairs are found on all sides of the stem except for the internode face directly below the opposite leaves. The narrowly oblanceolate leaves are 1½–3″ long.

The ¾″ flowers are pale purple to pale blue, sometimes to the point of appearing white from a distance. A dense ring of white hairs closes the throat of the ⅜–½″ calyx. Perennial.

Bloom Period: April and May.
*Bee Cave Rd., Travis Co.*

## Cedar Sage
*Salvia Roemeriana*

Cedar Sage prefers rocky, shaded woods, usually in or at the edge of a canyon. It will often have one to several erect to partially reclining stems 1–2' tall. Though it is scattered throughout our area, the greatest concentrations of plants are on the southern and south-eastern edges of the Hill Country.

The leaves are pubescent on both surfaces, with the longest hairs on the main veins of the underside of the blade. On the upper part of the plant, the leaves are simple, with a rounded kidney-shaped or heart-shaped blade at the end of a long petiole. On the lower part of the plant, the leaves are sometimes compound, with a pair of smaller lateral leaflets near the base of the petiole of the main leaf. The leaf margins have coarse, rounded teeth.

Brilliantly red, the 1–1¼" flowers are loosely spaced on the elongate raceme. The strongly two-lipped calyx is ¼–⅝" long. Perennial.

Bloom Period: March to July.
*Ranger Creek, Boerne, Kendall Co.*

## Shrubby Blue Sage, Mejorana
*Salvia ballotaeflora*

Of the *Salvia* species mentioned here, Mejorana is the only one with a woody habit. It forms a highly branched shrub up to 6' tall on dry, rocky soils on the southern edge of the Hill Country. A few specimens grow as far north as Blanco and Hays counties.

Ovate-deltoid to oblong-elliptic, the leaves are ½–1¼" long on petioles up to ½" long. They are coarsely dentate to crenate, with a rugose (wrinkled) surface.

The light blue ½" flowers have a flattened, funnel-like shape, and rise from a ⅜" calyx. The previous year's flowering stems persist as dead twigs, giving the plant a somewhat scraggly appearance.

Bloom Period: April to June.
*S. of Leakey, Real Co.*

## Mealy Sage
*Salvia farinacea*

Mealy Sage forms a low clump with one or a few flowering stalks rising 1–3' high from the base. A common plant, it is found on dry, limestone soils virtually throughout our area.

The leaves on the lower part of the plant tend to have longer petioles than those on the upper part. The 1–3" leaves are linear-lanceolate to ovate-lanceolate with coarsely toothed margins. Slender, leafy branchlets rise from the axils of the main leaves near the inflorescence.

Whorls of violet-blue flowers ½–1" long are spaced along the spike-like inflorescence. The calyces have a smokey violet-blue tinge. Perennial.

Bloom Period: April and May.
*S.W. of Brady, McCulloch Co.*

## Giant Blue Sage
*Salvia azurea*

Giant Blue Sage grows 3–6' tall, usually with a single erect, stout stem, branching in the upper half. It prefers dry soils in open, grassy situations.

The lowermost leaves are lanceolate to oblanceolate and up to 4" long, with serrate margins. These leaves often fall away during flowering. The uppermost leaves are linear, with entire margins.

Though the ½–1" flowers can vary from deep to light blue, in our area they are most often light blue. Unlike *S. farinacea*, the calyces are green. Perennial.

Bloom Period: September to October. *Kerrville, Kerr Co.*

## Tropical Sage
*Salvia coccinea*

Tropical Sage is an erect to reclining plant 6–30" tall. It is thinly scattered through the Hill Country area and is usually found on sandy soils or alluvium.

Long, spreading hairs cover the stems. The leaf blades are deltoid, with a cordate or truncate base and rounded or blunted teeth. The leaves on young plants have petioles ¼–1½" long; on older plants petiole length tends to be reduced to the point that the leaves are virtually sessile.

The scarlet-red flowers are 1" long, on a raceme with several well-separated whorls. Perennial.

Bloom Period: February to October. *Pedernales R., Blanco Co.*

## Basil Beebalm
*Monarda clinopodioides*

Basil Beebalm is most common in our area on the sandy soils of the Llano Uplift. It normally has one or a few simple stems 8–15″ high.

Minute, downwardly curved hairs cover the stems. The ¾–2″ leaves may be elliptic, lanceolate, or oblanceolate, with serrate or entire margins. The petioles tend to be short, averaging ¼–½″ in length.

The inflorescence is composed of several whorls of flowers in an interrupted spike. On a given day, a few light pink to white flowers ¾″ long will emerge from the densely clustered, numerous bracts. The bracts are elliptic, with raised veins. The calyx teeth reduce to threadlike tips ³⁄₁₆–¼″ long. Annual.

Bloom Period: April to July.
*Inks Lake State Park, Burnet Co.*

## Spotted Beebalm
*Monarda punctata*

Spotted Beebalm prefers the sandy soils of the Llano Uplift, but some of its varieties have been found on caliche in scattered locations across the Hill Country. It may have a few or several ascending branches 1–2′ tall.

The petiolate, lanceolate to oblanceolate leaves are up to 3″ long with subentire to serrate margins. Short, leaf-bearing branchlets often grow in the axils of the main stem leaves.

Yellow to whitish-cream in color, the flowers are dotted with light brown or purple spots. Unlike our other *Monarda* species, the calyx teeth of Spotted Beebalm are not threadlike, but are deltoid to lanceolate. Annual to perennial.

Bloom Period: May and June.
*Lake Buchanan, Llano Co. side.*

## Purple Horsemint, Lemon Beebalm
*Monarda citriodora*

Purple Horsemint grows 1–2½' tall, usually with several stems rising from the base. It is a common plant throughout Texas, often forming large, picturesque colonies up to several acres in extent. In the Hill Country area, *M. citriodora* is most abundant in the southeastern quadrant.

Small, stiff, downwardly curved hairs cover the stems. The lanceolate to oblanceolate leaves have blades 1–2½" long on petioles up to 1¼" long. The leaf margins vary from subentire to serrate.

Strongly two-lipped, the ¾" flowers are pink to light purple, and are often abundantly dotted with purple spots. Purple coloration on the upper surface of the elliptic to oblanceolate bracts compounds the beauty of the inflorescence. The calyces are light green with threadlike calyx teeth ⅛–¼" long. Annual to biennial.

Bloom Period: May to July.
*Hamilton Pool Rd., Travis Co.*

## Spearmint
*Mentha spicata*

## Common Horehound
*Marrubium vulgare*

This adaptable, weedy pest has a low, bushy habit (1–2' tall) with several erect to reclining-ascending stems branching from the base. Introduced from Eurasia, it can now be found throughout the state.

A fine white wool covers the stems, especially towards the base of the plant. The leaf blade and petiole together are about 2" long. Oval to broadly ovate, the blades have a crenate-dentate margin and a markedly rugose (wrinkled) surface.

The white to cream-colored flowers (³⁄₁₆" long) are in clusters in the axils of the uppermost leaves. Perennial.

Bloom Period: April to July.
*E. of Leakey, Real Co.*

Spearmint is an erect, branched plant 1–2' tall which has been introduced from Europe. It is a moisture-loving species that is found in seep areas and along streams.

The stems often have a purple tint, especially near the base. Up to 2" long, the leaves are oblanceolate to ovate-lanceolate with sharp serrations on the margins. The leaves are sessile to short-petiolate. Crushed leaves exhibit the characteristic "spearmint" odor.

Carried in slender, terminal spikes 1–2¼" long, the pale-lavender flowers are grouped in discreet whorls. Each whorl is subtended by linear bracts which are longer than the calyces. Perennial.

Bloom Period: June to September.
*Honey Creek, Llano Co.*

## Mock Pennyroyal
*Hedeoma Drummondii*

Mock Pennyroyal usually has few to numerous reclining-ascending stems 6–24″ long, commonly averaging about 1′ tall. It is found in grassy areas on dry, rocky soils.

Minute, stiff, downwardly-curled hairs cover the stems. The ¼–½″ leaves are linear-elliptic to obovate with short petioles. Most of the leaves have entire margins but a few are mildly crenate. At the time of flowering, many of the lower leaves fall away.

White to pale lavender, each flower is only ¼″ long, in a calyx ⅛–³⁄₁₆″ long. Annual to perennial.

Bloom Period: May to October.
*Medina Lake, Medina Co.*

## Annual Pennyroyal
*Hedeoma acinoides*

Annual Pennyroyal may grow 3–8″ tall, tending in the Hill Country area to the shorter side of that range. For a brief period in the Spring, it is common on dry limestone soils. Its stems may be erect or reclining-ascending and may be simple or multiple-branched.

A fine pubescence covers the stems in the upper half, while the lower half is bare. The ovate to elliptic leaves are ¼–1″ long and have short petioles. The leaf surfaces are glabrous and the leaf margins are entire to sparsely crenate-dentate. When crushed, the leaves have a very pleasant lemon-like odor.

The inflorescence is a crowded spike of axillary cymes, with 3–10 flowers per cyme. Individual flowers (¼–⅜″ long) are pink with a spreading lower lip. Annual.

Bloom Period: April and May.
*Lake Austin, Travis Co.*

## Purple Ground Cherry
*Physalis lobata*

Although uncommon in most of the
Hill Country, Purple Ground Cherry
can be found on dry caliche soils in the
Colorado River valley, in Kimble
county, and at the southern tip of our
area in Medina and Uvalde counties.
*P. lobata* is a low, spreading to reclining
plant 3–6″ high.

Under magnification, both the stems
and the leaves are found to be sparsely
covered with mineralized vesicles
(bubble-like structures). The 1–2″ leaves
are oblanceolate to linear-lanceolate
and are cuneately narrowed at the base
into a winged petiole. The leaf margins
are entire to sinuate to pinnatifid.

Blue to violet, the flowers are ½–¾″
across and have yellow anthers on purple filaments. A white-flowered variety
has been reported from Brown county.
The fruit is a berry enclosed in an expanded, papery calyx. Perennial.

Bloom Period: March to June.
*Near Bend, San Saba Co.*

## Yellow Ground Cherry
*Physalis viscosa* var. *cinarescens*
*(Physalis cinarescens)*

Yellow Ground Cherry is an erect to reclining plant 4–10″ tall. It is found on dry, rocky ground throughout our area.

The stems and leaves are covered in small, stellate (branched) hairs. The leaves are ovate to deltoid, with bluntly dentate to crenate margins.

The yellow corolla is ½–¾″ wide, with dark star-shaped markings in the center. An inflated calyx 1″ long by ⅝″ wide encloses the fruit, which is a berry ¼–⅜″ across. The fruiting pedicels are ½–1¾″ long. Perennial.

Bloom Period: April to October.
*N. of Troy, Bell Co.*

## False Nightshade
*Chamaesaracha sordida*
*(Chamaesaracha coniodes)*

This species of False Nightshade usually has several sprawling-reclining stems 2–5″ tall branching from the base. It is found on dry, rocky soils.

The pubescence is a mixture of a few long, spreading hairs with numerous very short hairs. The broadly lanceolate, subsessile leaves are 1–1½″ long, with margins varying from crenate to deeply pinnately lobed.

Solitary or in pairs from the axil, the yellow star-shaped flowers are ⅜–⅝″ wide on pedicels ¾–1¼″ long. Perennial.

Bloom Period: April and May.
*Lampasas, Lampasas Co.*

## Silver-Leaf Nightshade
*Solanum elaeagnifolium*

Common on dry soils throughout the Hill Country, Silver-Leaf Nightshade is an erect, bushy-branched plant 1–2½' tall.

A dense covering of tiny stellate hairs gives the stems and leaves a silvery-green or light gray-green appearance. The linear-lanceolate to oblanceolate leaves are 1½–6" long, with entire to very shallowly sinuate margins.

The 1" wide corolla is usually light blue to violet-purple, though white-flowered specimens are occasionally found. A few prickles can be found on the pedicels. The fruit is a berry ½–¾" in diameter that turns an off-yellow when mature. Perennial.

Bloom Period: April to September. *Rocksprings, Edwards Co.*

## Western Horse-Nettle
*Solanum dimidiatum*

Western Horse-Nettle is an erect, bushy plant 1–2' tall found on dry, rocky soils.

Large, stellate hairs loosely cover the stem and leaf surfaces, without altering the dark-green color of the plant. Ovate in gross outline, the 2–6" leaves are sinuately 5–7 lobed, each lobe having an entire margin. Stout prickles are distributed along the stems and on the main veins on the underside of the leaves.

The inflorescence is a few-flowered cyme with blue, violet-purple, or white flowers roughly 1" wide. The fruit is a berry ¾–1" in diameter. Perennial.

Bloom Period: April to September. *Brady, McCulloch Co.*

## Buffalo Bur
*Solanum rostratum*

Buffalo Bur grows 10–30″ tall and is found on dry, rocky soils and in waste places throughout our area.

Minute, stellate hairs cover the stems and leaves, which are well defended by numerous yellowish prickles. The leaves are 1 or 2 times pinnatifid, with rounded lobes.

The yellow 1″ flowers are arranged in racemes. The fruit is a capsule-like berry ⅜–½″ wide (enclosing numerous black seeds), protected by yellow prickles up to ⅜″ long. A similar plant, *S. citrullifolium*, which has violet-purple flowers, is found in the southwestern part of the Hill Country. Annual.

Bloom Period: May to October.
*Near Priddy, Mills Co.*

## Texas Nightshade
*Solanum triquetrum*

Texas Nightshade is an erect, single-stemmed to multiple-branched plant of dry soils. This highly variable species is commonly 1–2′ tall, but sometimes becomes a semi-climbing shrub up to 7′ tall.

The glabrous, 2″ leaves are narrowly deltoid to cordate. Some leaves may be hastately 3–5 lobed, with a lanceolate to linear middle lobe.

Five twisted, reflexed petals form a star-shaped white to violet-tinged corolla. The flowers are ⅜–⅝″ wide and tend to hang towards the ground on slender pedicels ¼–½″ long. The fruit is a bright red berry 3/16–⅜″ in diameter. Perennial.

Bloom Period: April to November.
*Zilker Park, Austin, Travis Co.*

### Jimson-Weed, Indian Apple
*Datura inoxia*

Jimson-Weed is a widely branching, bushy plant 2–4' tall. It is covered with spreading hairs. With age, the lower leaf surface becomes almost glabrous, except for the primary veins, which remain pubescent. Ovate with an asymmetric base, the leaves are up to 8" long. The white, funnel-like corolla is up to 8" long. Perennial.
    Bloom Period: April to October.
*Near McGregor, McLennan Co.*

### Desert Tobacco
*Nicotiana trigonophylla*

More common in West and South Texas, Desert Tobacco is occasional on ledges in the Hill Country. Covered in sticky, glandular hairs, it grows 3' tall, with sessile, elliptic-lanceolate leaves up to 3½" long. The inflorescence is a loose panicle-like raceme, with greenish-white to creamy-yellow flowers ½–¾" wide. Biennial to perennial.
    Bloom Period: April to October.
*Pedernales R., Travis Co.*

### Fiddle-Leaf Tobacco
*Nicotiana repanda*

Fiddle-Leaf Tobacco grows 2½' tall, with several loose branches from a central stem. The leaves are ovate to obovate, and are sometimes constricted in the middle of the blade to a fiddle-like shape. The white flowers are up to 2½" long and 1–1½" wide, emerging from a calyx up to ½" long.
    Bloom Period: March to September.
*Johnson City, Blanco Co.*

## Monkey-Flower
*Mimulus glabratus*

Monkey-Flower is an erect to reclin-ing-ascending plant 6–15″ high. It can be found in moist soils at streamside or in shallow water, and is most common in our area on the Llano Uplift.

Broadly ovate to rounded, the 1–2½″ leaves have 3–5 prominent veins and dentate margins. The uppermost leaves are sessile on the hollow stems, while the lowermost leaves have petioles which may be longer than the leaf blade.

The tubular yellow flowers are about ½–¾″ long, emerging from a bell-shaped ¼–⅜″ calyx which is red-spotted and red tinged. Perennial.

Bloom Period: March to June.
*Under Buchanan Dam, Llano Co.*

## Common Mullein
*Verbascum Thapsus*

Sending up a single erect stem as much as 6′ tall from a basal rosette of leaves, Common Mullein is easily rec-ognizable in the open fields and prai-ries of the Hill Country.

The entire plant is densely covered in a soft, woolly pubescence composed of branched hairs. At the base, the oblong to spatulate leaves reach 12″ in length and are petiolate. Towards the top of the plant, the leaves become smaller and sessile. The lower leaf margins often extend down the stem, below the point of attachment of the leaf to the stem.

Dozens of yellow flowers are carried on a crowded, elongate spike which may be up to 2′ long, if not longer. The individual flowers are about 1″ wide. Biennial.

Bloom Period: April to October.
*Meridian, Bosque Co.*

## Purple Sage, Cenizo
*Leucophyllum frutescens*

Cenizo is a shrub up to 8' tall that is found on rocky limestone hills and bluffs. In the Hill Country area, it is most common south of a line drawn between Menard and Travis counties.

An extremely dense layer of fine hairs on the leaves and young stems gives them a silvery-gray appearance. The elliptic-obovate leaves are up to 1" long, and have a rounded apex and a cuneate base. They are alternate and may be sessile or subsessile.

The lavender to light purple flowers rise from the axils of the leaves. Almost bell-shaped, they have 5 rounded corolla lobes and are about ¾" long by ¾" wide.

Bloom Period: May to October.
*Junction, Kimble Co.*

## Fox-Glove
*Penstemon Cobaea*

A common roadside plant, Fox-Glove grows 1–2½' high and is found on rocky, calcareous soils throughout the Hill Country area.

At the base, the leaves are petiolate to long petiolate. From the midstem up, they are sessile. The leaves are 2–3½" long with a waxy-shiny luster and have coarse teeth on the margins.

Inside the calyx, the corolla tube is very narrow, but once past the calyx, the tube inflates broadly. The flowers are 1½–2" long and may be white, pale lavender, or pale violet. Inside the inflated tube are several purple lines which extend, more or less, out onto the 5 corolla lobes. Yellow hairs lightly beard the staminode. Perennial.

Bloom Period: April and May.
*Brownwood, Brown Co.*

### Cut-Leaf Penstemon
*Penstemon baccharifolius*

This is a rock-loving plant that is often found growing in small crevices on sheer bluffs. Cut-Leaf Penstemon is erect to reclining-ascending, with several stems 6–24″ high. Though common in West Texas, it occurs in our area at only a few scattered locations in Bandera, Edwards, and Medina counties.

Minute gland-tipped hairs cover the uppermost part of the stem. The opposite, oblanceolate to obovate leaves are ½–1¾″ long, and may be entire or toothed in the upper half of the blade. The scarlet-red 1″ flowers have a partial white ring at the throat of the corolla, on the lower three lobes. The inflorescence is in a panicle-like arrangement, with pairs of stems (and/or pedicels) rising from the axils of reduced leaves. *P. baccharifolius* is well adapted to dry, rocky environments and is appropriate for xeric landscaping applications. It will bloom from Spring through Fall if given a little water. Perennial.

Bloom Period: May to September.
*Near Bandera Falls, Bandera Co.*

## Loose-Flowered Penstemon
*Penstemon laxiflorus*

Though the majority of its range is in East Texas, *P. laxiflorus* (12–24″ tall) is occasionally found in sandy or alluvial soils in the northern half of the Hill Country.

To the naked eye, the stems appear glabrous, but magnification reveals a covering of exceedingly minute hairs. The narrowly lanceolate leaves are 1¼–3½″ long, with sharply toothed margins. Pigments often concentrate at the margins and in the veins, giving them a red tinge.

White to light pink, the ⅝–1″ flowers are mildly inflated to only 2 or 3 times the diameter of the corolla tube as it emerges from the calyx. The floor of the tube is pleated or folded and has several purple lines. A prominent staminode, made conspicuous by its dense coat of golden hairs, lies on the lower lip of the corolla. In this species, the clusters of flowers are offset from the main axis of the inflorescence by short peduncles ½–1¼″ long. Perennial.

Bloom Period: April and May.
*Near Honey Creek, Llano Co.*

## White Penstemon
*Penstemon guadalupensis*

White Penstemon is a colonial plant 6–12″ tall that spreads by underground stems. Found on dry soils, it is common in our area only in Brown and Comanche counties, with a few scattered locations in Llano and Gillespie counties.

This species has two distinct leaf types. The basal (overwintering) leaves are linear to linear-spatuluate and are 2–4″ long by 1⁄16–⅛″ wide. The leaves of the flowering stem are lanceolate, tending to be widest in the lower third of the blade, and up to 2¼″ long. Both leaf types are essentially glabrous and smooth to the touch.

The mildly inflated white flowers are ⅝–⅞″ long. Perennial.

Bloom Period: March to May.
*Comanche, Comanche Co.*

## Scarlet Penstemon
*Penstemon triflorus*

Arguably the most beautiful Penstemon in the Hill Country, *P. triflorus* grows to 2' in height on dry limestone soils in the southwestern third of our area. Though found as far north as Gillespie county and as far east as Kendall and Bexar counties, it apparently is most abundant in Uvalde, Real, Bandera, and Edwards counties.

At the midstem, the lanceolate to oblanceolate leaves are 1½–3⅓" long and sessile, with subentire to sharply dentate margins.

Only slightly inflated, the brilliantly red to pinkish-red flowers are 1–1¼" long and are lined inside the corolla tube. The staminode is glabrous to nearly glabrous, a quality that distinguishes this species from a close relative, *P. Helleri*, which has a staminode lightly bearded with golden hairs for half its length. A comparison of herbarium specimens of both species reveals that, staminodes aside, all other morphological characteristics are interchangeable between the two. It may be equally valid to consider both to be a single species, with one or the other relegated to the level of a subspecies or variety. Perennial.

Bloom Period: April to May.

*S. of Leakey, Real Co.*

## Snapdragon Vine
*Maurandya antirrhiniflora*

Snapdragon Vine is a handsome plant that can be found hanging on bluffs and roadcuts or climbing on fences and shrubs. It lives on rocky, calcareous soils in the southern half of the Hill Country area.

A loose mass of twining stems comprises the main body of the plant. Nearly triangular, the numerous, glabrous leaves have 3 lobes and are ½–1" long. They are cordate at the base of the leaf blade, where they attach to petioles up to ¾" long.

The flowers are ½–¾" long (on pedicels ½–1" long), each with a cream-colored corolla tube and 5 brightly colored violet or purple corolla lobes. At the throat of the tube, the floor (or palate) is raised and is a bright creamy-yellow. The fruit is a round capsule about ¼" in diameter. Perennial.

Bloom Period: March to September. *Castroville, Medina Co.*

## Texas Toad-Flax
*Linaria texana*

Texas Toad-Flax is a slender, delicate plant with one or several stems, growing up to 2' tall. It prefers sandy soils and is abundant in the Llano Uplift region, but can also be found on limestone soils throughout our area.

Short (1–3"), reclining, spreading branches grow at the base of the otherwise erect stems. Narrowly linear, the leaves are ¾–1½" long.

The pale violet to pale blue flowers are pastel to the point of almost appearing off-white. They are ¼–½" long, with slender, curved spurs ¼–⅜" long. Annual to biennial.

Bloom Period: March and April. *Fairland, Burnet Co.*

## Water Speedwell
*Veronica Anagallis-aquatica*

As its common name suggests, Water Speedwell is found in or near water. Growing 6–12″ tall, it is erect to basally reclining, often rooting at the nodes when they touch the ground. *V. Anagallis-aquatica* has been introduced from Eurasia, and seems, in our area, to be confined to Travis, Burnet, Blanco, Kendall, and Gillespie counties.

The sessile, oblanceolate leaves are glabrous, with shallow sharp or blunt teeth on the margins.

The inflorescence is an axillary raceme up to 4″ long. Individual flowers (³⁄₁₆–¼″ wide) have 4 pale lavender corolla lobes, streaked with dark violet lines. They are underlain by 4 lanceolate sepals, and are carried on a ¼–⅜″ pedicel. Perennial.

Bloom Period: April and May.
*Pedernales R., Gillespie Co.*

## Persian Speedwell
*Veronica persica*

Persian Speedwell is another introduced species from Eurasia. On the dry, caliche soils of the Hill Country, it grows 1–5″ tall, often in waste places or as a lawn weed.

The broad, ovate leaves are ¼–⅝″ long and have several large, rounded teeth on their margins.

The flowers are ¼–⅜″ wide, with 4 lobes. The upper lobe is violet blue with dark violet lines; the side lobes are white with a violet blush at the tip and also are streaked with dark violet lines; the lowermost lobe is white with only a suggestion of streaking caused by its veins. Note that the flower pedicels are much longer than the leaves. Annual.

Bloom Period: January to May.
*Near Lake Austin, Travis Co.*

## Prairie Agalinis
*Agalinis heterophylla*

Prairie Agalinis is an erect plant 1–2′ tall, with numerous ascending branches. It is found growing on moist soils or at the edge of streams and rivers.

The stems are smooth, with leaves that may either spread or run parallel to the stems. Some of the larger leaves may be 1¼″ long by ⅛″ wide. Near the ends of the branches, the leaves typically are only ½–1″ long.

The flowers are ¾–1¼″ long and vary in color from pink to white with a lavender tinge. They are on short pedicels ¹⁄₁₆–⅛″ long. Annual.

Bloom Period: September and October.

*Pedernales R., Blanco Co.*

## Plateau Agalinis
*Agalinis edwardsiana*

Plateau Agalinis is a bushy plant 1–3′ tall found on dry caliche soils of the Edwards Plateau.

The stems and leaves are light green, often with a reddish-purple tint that may give the plant only a slight tinge or, in some cases, so strongly color the plant that it is dark purple. The narrowly linear, spreading leaves are ¾–1¼″ long.

The pink flowers are about ¾″ long, on ascending pedicels as much as 1¼″ long. Annual.

Bloom Period: September to November.

*Near Bee Cave, Travis Co.*

## Prairie Paintbrush
*Castilleja purpurea*

Prairie Paintbrush is an extremely attractive resident of Central Texas, but is relatively unknown. It grows in clumps consisting of several stems, each 6–18″ high. Adapted to dry, rocky, caliche soils, it can be found throughout the Hill Country, except in the sandy soils of the Llano Uplift.

Soft hairs coat the stems and leaves, giving the plants a slight gray-green cast. The leaves are up to 2½″ long, with 1–3 pairs of spreading lateral lobes.

The striking coloration of the inflorescence is due to the bracts, which are brightly colored on the upper part of the blade. The actual flowers, hidden within the bracts, are yellow-green and rather inconspicuous. We have three varieties (all perennial) in the Hill Country area:

Var. *purpurea*—Purple to rose-pink. Found N.W. of a line from McLennan Co. to central McCulloch Co.

Var. *citrina*—Yellow. In Edwards, Kimble, Menard, and southwestern McCulloch counties.

Var. *Lindheimeri*—Light to dark orange. Mostly S.E. of a line from McLennan Co. to Real Co.

Bloom Period: March to May.
*Var. purpurea—Brady, McCulloch Co.*
*Var. citrina—Near Mason Co./Menard Co. line.*
*Var. Lindheimeri—Near Bee Cave, Travis Co.*

## Texas Paintbrush
*Castilleja indivisa*

In its natural state, Texas Paintbrush prefers to grow on the sandy soils that are found in the Llano Uplift region. It is also found in calcareous soils along roadsides throughout the rest of the Hill Country, where it has been distributed by the Texas Dept. of Highways since the early 1930's. It grows in few-stemmed clumps 6–18″ tall.

Long, soft, spreading hairs cover the stems. The linear to lanceolate leaves usually have entire margins, but sometimes have one or two pairs of spreading lobes.

The upper half of each leaflike bract is bright red. The actual flowers are about 1″ long, slender, and yellowgreen. Annual.

Bloom Period: March to May.
*Bluffton, Llano Co.*

## Bluehearts
*Buchnera floridana*

Bluehearts is a slender plant 6–24″ tall, found in moist soils near or at the edge of streams. Its roots are thought to be parasitic on the roots of other plants.

Individuals in a single population may contain variable supplies of reddish-purple pigmentation, resulting in some plants that are light green with a slight purple tinge and others that are dark purple-red. The slender, opposite, oblanceolate leaves are as long as 3½″, and often bear white mineralized dots on the surface.

Carried on terminal spikes, the pink flowers are about ⅜″ long. Each flower is underlain by a bract 1/16–⅛″ long. Perennial.

Bloom Period: April to October.
*Slaughter Creek, Travis Co.*

## Trumpet Creeper
*Campsis radicans*

Trumpet Creeper is a climbing vine or vine-like shrub. Although it is commonly seen as an ornamental around habitations, wild colonies can be found in a few locations in our area, primarily in deep alluvial soils.

The pinnately compound leaves consist of 5–11 lanceolate leaflets, each 1¼–2″ long. Small tufts of hair are found on the rachis of the leaf, at the point where the pairs of leaflets attach.

Carried in terminal panicles, the orange to red-orange flowers are about 2½″ long. The calyx mimics the color of the corolla and is ½–¾″ long.

Bloom Period: May to September.
*Near San Saba, San Saba Co.*

## Desert Willow
*Chilopsis linearis*

The normal range of Desert Willow is in West Texas and the Rio Grande Valley, but, since it makes such a beautiful spreading bush or small tree, it has been cultivated and used as an ornamental in Central Texas. It has escaped cultivation in several locations and is now randomly distributed through the Hill Country.

The linear to linear-lanceolate leaves of Desert Willow are 2½–4″ long, with entire margins.

Flower color varies; some specimens have white flowers with pale purple lines while others display bright violet-purple mottling and strong purple lines. The flowers are ¾–2″ long.

Bloom Period: May to September.
*E. of Lampasas, Lampasas Co.*

## Devil's Claw
*Proboscidea louisianica*

Through most of the Hill Country, Devil's Claw is an occasional plant of roadsides and waste places. In a few localities (particularly in Mason Co.), it is a common weed of cultivated fields. It is a low, spreading, bushy plant 1–2' high.

Sticky hairs cover the stems and leaves, making them unpleasant to handle. The leaves are broadly ovate to reniform, with an asymmetrically cordate base. They may be 3–10" wide, and are usually wider than long, with an entire to slightly sinuate margin.

The inflorescence is an open, loose raceme of 6–15 flowers, though only 2–4 may bloom at the same time. Individual flowers (1–1½" long) vary in color from pink to white, and are dotted with purple or brown spots. The fruit is a fleshy, curved pod that splits into two "claws" when it dries, hence the common name. Annual.

Bloom Period: June to September.
*Mason, Mason co.*

## Drummond's Wild Petunia
*Ruellia Drummondiana*

Found on deep soils in canyons and along waterways, Drummond's Petunia is a coarse, erect plant 1–3' tall. In our area, it is generally confined to the eastern and southern edges of the Hill Country, in an arc from McLennan Co. to Uvalde Co.

Short, stiff, slightly rough hairs cover the 4-angled stem. The ovate to ovate-elliptic leaves are 2–6" long, with undulate margins, on petioles ½–1" long. They are usually dark green on the upper leaf surface and pale green on the underside.

Bundles of 2–7 flowers occur in the axils of the leaves. Each purple to light purple flower is approximately 1½" long. The calyx lobes are linear, reaching ¾–1¼" in length. Perennial.

Bloom Period: June to November.
*Twin Sisters, Blanco Co.*

## Snake Herb
*Dyschoriste linearis*

Snake Herb is 4–18" tall (tending to the short side of that range), with several simple stems rising from the base. It is found throughout our area on dry caliche soils.

Narrowly oblanceolate to oblong-spatulate, the opposite leaves are 1–2½" long, with entire margins and a few sparse hairs on the midrib and veins.

Born in the axils of the leaves, the light purple flowers are about 1" long. Unopened flowers are usually exceeded by the linear calyx lobes, which are up to ¾" long. Perennial.

Bloom Period: May and June.
*Bluff over Lake Austin, Travis Co.*

## Common Wild Petunia
*Ruellia nudiflora*

Common Wild Petunia grows 1–2' tall, with one or several erect to reclining-ascending stems rising from the base. It is found throughout the Hill Country area.

The leaves are elliptic to obovate and 2–5" long, with undulate-dentate margins. An obviously netlike pattern of veins is found on the underside of the leaf.

The purple flowers are 1½–2½" long, in terminal panicles. A white-flowered variety, *R. nudiflora* var. *Metzae*, is found south of a line drawn from northernmost Travis Co. to Menard Co. Perennial.

Bloom Period: April to October.

*R. nudiflora—Stonewall, Gillespie Co.*
*R. nudiflora var. Metzae—Center Point, Kerr Co.*

*Ruellia nudiflora* var. *Metzae*

## Low Wild Petunia
*Ruellia humilis*

Low Wild Petunia occurs, in our area, on the southern and eastern edge of the Hill Country, from McLennan Co. to Real Co. Though usually only 8–12″ tall, it can reach 2′ in height. Locally, it shows a preference for partial shade, growing in open woods, brushy areas, and along weedy fencerows.

Both the stems and the leaves are pubescent. Elliptic to ovate in outline, the leaves are 1–2½″ long and are either sessile or on short petioles ⅛″ long.

The flowers are one to few in the axils of the leaves. They are light purple, with purple-red lines in the throat, and are about 2¼″ long. Perennial.

Bloom Period: June to September.
*Near Slaughter Creek, Travis Co.*

## Flame Acanthus
*Anisacanthus Wrightii*

Flame Acanthus is becoming popular in native plant landscaping both for its ornamental qualities and its ability to attract hummingbirds. The natural range of this plant extends from Mexico up to the edge of the Hill Country in Uvalde Co., where it is found along streams or in dry arroyos. It is a small, bushy shrub 2–4′ tall.

Soft hairs descend in a line on the stem from between one pair of leaves to the axils of the next lower pair (and also down the leaf midrib onto the petiole). The lanceolate leaves are up to 2¼″ long.

In bloom, *A. Wrightii* produces orange flowers about 1½″ long, in terminal spikes.

Bloom Period: June and July.
*Near Concan, Uvalde Co.*

## Tube-Tongue
*Siphonoglossa pilosella*
*(Justicia pilosella)*

Under favorable circumstances, Tube-Tongue can reach 12″ in height, but it is usually only 2–5″ tall. It is found in colonies in a variety of habitats, from alluvial soils at streamside to dry caliche soils under brush on hilltops.

Spreading hairs are found on the stems, main leaf veins, and along the margins of the leaves. The ovate to oval leaves are normally ½–¾″ long, but can be as long as 1¼″.

Strongly 2-lipped, the 1″ flowers are lavender-pink, with a long white floral tube. They may be terminal or axillary. Perennial.

Bloom Period: April to October.
*Near Pedernales R., Travis Co.*

## American Water-Willow
*Justicia americana*

American Water-Willow is an erect plant 6–24″ tall and is found in mud or shallow water throughout our area. Where found, it is usually in large colonies which have spread by underground stems.

Linear to lanceolate, the leaves are 2½–4″ long and may be short petiolate or sessile. The smooth stems and leaves are glabrous.

The inflorescence is a capitate spike as much as 1¼″ long, on an axillary peduncle up to 6″ long. Individual flowers are ¼–⅝″ long, and may vary from white to pale violet. The middle lobe of the lower lip is attractively marked with dark purple lines or spots. Each flower has only 2 stamens. Perennial.

Bloom Period: April to October.
*Llano R., Castell, Llano Co.*

## Small Bluets
*Hedyotis crassifolia*
*(Houstonia crassifolia)*

Small Bluets are often among the first wildflowers of Spring. They are easily overlooked because they are low, diffuse plants averaging 1–2" in height (though they can grow to 5"). Look for them in open grasslands, open woods, and pastures, where they sometimes form extensive colonies.

The lowermost leaves are oblanceolate to spatulate, growing to ⅝" in length. At midstem or higher, the leaves become elliptic to oval, and smaller, averaging ⅛–³⁄₁₆" long.

Blue or blue-violet flowers ⅛–³⁄₁₆" wide, with 4 corolla lobes, are terminal on the stems. Annual.

Bloom Period: January to March.
*Krause Spring, Spicewood, Burnet Co.*

## Baby's Breath, Bluets
*Hedyotis nigricans*
*(Houstonia nigricans)*

Baby's Breath is a much-branched, erect to reclining-ascending plant 3–18" tall. It prefers dry soils and is common on open ground along roadsides.

Threadlike to narrowly linear, the leaves may be up to 1½" long, but are usually smaller. The opposite leaves and stems are glabrous.

Arranged in cymes, the flowers may be sessile or short-peduncled, with funnel-like corollas. The numerous flowers are ³⁄₁₆–¼" long and may be white, light pink, or pale violet. Perennial.

Bloom Period: April to November.
*Lampasas, Lampasas Co.*

### Buttonbush
*Cephalanthus occidentalis*

Though it is most common locally in the northern half of the Hill Country, Buttonbush can be found at the margins of streams, ponds, and lakes throughout our area and the rest of Texas. It is a bushy, much-branched shrub 3–7' tall.

A good deal of variation is found in the leaves. They may be ovate, ovate-oblong, or narrowly lanceolate, and up to 6" long with petioles ⅛–1" long. Their arrangement may be opposite or ternate (three at a node). The leaf surfaces may be glabrous or covered in very short, soft hairs.

The inflorescence is a creamy-white, globe-like head ½–1¼" in diameter. It is composed of many individual flowers, each about ¼" long, with 4 stamens extending well past the throat of the flower. The bright yellow anthers create something of a halo effect around the flower heads.

Bloom Period: June to September.
*Lake Travis, Travis Co.*

### Elder-Berry
*Sambucus canadensis*

### Rusty Black-Haw, Southern Black-Haw
*Viburnum rufidulum*

In the rockier parts of the Hill Country, Rusty Black-Haw may be an attractive shrub or small tree 4–12′ tall. It reaches 10–20′ in height under moist conditions in alluvial soils. *V. rufidulum* is found along fencerows and streams, and in canyons and open woods.

Square plates of gray bark arranged in a checkered pattern cover the trunk. The waxy-shiny 1–3″ leaves are elliptic, obovate, or oblanceolate, with finely toothed margins. Fine rusty-red hairs cover the winter buds, the petioles, and the primary vein on the underside of the leaves.

The inflorescence is a large cyme up to 4″ wide, composed of numerous creamy-white flowers ⅛–¼″ wide. The fruit is a glaucous, blue-black to reddish purple drupe ⅜–½″ long.

Bloom Period: March to May.
*Rafter Hollow, Gillespie Co.*

Elder-Berry is a large, erect, herbaceous plant 3–10′ tall, found in moist soils or along streams. Though primarily found in East Texas and on the eastern edge of the Hill Country, it also has a scattered distribution in appropriate habitats in the rest of our area.

The pinnate leaves have 5–11 ovate-elliptic to lanceolate leaflets, each leaflet approximately 2½–3½″ long. The leaf margins are sharply toothed.

The inflorescence is a large, flattened cyme up to 10″ across, composed of numerous white flowers ⅛–¼″ wide. Each flower has 5 stamens. Birds are fond of the fruits, which are berry-like drupes ⅛–³⁄₁₆″ in diameter. Perennial.

Bloom Period: May to July.
*Blanco State Park, Blanco Co.*

## Texas Honeysuckle, White Honeysuckle
*Lonicera albiflora*

Texas Honeysuckle takes the form of a shrub (3–6' tall) which has a few vine-like branches in its upper half. Unlike the introduced Japanese Honeysuckle, it is non-aggressive and non-invasive.

The glabrous, somewhat stiff leaves are suborbicular to oval to obovate and are ½–1½" long. Directly below the inflorescence, the uppermost opposite leaves have their bases fused together, forming a cup-like structure pierced in the middle by the stem.

White to yellowish-white flowers ½–¾" long form sessile clusters at the ends of the stems. In the Fall, the leaves drop away, accenting the clusters of bright red, translucent berries.

Bloom Period: April.

*Wolf Creek, Kerr Co.*

## Corn-Salad
*Valerianella amarella*

Corn-Salad is an erect plant 4–12″ tall. It is found in colonies on prairies and open ground. Some colonies west of Waco, in McLennan Co., cover several acres.

Its stems exhibit dichotomous branching, that is, the stems divide into successive, symmetrical pairs of branches going towards the inflorescence. Near the base, the leaves are obovate to spatulate. Farther up the stem, they are oblong to ovate. Both the leaves and the stems are glabrous.

The inflorescence is an aggregation of cyme-like clusters. Individual flowers are white, with a funnel-like corolla, and are 1/16–1/8″ wide. Annual.

Bloom Period: March to May.
*W. of Waco, McLennan Co.*

## Meloncito, Speckled Gourd
*Melothria pendula*

A species of the Gulf Coast and South Texas, Meloncito can be found along the eastern edge of the Hill Country as far north as Bell Co. It is a climbing vine found in moist canyons and along watercourses.

Palmately veined, the 1–2½" leaves are orbicular in outline with 3–5 lobes and a cordate base. A distinctive identifying feature is the roughness of the leaf surfaces, both upper and lower, which feel like fine sandpaper.

The flower is yellow and has 5 lobes. The fruit is a small gourd ¾" long, which is green with greenish-white speckles when immature. As it ripens, it turns dull black. Perennial.

Bloom Period: April to September.
*Krause Spring, Spicewood, Burnet Co.*

## Buffalo Gourd, Stinking Gourd
*Cucurbita foetidissima*

This coarse, prostrate to low-climbing vine may have runners up to 20' long. Buffalo Gourd is common in our area in waste places, fields, and along roadsides.

The gray-green leaves are triangular-ovate, with shallow lobes, and may grow to 12" long or longer. Commonly, the leaf blade is folded upward parallel to the midvein.

Opening in the early morning, the yellow flowers are 3–4" long and 1–2" wide. The fruit is a gourd (2–3" in diameter) which is dark green with light green stripes. As it ripens, it turns yellow. Perennial.

Bloom Period: May to September.
*Medina R. floodplain, Bandera Co.*

## Balsam-Gourd, Snake-Apple
*Ibervillea Lindheimeri*

Balsam-Gourd is a climbing vine that can be found growing on brush in open woodlands and on fences.

The leaves are shallowly or deeply 3 to 5 lobed. Any or all of the 4 possible combinations derived from the foregoing information are likely to be found on the same plant. The lobes or margins of the lobes may be coarsely toothed or undulate.

Thin-skinned, soft, and fleshy, the fruit is a bright red globe 1–2″ in diameter. When hanging from a vine growing on a barbed wire fence, these fruits are very picturesque. The yellow flowers are ¼–½″ in diameter. A close cousin, *I. tenuisecta*, has been re-assigned and is now known as *I. Lindheimeri* var. *tenuisecta*. Perennial.

Bloom Period: April to September.
*Near Fool Mt., Llano Co.*

## Texas Bluebell, Basin Bellflower
*Campanula Reverchonii*

Truly rare, Texas Bluebell is known from only a few sites in Llano, Mason, and Burnet counties (its entire range). It seems to prefer freshly eroded soils (granite grus) on or near granite domes. Unfortunately, some of its former locations have become quarries.

*Campanula Reverchonii* is a small, diffusely branched plant 1–8″ tall. Near the base of the plant, the ¼–½″ leaves are spatulate to oblanceolate, with a few coarse teeth on the margins. Going up the stem, the leaves rapidly become linear and then threadlike.

The light violet-blue flowers have a funnel-like corolla and are ¼–½″ long and about ⅜–½″ wide. Texas Bluebell is relatively unknown, unstudied, and unappreciated. One of only two true Bluebells in the state of Texas, and by far the most rare, *Campanula Reverchonii* deserves more protection than it currently is receiving. Annual.

Bloom Period: May to July.
*Near Granite Mt., Burnet Co.*

## Venus' Looking Glass
*Triodanis perfoliata*

Venus' Looking Glass is an inconspic-uous but attractive plant with slender, unbranched stems 6–18″ high. It is usually found in disturbed soils or in moist areas such as ditches along roadways.

The round to ovate leaves clasp the stems and have a bract-like appearance. They commonly have toothed margins.

Each leaf node may bear 1 or several flowers in its axil. Across the Hill Coun-try, the blue flowers are widely variable in width, ranging from ¼–¾″ in diame-ter. Annual.

Bloom Period: April and May.
*New Braunfels, Comal Co.*

## Western Venus' Looking Glass
*Triodanis coloradoensis*

Of our *Triodanis* species, Western Venus' Looking Glass is probably the most beautiful. It has erect stems, which may be simple or with a few as-cending upper branches, and grows 6–24″ tall on bluffs, dry hillsides, and alluvium.

On the lower part of the stem, the leaves are petiolate. Above that, the leaves are sessile, with an oblanceolate to narrowly elliptic shape, growing ½–2½″ long.

The blue flowers rise from the axils of the leaves and may be sessile or short-peduncled. The calyx averages ½″ long, with narrowly lanceolate calyx lobes up to ⅝″ long. Annual.

Bloom Period: April to June.
*Near Concan, Uvalde Co.*

## Cardinal Flower
*Lobelia Cardinalis*

For sheer visual impact, it would be hard to beat a good stand of Cardinal Flower. Though commonly scattered along watercourses, they sometimes form large colonies in the beds of shallow streams, creating a vivid spectacle at peak bloom. The simple, erect stems grow 1–4' tall and are found in moist soils in or very near streams.

Numerous ovate to oblanceolate leaves 3–5" long line the stems. The leaves are finely to somewhat coarsely toothed. In our area, the stems and leaves tend to be sparsely covered in short, spreading hairs, though essentially glabrous specimens may be found.

The bright scarlet flowers are in terminal racemes as much as 18" long. Individual flowers are about 1¼" long. Extending beyond the corolla lobes is a red filament tube 1–1¼" long (formed by fusion of the filaments), capped with a gray anther tube (formed by fusion of the anthers) about ³⁄₁₆" long. Perennial.

Bloom Period: July to October.
*Pedernales R. at LBJ Ranch, Gillespie Co.*

## Woolly Ironweed
*Vernonia Lindheimeri*

In our area, Woolly Ironweed is found on dry caliche or limestone slopes, generally east of a line between Bosque and Uvalde counties.

It may have one or several erect stems 10–30″ tall, with narrowly linear leaves 1½–3″ long. Locally, the leaves are usually glabrous on the upper surface and densely woolly on the lower surface. Some plants will be found that are woolly on both leaf surfaces.

Each reddish-purple flower head may bear 20–60 individual flowers ³⁄₁₆–¼″ long. The achenes have purple, bristle-like pappus awns. Perennial.

Bloom Period: June to September.
*Near Bee Cave, Travis Co.*

## Western Ironweed
*Vernonia Baldwinii*

Western Ironweed has simple, erect stems 2–5′ tall that are much-branched at the top, near the inflorescence. It prefers calcareous clay soils and is found scattered throughout the Hill Country area.

Minute hairs coat the undersides of the finely serrate leaves and the striate stems, while the upper leaf surface is essentially glabrous. The ovate-lanceolate leaves are sessile or nearly so, reaching 6″ in length.

Numerous purple flower heads ¼–³⁄₈″ long aggregate in a well-branched inflorescence. *V. Baldwinii* hybridizes with *V. Lindheimeri* to form an intermediate species known as *V. guadalupensis*. Perennial.

Bloom Period: June to September.
*Near Henly, Hays Co.*

## Gay-Feather, Blazing Star
*Liatris mucronata*

One of our more attractive Fall bloomers, Blazing Star may have one or several erect to ascending stems 1–2½' tall. It lives on poor limestone soils and bare caliche, and can be found in the eastern two-thirds of the Hill Country area.

Narrowly linear leaves 2–4" long are whorled around the stem. On some plants the leaves are punctate, on others they are not.

The purple flower heads are arranged in a spike-like inflorescence 3–12" long, with each head surrounded by ovate to obovate phyllaries with pointed tips. Individual flowers are ¼–⅜" long, maturing into achenes with plumose pappus bristles. Perennial.

Bloom Period: August to October.
*Kendalia, Kendall Co.*

## Brickell-Bush
*Brickellia cylindraceae*

Brickell-Bush is not very striking but it is a common member of our flora. It normally has several erect, unbranched stems up to 3' tall, growing in rocky, limestone soils.

Variable to a fault, the ½–1" leaves may be opposite or alternate, sessile or short petiolate, and ovate to lanceolate with blunt-toothed margins.

The inflorescence may be raceme-like or panicle-like, with numerous ½" long flower heads that are each constricted into a tight column. Minute hairs coat the achenes, which have simple pappus bristles. Perennial.

Bloom Period: September to November.
*Bee Cave Rd., Travis Co.*

## White Boneset
*Eupatorium serotinum*

Boneset spreads by rhizomes to form colonies of plants 1½–4' tall. It is usually found in moist soils near streams. The mostly opposite leaves are ovate to lanceolate and are 2–5" long with coarsely toothed margins. The white flower heads are in much-branched, flat-topped terminal clusters. Perennial.
   Bloom Period: August to October.
*Sandy Creek, Llano Co.*

## Blue Mist-Flower
*Eupatorium coelestinum*
*(Conoclinium coelestinum)*

Blue Mist-Flower forms bushy, reclining-ascending plants 1–4' tall on moist soils. The opposite leaves (1–3" long) are deltoid or triangular with coarsely blunt-toothed margins. The blue flower heads are in corymb-like clusters. Perennial.
   Bloom Period: July to October.
*Salado Creek, Bell Co.*

## Thoroughwort
*Eupatorium havanense*
*(Ageratina havanensis)*

Thoroughwort is an open, woody shrub 1–5' tall, found on rocky hillsides and bluffs in the southern half of the Hill Country. The opposite, deltoid leaves are 1–2" long, with 5–9 large teeth on each margin. The clusters of white flower heads are very fragrant. Perennial.
   Bloom Period: May to November.
*Kerrville, Kerr Co.*

## Roosevelt Weed, Poverty Weed
*Baccharis neglecta*

Poverty Weed forms a weak, open bush 3–9′ tall, mainly on calcareous soils throughout the Hill Country, but sometimes also on granitic soils. It is especially likely to be found on disturbed ground and in waste areas.

Narrowly linear to narrowly elliptic, the leaves are 1–2½″ long and are sessile on the striate branches. The margins of the leaves may be entire or sparsely serrate.

This plant becomes somewhat attractive in the Fall, due to the masses of long, silvery, silky pappus hairs produced by the female flowers. Perennial.

Bloom Period: September and October.
*Copperas Cove, Coryell Co.*

## Scratch Daisy, Granite Daisy
*Croptilon divaricatum*
*(Croptilon Hookerianum* var. *graniticum)*

Found on granitic soils of the Llano Uplift, Scratch Daisy has one to several erect or ascending branches rising from the base. It averages 6–12″ high.

Most of the leaves are basal. They are alternate, linear, 1–1½″ long, and have glandular hairs on the margins.

The yellow flower heads are ⅜–⅝″ in diameter, arranged in a very loose panicle-like inflorescence. Together, an achene and its straw-colored pappus bristles measure about ⅛″. The linear-lanceolate phyllaries have membrane-like margins. Annual.

Bloom Period: June to December.
*Coal Creek, Gillespie Co.*

## Gray Golden-Aster
*Heterotheca canescens*

Gray Golden-Aster is a low, bushy, much-branched plant 4–18″ tall. The lower stems are woody, as is the tap-root. A common roadside flower, it can be found in colonies on dry, calcareous soils throughout the Hill Country.

A dense coat of hairs on the leaves and stems gives it an overall light gray-green color. The oblanceolate leaves are ¼–2″ long and often have bundles of smaller leaves in their axils.

The yellow flower heads are terminal and are ⅜–⅝″ in diameter. Minute hairs cover the achenes, which have straw-colored pappus bristles. Perennial.

Bloom Period: July to September.
*Mason, Mason Co.*

## Camphor Weed
*Heterotheca latifolia*

Crush the leaves of this plant, and you will release a strong camphor-like scent. Camphor Weed is an open, bushy, herbaceous plant 1–5′ tall. It prefers the sandy soils of the Llano Up-lift, but will also grow in alluvial soils elsewhere in the Hill Country.

The stems and leaves are covered in spreading white hairs. The leaves are ovate to elliptic with entire or serrate margins. On the lower stem, the leaves are long-petiolate, and are often winged at the base. Leaves on the upper stem are sessile, with truncate bases.

The yellow flower heads are ¾–1″ wide and are terminal. Annual.

Bloom Period: May to October.
*Near Enchanted Rock, Llano Co.*

## Sticky Granite-Daisy
*Heterotheca stenophylla*

Sticky Granite-Daisy grows 6–18″ high with several erect to ascending stems rising from a semi-woody root. In our area, it is found primarily on sandy soils and granite outcrops of the Llano Uplift.

Broadly linear to oblanceolate, the leaves are ½–1½″ long and are covered with short, stiff hairs. Resin glands on the leaves make them sticky to the touch.

The yellow flower heads are terminal on leafy stalks and are ¾–1¼″ in diameter. Each head is closely subtended by one to several linear, reduced leaves. Perennial.

Bloom Period: April to September.
*Llano River, Llano, Llano Co.*

## Sleepy-Daisy
*Xanthisma texanum* var. *Drummondii*

Sleepy-Daisy has the habit of folding up its ray flowers at night and in cloudy weather, thus its common name. It is an erect plant 1–3′ tall, branching in its upper half, found mainly on the Llano Uplift, but also in Mills, Brown, and Comanche counties.

The lowest leaves are pinnately lobed, becoming merely dentate a little higher up. At the midstem and above, the leaves (½–2″ long) are entire and narrowly lanceolate or narrowly elliptic. They are essentially glabrous, with a minute ciliate fringe on the margins.

The yellow, terminal flower heads are ¾–1½″ wide. Annual.

Bloom Period: May to September.
*Marble Falls, Burnet Co.*

## Gumweed
*Grindelia microcephala*

## Fall Gumweed
*Grindelia lanceolata*

Fall Gumweed normally has one to several erect-ascending stems 1–3' tall, each branching near the inflorescence. It is a perennial species found on calcareous soils throughout our area.

The lanceolate to deltoid leaves are stiff, with a few teeth sparsely distributed along the margins.

The yellow flower heads (about 1" across) are solitary and terminal. Note the presence of ray flowers. An annual species, *G. squarrosa*, is also found blooming in this area at the same time, but generally lacks ray flowers.

Bloom Period: July to October.
*Twin Sisters, Blanco Co.*

Gumweed is a bushy, erect plant 6–36" high found on calcareous and sandy soils along the southern and eastern rim of the Hill Country.

The lower leaves are long-petiolate and sometimes pinnately lobed. Farther up the stem, the leaves become sessile and oblong to oblanceolate, with small teeth lining the margins. Resinous glands cause the plant to be sticky, especially at the inflorescence.

The yellow flower heads are terminal and are ½–1½" in diameter. The phyllaries are very narrowly lanceolate to linear, with slender, pointed tips. Annual.

Bloom Period: April to August.
*Castroville, Medina Co.*

## Saw-Leaf Daisy
*Prionopsis ciliata*

This stout, erect, unbranched plant grows 2–5′ tall. Locally, it is found on calcareous soils in Brown, San Saba, and McCulloch counties.

Elliptic to obovate, the glabrous leaves are alternate on the tough, striate stems. They are stiff and sessile, with sharp, coarse teeth on the margins.

Saw-Leaf Daisy has yellow flower heads 1–2″ across. They are solitary and terminal on the numerous short branchlets at the end of the stem. A sticky resin covers the linear to narrowly lanceolate phyllaries. The achenes are ellipsoid, with a pappus of bristles ¼–½″ long. Annual.

Bloom Period: August to November.
*Brady, McCulloch Co.*

## Tatalencho
*Gymnosperma glutinosum*

Tatalencho is an open, semi-woody plant consisting of several stems rising 1½–5′ high. It is common on dry caliche soils on the southern and southeastern edge of the Hill Country.

Most of the main stems are unbranched and naked in their lower half, since the leaves fall away as the stem becomes more woody. The alternate, sessile leaves are linear to narrowly lanceolate and are ¾–2″ long by ¹⁄₁₆–¼″ wide. They have entire margins.

The yellow flower heads are in somewhat flat-topped, corymb-like masses. Individual flowers are only about ³⁄₁₆″ long. Perennial.

Bloom Period: September to November.
*W. of Johnson City, Blanco Co.*

## Broomweed
*Xanthocephalum dracunculoides*
*(Amphiachyris amoenum)*

Broomweed rises 6–36″ high on a single stem which is highly branched in its upper two-thirds. It can be found on poor caliche soils and dry calcareous uplands throughout our area.

The glabrous, linear to linear-lanceolate leaves are ¼–1¼″ long.

The numerous yellow flower heads are terminal on short branchlets. They are small, averaging ¼–⅜″ in diameter. Annual.

Bloom Period: July to November.
*Rumley, Lampasas Co.*

## Broom Snakeweed
*Xanthocephalum Sarothrae*
*(Gutierrezia Sarothrae)*

Broom Snakeweed is common in West Texas, but uncommon in our area. It can be found in scattered locations in Edwards, Travis, and Kendall counties. It is a low, several-branched species 6–18″ high, found on dry, calcareous uplands.

At flowering time, the leaves on the lower part of the stem either die and dry up or fall away. The majority of the glabrous, linear leaves (¼–2½″ long) are found directly under the inflorescence.

The yellow flower heads are massed in a corymb-like inflorescence. There are 3–7 ray flowers and 2–6 disk flowers in a head. Perennial.

Bloom Period: September and October.
*Bee Cave Rd., Travis Co.*

## Tall Goldenrod
*Solidago altissima*
*(Solidago canadensis)*

This species of *Solidago* will almost always be found growing on moist soils in or near streams. It is an erect, robust plant 3–6' tall, which spreads by rhizomes.

A fine, rough pubescence covers the stems and leaves. Lanceolate to elongate-elliptic, the leaves are 1–5" long by ⅛–½" wide, with sharp, shallow teeth along the margins.

The numerous yellow flower heads are usually crowded onto one side of the floral branchlets. Perennial.

Bloom Period: September and October.
*Johnson City, Blanco Co.*

## Prairie Goldenrod
*Solidago nemoralis*

Prairie Goldenrod is the common, abundant *Solidago* seen along the roadside in dry caliche, uplands, and grassy areas. It has one to several erect, unbranched stems 8–24" high.

Very minute hairs cover the stems and leaves, generally making them smooth to the touch (although some specimens are slightly rough). The 1–3" leaves are narrowly oblanceolate at the midstem, diminishing in size going up the stem. Most of the leaves are entire, though a few will have scattered teeth near the apex of the blade.

The yellow flower heads tend to be crowded on one side of the curved branchlets. Perennial.

Bloom Period: September and October.
*Dripping Springs, Hays Co.*

## Tall Aster
*Aster praealtus*

Tall Aster grows 1–4′ tall, with erect, simple stems, in moist soils. Linear-lanceolate to narrowly elliptic, the stem leaves are sessile and are 1½–4″ long by up to ⅜″ wide. The numerous purple flower heads are ¾–1¼″ wide. It is found in Brown, Comanche, Real, and Uvalde counties. Perennial.
    Bloom Period: October.
*Energy, Comanche Co.*

## Texas Aster
*Aster texanus*

Texas Aster is an erect plant 1–3′ tall found on calcareous clays on the eastern edge of the Hill Country. Its ovate, dentate leaves are 2–5″ long, with a winged petiole and a blade that is cordate or truncate at its base. The numerous purple flower heads are ½–¾″ wide, on branchlets lined with much reduced leaves. Perennial.
    Bloom Period: September to November.
*Oak Hill, Travis Co.*

## Spread-Leaf Aster
*Aster patens*

Spread-Leaf Aster grows 1–2′ tall on dry sandy soils, preferably near light shade. The lower leaves are obovate with a winged, subpetiolar clasping base. Sharply truncate at their base, the upper leaves are ovate to short lanceolate. The blue-purple flower heads are ¾–1″ wide and are not crowded together. Perennial.
    Bloom Period: October.
*Near Hye, Gillespie Co.*

### White Aster
*Aster ericoides*

Spreading by rhizomes, White Aster grows into a much-branched erect to reclining or arching plant 4–30″ high. Its leaves are linear to narrowly lanceolate (sometimes oblong), and at midstem are ⅜–¾″ long. The numerous white flower heads are about ¼″ wide, on branchlets covered with leaves ¹⁄₁₆–⅛″ long. Perennial.
Bloom Period: October and November.
*Comfort, Kendall Co.*

### Hierba del Marrano
*Aster subulatus*

This species of *Aster* grows in colonies in moist soils, ditches, and wet low places. It is a much-branched plant 1½–5′ tall. The linear, pointed leaves are 2″ long at the base, and ¼–1″ long elsewhere. The white flower heads (¼–⅜″ wide) are often suffused with a light purple blush. Annual.
Bloom Period: July to November.
*Lake Austin, Travis Co.*

### Dwarf White Aster
*Chaetopappa bellidifolia*

Usually abundant where found, Dwarf White Aster grows 2–6″ high on dry calcareous soils and up to 15″ high on creek soils, mainly in the southern half of our area. Its oblanceolate to spatulate leaves are ¼–1½″ long. The small flower heads are ³⁄₁₆–¼″ wide and may be white, pale lavender, or light blue. Annual.
Bloom Period: April to July.
*Center Point, Kerr Co.*

### Philadelphia Fleabane
*Erigeron philadelphicus*

Philadelphia Fleabane grows on moist soils along the eastern edge of the Hill Country. It stands 8–30″ tall, usually with a single stalk. The basal leaves are narrowly oblanceolate to obovate. The flower heads are ½–¾″ wide, with thread-like white ray flowers and yellow disk flowers. Annual to short-lived perennial.
Bloom Period: March to May.
*Miller Creek, Blanco Co.*

### Prairie Fleabane
*Erigeron modestus*

Prairie Fleabane grows on dry, calcareous soils throughout our area. It forms a low clump 3–6″ high and 4–10″ wide. The oblanceolate leaves are sometimes few pinnately-lobed or toothed. The ½–¾″ flowers are carried above the foliage on peduncles 3–7″ long, on which the young, unopened flowers characteristically nod. Perennial.
Bloom Period: February to May.
*West Lake Hills, Travis Co.*

### Lazy Daisy
*Aphanostephus* sp.

We have two similar species of Lazy Daisy in the Hill Country. Both are erect plants 4–16″ tall that branch in their upper half. *A. skirrhobasis* has an achene with a scaly, uneven pappus less than 2 mm. long. *A. ramosissimus* has a ciliate, even pappus less than 2.5 mm. long. The flower heads are ½–1½″ wide. Annual.
Bloom Period: March to June.
*Marble Falls, Burnet Co.*

## Marsh Fleabane
*Pluchea purpurascens*
*(Pluchea odorata)*

Marsh-Fleabane is a bushy plant
1–4′ tall, found in moist soils of streams
and ditches throughout the Hill Country area.

Its ovate to broadly lanceolate leaves
(sometimes elliptic) may be sessile or
short-petiolate and may be entire to
shallowly toothed. The leaf blades vary
from glabrous to finely and minutely
pubescent.

The pinkish-purple flower heads are
in cyme-like clusters that are flat-
topped to rounded. Individual flower
heads are 3/16–1/4″ high. There are no ray
flowers present, only disk flowers.
Annual.

Bloom Period: August to October.
*Bull Creek, Austin, Travis Co.*

## Black-Foot Daisy
*Melampodium leucanthum*

Black-Foot Daisy is one of the few plants that blooms through the hot Texas summer. It is a bushy perennial or subshrub (with a woody base), growing 6–18″ tall on dry caliche soils throughout our area. Normally, it has a flattened shape and is wider than tall.

Very short, rough hairs coat the stems and leaves. The linear-oblong leaves are ¾–1¾″ long and may be entire to pinnately few-lobed.

The flower heads are ¾–1¼″ wide, with 8–10 white ray flowers and numerous yellow disk flowers. Dark veins are conspicuous on the underside of the ray flowers. Each head has 5 broadly ovate phyllaries which are covered in a combination of short, stiff hairs and longer, woolly hairs. An oddly shaped structure at the base of each ray flower can be examined by pulling back one of the outer phyllaries. It is apparently an inner phyllary modified into a cup-like configuration to protect the achene of the ray flower. Perennial.

Bloom Period: April to October.
*Near Knight Mt., Lampasas Co.*

## White Rosin-Weed
*Silphium albiflorum*

Harsh conditions produce tough plants. A good example of this is White Rosin-Weed, which is a rough, coarse plant 1½–3' tall that can be found growing on dry, barren caliche soils north of a line drawn between Travis and Kimble counties.

Its alternate leaves are very rigid and are covered with stiff hairs. The leaves are deeply pinnatifid in the same manner as a Staghorn fern, and are almost as broad as long.

Stout, rigid stems carry the white flower heads in a raceme-like arrangement. The heads are 1½–2½" wide. Perennial.

Bloom Period: May to July.
*Norse Community, Bosque Co.*

## Simpson Rosinweed
*Silphium Simpsonii* var. *Wrightii*

Simpson Rosinweed is a robust plant growing 2–6' tall, usually with unbranched stems. It can be found scattered in a few locations on the eastern edge of the Hill Country, usually in alluvial soils.

Near the base, the leaves are opposite, long-petiolate, lanceolate-bladed, and large (up to 10" long). In the upper two thirds of the plant, the leaves become alternate, sessile, lanceolate, and smaller (2½–5" long).

Solitary and terminal on short branchlets of irregular length, the yellow flower heads grow 1½–2½" wide. *Silphium* species hybridize freely with one another, giving rise to many intermediate forms. Perennial.

Bloom Period: July to September.
*Twin Sisters, Blanco Co.*

## Texas Green-Eyes
*Berlandiera texana*

Texas Green-Eyes has erect, unbranched stems 2–4′ tall. It prefers deep soils and can be found on highway embankments, in river valleys, and at the edge of woods in the southern half of the Hill Country.

Soft hairs cover the stems and the alternate leaves. At the midstem, the leaves are triangular to ovate and may be sessile or short-petiolate. The leaf margins are evenly toothed (sometimes doubly toothed).

The flower heads are up to 2″ wide, with yellow ray flowers and dark red to maroon disk flowers. Each disk flower is subtended by a green phyllary, causing the disk to be green. Perennial.

Bloom Period: May to July.
*Blanco River, Blanco Co.*

## Texas Star, Lindheimer Daisy
*Lindheimera texana*

Named in honor of Ferdinand Lindheimer (an important early Texas botanist), Lindheimer Daisy is a common plant 4–12″ high and is found in open grassy areas throughout the Hill Country.

Highly variable in appearance, it may have a simple stem or multiple branches. Its alternate leaves may be lanceolate, ovate, or oblanceolate and up to 5″ long (though usually ⅝–1½″ long). They are usually sessile and may be entire to coarsely toothed.

The yellow flower heads have 5 ray flowers and about 2 or 3 times as many disk flowers. The ray flower achenes are very broad and flat and have two horns near the top. Annual.

Bloom Period: March to May.
*Laguna Community, Uvalde Co.*

## Nerve-Ray
*Tetragonotheca texana*

Nerve-Ray is a multiple-branched open-bushy plant 1–2′ tall. It is found on rocky ground in the southern half of our area.

The opposite leaves (1–5″ long) are elliptic to ob-elliptic or obovate in outline, with pinnately incised or coarsely toothed margins. Most of the leaves are long-petiolate and clasping, but the uppermost opposite leaves have their bases fused together with the stem piercing the center.

Each flower head bears 6–15 yellow ray flowers and numerous brownish-red disk flowers. The heads are 1–1¾″ across and are solitary at the end of long peduncles. There are 4 very large outer phyllaries and 6–15 small inner phyllaries. Perennial.

Bloom Period: April to September.
*Near Medina Lake, Bandera Co.*

## Engelmann Daisy
*Engelmannia pinnatifida*

Engelmann Daisy grows 6–24″ tall with one to several erect stems. It is a common roadside plant found throughout our area.

Stiffish hairs coat the stems and leaves. At the base, the leaves are 6–12″ long and deeply pinnatifid. Going up the stem, the leaves become smaller.

The inflorescence is composed of numerous yellow flower heads 1–1½″ wide. Normally, there are 8 ray flowers, which are fertile and 3-toothed, and numerous disk flowers, which are infertile and 5-toothed. The phyllaries are in 3 series, the outermost being linear, the next slightly broader, and the innermost broadly obovate. Perennial.

Bloom Period: March to July.
*Evant, Coryell Co.*

## Purple Cone-Flower
*Echinacea angustifolia* var. *angustifolia*

In the past, Purple Cone-Flower was found in most of the Hill Country area. Currently, it is restricted to a few small local populations. Grazing, habitat destruction, and gathering have probably all contributed to its decline. It grows 1–2½' tall, on calcareous clays and in prairie situations.

Most of the leaves are basal and are covered in rough, stiff hairs. They are long-petiolate, narrowly oblanceolate, and 3–10" long. Each leaf has 3–5 main veins. The leaves of the upper stem are much smaller.

Given the striking appearance of the large flower heads, it would be a worthwhile project to re-establish the species in our public parks. The ray flowers are a beautiful shade of pale reddish-purple, surrounding a dark reddish-purple disk, making a flower head 2–3½" across. Perennial.

Bloom Period: May and June.
*Near Lamkin, Comanche Co.*

## Brown-Eyed Susan
*Rudbeckia hirta*

Brown-Eyed Susan grows 1–2½' tall with unbranched or few-branched stems. It is often found in large, showy colonies in open grassy areas on sandy or calcareous soils, mainly in the southern half of our area (but scattered elsewhere).

Rough spreading hairs cover the stems and leaves. The leaves are ovate to oblanceolate and may be sessile or short-petiolate. Their margins may be entire or toothed.

Ordinarily drooping downwards, the ray flowers are yellow with a red-brown spot at the base. The disk flowers are tightly packed in a purple-brown cone ⅜–1½" high. Annual to short-lived perennial.

Bloom Period: April to July.
*New Braunfels, Comal Co.*

## Clasping-Leaf Coneflower
*Dracopis amplexicaulis*
*(Rudbeckia amplexicaulis)*

A common species in East Texas, Clasping-Leaf Coneflower occurs locally in the northeastern part of the Hill Country on the moist soils of ditches, low places, and roadsides. It grows 1–2½' tall, with a simple or few-branched stem.

From the midstem up, the glabrous leaves are alternate, ovate to broadly lanceolate, entire to mildly toothed, and clasping.

The flower heads have a green columnar disk (with brown disk flowers) up to 1¼" high and 5–9 yellow ray flowers, each with a red-brown basal spot. Annual.

Bloom Period: April and May.
*Near Gustine, Comanche Co.*

## Mexican Hat
*Ratibida columnaris*

Mexican Hat is a bushy, herbaceous plant 1–4′ tall with numerous spreading branches. It is common on dry calcareous soils along roadsides throughout our area.

Its leaves are 1–6″ long and are pinnately divided to the midrib into 5–13 linear lobes. Each lobe may be entire or three-parted, and occasionally some are broad or oblanceolate.

The flower heads have green columnar disks ½–1½″ tall with brown disk flowers. There are 3–7 ray flowers, which are yellow with brown markings, though the proportions of the two colors are variable. Biennial or perennial.

Bloom Period: April to July.

*Georgetown, Williamson Co.*

## Golden-Eye
*Viguiera dentata*

Golden-Eye is an open, bushy, much-branched plant 3–6′ tall that tends to grow in colonies. It is extremely common on dry caliche soils on the eastern edge of our area and is scattered elsewhere.

Its leaves are opposite below and alternate above. They are ovate to broadly ovate and are basally cuneate to truncate with margins that are entire to shallowly toothed. Leaf length varies from 1–6″, though most average around 3″.

The numerous yellow flower heads are ¾–1¼″ wide with a disk ¼–⅜″ high. Perennial.

Bloom Period: September and October.

*River Hills Rd., Travis Co.*

## Rough Sunflower
*Helianthus hirsutus*

A common plant in East Texas, *Helianthus hirsutus* occurs in streamside habitats in a few Hill Country counties. Spreading by rhizomes, it forms colonies with stems 1½–5' tall.

Its opposite leaves are 1–3" long and are ovate to ovate-lanceolate. Covered in stiff hairs, they are rough to the touch. They may be sessile or short-petiolate with entire to finely toothed margins.

The yellow flower heads are 1¼–2½" in diameter and have red veins on the underside of the ray flowers. The green phyllaries are lanceolate to linear-lanceolate. Perennial.

Bloom Period: June and July.
*Little Blanco River, Blanco Co.*

## Maximilian Sunflower
*Helianthus Maximiliani*

Maximilian Sunflower grows 1–6' tall with several erect, unbranched stems. It occurs in colonies on the dry ground of prairies or the moist ground of ditches and low places. It is most common on the eastern edge of our area, but is scattered throughout the Hill Country.

Short, somewhat rough hairs cover the stems and leaves. The alternate, narrowly lanceolate leaves are pointed at both ends and may be 1½–10" long, averaging 2–4" long.

The bright yellow flower heads (1½–3" wide) are carried in terminal raceme-like arrangements or in the axils of the leaves. Perennial.

Bloom Period: September and October.
*San Marcos, Hays Co.*

## Common Sunflower
*Helianthus annuus*

Common Sunflower grows 1½–8' tall on dry soils, especially disturbed soils, throughout our area.

Various parts of the stem may be green or dark purple. Both the stems and the leaves are covered in rough, coarse hairs. The alternate leaves have ovate blades that are basally truncate to cordate on petioles nearly as long as the blades. The blades are 2½–10" long and are often nearly as broad as long.

The flower heads are up to 4" across, with yellow ray flowers and brown disk flowers. The broadly ovate phyllaries narrow abruptly at the apex to a thread-like tip. Annual.

Bloom Period: May to October.
*Bee Cave Rd., Travis Co.*

## Zexmenia
*Zexmenia hispida*
*(Wedelia hispida)*

Zexmenia forms bushy clumps 1–2½' high that are basally woody. It is found on dry ground, mainly in the southern two-thirds of our area.

Rough, stiff hairs cover the stems and leaves. The ovate-lanceolate leaves are pointed at both ends and are sessile or nearly so. There are a few teeth on either margin, the lower pair of which may be more prominent or even lobed.

Long peduncles carry the yellow-orange flowers well above the foliage. The outer phyllaries are lanceolate. Perennial.

Bloom Period: May to September.
*Smithson Valley, Comal Co.*

## Bush Sunflower
*Simsia calva*

True to its name, Bush Sunflower makes a low, scraggly bush 6–24" high. It prefers the dry soils of uplands and can be found throughout our area.

Both the stems and the leaves are rough to the touch, due to stiff, spreading hairs. The opposite leaves have shallowly lobed deltoid blades on petioles ¼–½ as long as the blade. On average, the blade is 1¼" long with a petiole ½" long. The petioles are often broadly winged where they meet the stem.

The yellow flower heads are solitary on peduncles up to 6" long. They are 1–1½" wide. Perennial.

Bloom Period: April to October.
*Blanket, Brown Co.*

## Frostweed
*Verbesina virginica*

In the Winter, as the temperature falls a few degrees below freezing, the dead stems of Frostweed split at the base and extrude a thin, curling shaving of ice. If you will carefully note the location of a blooming colony, you can go back one morning a few months later (after a hard freeze), and observe this effect. Frostweed has erect, unbranched stems 3–6' tall and is found in rich loamy soils near creeks or in the shade of large trees. It grows throughout our area.

Wing-like ribs run the length of the green stems.

The numerous, small flower heads are arranged in a massive inflorescence up to 6" across. Both the ray and disk flowers are dull white to greenish-white. Perennial.

Bloom Period: August to November.
*Shoal Creek, Austin, Travis Co.*

## Cowpen Daisy
*Verbesina encelioides*

Cowpen Daisy grows 1–4' tall, with much-branched, bushy stems. It is common throughout the Hill Country, where it is found on disturbed soils.

A dense covering of minute hairs gives the plant a gray-green appearance. The coarsely toothed leaves may be opposite or alternate and have a long deltoid blade which narrows to a sub-petiolar base which is broadly winged where it attaches to the stem.

The yellow flower heads are up to 2½" wide. Minute hairs line the ribs of the achene, which has a pappus of two bristles. Annual.

Bloom Period: April to October.
*Near Enchanted Rock, Llano Co.*

*Coreopsis basalis*

*Coreopsis tinctoria*

## Golden-Wave
*Coreopsis* sp.

Two common species of *Coreopsis* grow in the Hill Country. Both are erect, well-branched plants which are tolerant of a wide range of soil types.

Both species have opposite leaves which are 1–3 times pinnately divided into linear or linear-lanceolate segments. Occasionally, the segments will be broader, with an elliptic or obovate shape.

The flower heads are ½–1" in diameter, with three-toothed yellow rays which have a red-brown basal spot. *Coreopsis basalis* has linear, green outer phyllaries ¼–⅜" long which are much longer than the dark purple inner phyllaries. In contrast, *Coreopsis tinctoria* has green to dark colored outer phyllaries less than ¹⁄₁₆" long which are much shorter than the dark purple inner phyllaries. Either species, given moisture, rich soil, and the protection of partial shade, will reach a height of 3–4'. Otherwise, they will average about 1–1½' high. Annual.

Bloom Period: April to June.

C. *basalis*-Panther Canyon, New Braunfels, Comal Co.

C. *tinctoria*-Hwy. 183, Williamson Co.

## Navajo Tea
*Thelesperma simplicifolium*

Navajo Tea grows 1–2½' tall with one to several erect, slender stems. Spreading by rhizomes, it forms colonies on dry calcareous outcrops throughout the Hill Country.

There are relatively few leaves on the stems, making them appear somewhat naked. The linear leaves are 1–3" long, and are pinnately divided into linear segments at the base of the plant, becoming three-parted to simple and entire going up the stem. Both the stems and the leaves are glaucous.

The yellow flower heads are ¾–1¼" wide, on peduncles 1–6" long. Each head has 8 ray flowers. Perennial.

Bloom Period: May to November.
*Bushwhack Creek, Kerr Co.*

## Greenthread
*Thelesperma filifolium*

Greenthread is a few-branched to multiple-branched bushy plant 6–24" tall. It grows on dry, calcareous soil and can be found in all counties in our area.

The leaves are once, twice, or three times pinnately divided into narrowly oblanceolate or linear segments. Towards the top of the plant, the segments become more linear and the leaves become either three-parted or simple.

The flower heads are 1–1½" wide, with 8 yellow ray flowers and numerous brown disk flowers. They are carried on peduncles 2–10" long. Annual to short-lived perennial.

Bloom Period: April to June.
*Belton, Bell Co.*

## Barbara's Buttons
*Marshallia caespitosa*

## Straggler Daisy
*Calyptocarpus vialis*

Straggler Daisy is a low-growing plant 1–4″ high, with sprawling stems 4–18″ long. Common throughout our area, it prefers some shade and can be found at the edge of woods in the wild and as a common lawn pest in town.

Its opposite leaves have slightly serrate, deltoid blades ⅜–1¼″ long, on petioles about ⅓ as long as the blade.

The solitary yellow flower heads are roughly ¼″ in diameter and have 5 phyllaries. The fruit is a flattened achene which has two horn-like pappus awns. Perennial.

Bloom Period: April to November.
*Fischer Hall, Comal Co.*

Barbara's Buttons grows 6–18″ tall on sandy or calcareous soils throughout our area.

Near the base, its narrowly oblanceolate leaves are 1–4″ long. At the midstem and above, the leaves become sparse, linear, and smaller (½–1½″ long).

The rounded flower heads are solitary at the ends of the stems. Each head consists of numerous green, narrowly lanceolate phyllaries ¼–⅜″ long and numerous white to cream-colored disk flowers about ½″ long. There are no ray flowers. Perennial.

Bloom Period: April and May.
*Bee Cave Rd., Travis Co.*

### Firewheel, Indian Blanket
*Gaillardia pulchella*

In May, Firewheel produces beautiful, massive displays of color in fields and along roadsides throughout the Hill Country. Easily grown from seed, it can be an easy and satisfying initial project for anyone trying to re-vegetate worn-out land.

Firewheel is a somewhat bushy plant 1–2' tall. Its oblanceolate leaves are 1–3½" long and may be lobed, coarsely toothed, or entire. The apex of the leaf may be pointed or rounded while the base may be sessile or clasping. It is difficult to tell without a dissecting microscope, but the hairs of this plant (especially on the flower head) are segmented, like a string of rectangular beads.

The brightly colored flower heads are 1¼–2" in diameter, with 6–10 red ray flowers that are tipped with yellow. Unopened disk flowers are yellow, turning dark red in bloom. The linear to narrowly lanceolate phyllaries are about ½" long. Annual.

Bloom Period: April to June.
*Blanco, Blanco Co.*

## Pincushion Daisy
*Gaillardia suavis*

Pincushion Daisy is a low plant 1–3″ tall that throws up a naked flower stalk 1–2½′ tall. It is found throughout our area, on sandy and calcareous soils.

The oblanceolate to spatulate leaves form a dense basal rosette. They are 2–6″ long and may be entire or deeply pinnately lobed.

Solitary at the end of the long, naked flower stalk, the globe-shaped flower head (¾″ wide) consists mainly of reddish-brown disk flowers. Normally, the orange ray flowers are absent. When they are present, there tend to be 12–18 of them. Perennial.

Bloom Period: March to May.
*Medina, Bandera Co.*

## Sneezeweed
*Helenium quadridentatum*

Sneezeweed is an erect, usually single-stemmed plant 1–3′ tall. It is found on wet soils, mainly in the southern half of our area.

The linear to narrowly lanceolate leaves are 2–4″ long, with entire margins that extend onto and down the stem, causing it to be winged.

At the top of the plant, the stem divides into several branchlets, each of which carries a single flower head. The flower head consists of a reddish-brown disk (usually a little wider than tall) and numerous yellow ray flowers (⅛–⅝″ long) which are basally red. If the ray flowers are absent or less than ⅛″ long, then the plant is probably *H. microcephalum*. Annual.

Bloom Period: May to July.
*Commons Ford Rd., Travis Co.*

## Fall Sneezeweed
*Helenium autumnale*

Fall Sneezeweed is an erect, branched plant 1–4' tall found locally in moist creek soils in Travis, Blanco, and Kerr counties. The narrowly elliptic or lanceolate leaves (1–6" long) are shallowly toothed, with margins that extend down the stems, making them winged. It is an attractive but uncommon plant. Perennial.
  Bloom Period: September and October.
*Bull Creek, Travis Co.*

## Brown Bitterweed
*Helenium badium*

Brown Bitterweed grows 6–8" tall on dry soils, with a single stem that is much-branched in its upper two-thirds. Most of its leaves are linear, but a few near the base are pinnately lobed. The terminal flower heads each have about 8 yellow ray flowers and numerous brown disk flowers arranged in a globe-like configuration. Annual.
  Bloom Period: April to July.
*Inks Lake State Park, Burnet Co.*

## Yellow Bitterweed
*Helenium amarum*

Yellow Bitterweed, *Helenium amarum*, is essentially identical to Brown Bitterweed, *Helenium badium*, the major difference being that the disk flowers in this species are yellow. It may be that one of these two species should be downgraded and considered a variety of the other. Annual.
  Bloom Period: April to November.
*Brownwood, Brown Co.*

## Huisache-Daisy
*Amblyolepis setigera*

Huisache-Daisy is a few-branched plant 6–18" tall that is found in colonies throughout the Hill Country, except for the northeastern corner of our area.

Some plants are glabrous while others are sparsely covered with very long spreading hairs. Near the base of the plant, the alternate, sessile leaves are oblanceolate and up to 4" long. Going up the stem, the leaves become smaller, ovate, and clasping. The leaf margins are entire, but those plants covered in long hairs may appear to be very finely toothed on the margins due to a ciliate fringe.

The yellow flower heads are terminal and solitary on long peduncle-like stalks. Each head consists of 8–10 ray flowers ½–1" long and numerous disk flowers. The ray flowers are prominently 3–4 toothed terminally. Eight lanceolate to broadly-ovate outer phyllaries underlie the flower head. Annual.

Bloom Period: April to June.
*Junction, Kimble Co.*

## Rock Daisy
*Perityle Lindheimeri*

Endemic to the Edwards Plateau, Rock Daisy is found in the southern third of our area, growing from small crevices in cliffs. Small in stature, it is a low, spreading, bushy plant 6–15″ high.

Near the woody base of the plant, the leaves are opposite. Going up the stems, they become alternate. They are ovate-lanceolate to almost deltoid and are ½–2″ long, with 3–5 tooth-like lobes per margin.

The numerous yellow flower heads are carried at the ends of the branches in a cyme-like arrangement. Each head (¼–⅜″ in diameter) consists of 3–5 ray flowers and 10–15 disk flowers. The pappus of the achene is a single bristle. Perennial.

Bloom Period: April to September.
*Pedernales R., Travis Co.*

## Slender-Stem Bitterweed
*Hymenoxys scaposa*

The leafy clumps of this plant are common on dry calcareous soils and caliche banks throughout the Hill Country. The leafy part of the plant is usually only 3–6″ tall, but the erect flower stalks may reach 18″ in height.

Narrowly oblanceolate to linear, the basal leaves are up to 3″ long. Most are entire, but some have a few short lobes. All are covered with long, fine, soft hairs.

Each stem sends up a single, naked flower stalk (3–16″ long) which carries a single flower head ¾–1¼″ wide. Red-brown veins are often visible on the underside of the rays. Perennial.

Bloom Period: March to October.
*Hunt, Kerr Co.*

### Slender-Leaf Hymenoxys
*Hymenoxys linearifolia*

Actually very common, *H. linearifolia* is abundant in grassy areas in the southern two-thirds of the Hill Country. Its stems have multiple branches and each may carry more than one flower head. The yellow heads are ⅜–⅝″ wide on peduncles 1–6″ long. The linear to oblanceolate leaves are ¼–1¼″ long. Annual.
Bloom Period: March to June.
*Near Concan, Uvalde Co.*

### Dogweed
*Dyssodia tagetoides*

Found on caliche soils in the eastern half of our area, Dogweed is an erect, much-branched plant 1–2½′ tall. Its alternate, linear leaves are 1–3″ long, with well-spaced coarse teeth on the margins. The yellow flower heads are ⅝–1″ wide. Pale orange glands dot the phyllaries and leaves. Annual to short-lived perennial.
Bloom Period: June to August.
*Spicewood, Burnet Co.*

### Parralena
*Dyssodia pentachaeta*

Parralena is a low, bushy, densely leafy plant 2–8″ tall that is found on dry caliche throughout our area. Its opposite leaves are pinnately divided into 3–11 lobes and are sometimes stiff to the touch. Peduncles 1–4″ long carry the yellow flower heads, which are ¼–½″ in diameter. Perennial.
Bloom Period: Spring to Fall.
*Rio Frio, Real Co.*

## Damianita
*Chrysactina mexicana*

Damianita is a short, spreading shrub 8–16″ tall found on caliche and limestone outcrops in the southern half of the Hill Country.

Alternate, dark green, linear leaves ¼–⅜″ long crowd the stems. The leaves are dotted with glands and are aromatic when crushed.

The yellow flower heads are solitary on peduncles 1–2″ long that raise them above the foliage. Each head (⅜–¾″ in diameter) has about 12 ray flowers, numerous disk flowers and about 12 phyllaries. The ray flowers are 3-toothed and the disk flowers are 5-toothed. Under normal conditions, Damianita has a rather nondescript shape. Under harsh conditions, such as a dry, barren rock outcrop, it takes on a twisted, gnarled appearance similar to a fine bonsai. Perennial.

Bloom Period: April and May.
*Lakeway, Travis Co.*

## Palafoxia
*Palafoxia callosa*

Palafoxia is an erect, open, diffusely branched plant 1–2½' tall that can be found on all soil types throughout the Hill Country.

Its narrowly lanceolate to linear leaves are 1–2" long. They are densely covered with fine, minute hairs which give the plant a gray-green appearance.

There are no ray flowers, only white to pink disk flowers. The linear phyllaries are less than 1.3 mm. wide and the pappus less than 2 mm. long. *P. rosea*, an almost identical relative found in the Llano Uplift region, has phyllaries over 1.3 mm. wide and pappus over 2 mm. long. Annual.

Bloom Period: June to November.
*Honey Creek, Llano Co.*

## Woolly-White, Old Plainsman
*Hymenopappus scabiosaeus*

Old Plainsman is a single-stemmed plant 1–3' tall that grows on the calcareous clay soils of grasslands and prairies throughout our area.

Some plants are densely covered in white hairs, while others are nearly glabrous. In any case, the pubescence on the underside of the leaf will be more dense than that on the upper surface. The leaves may be once or twice pinnately lobed and up to 5" long.

The stem divides into numerous small branches and branchlets at the inflorescence, which is white to creamy-white. A white and pink flowered species, *H. artemisiaefolius*, is common on sandy soils in the Llano Uplift region. Biennial.

Bloom Period: April to June.
*Moody, McLennan Co.*

## Yarrow, Milfoil
*Achillea millefolium*

Yarrow is an attractive, delicate-look-ing plant (6–36″ tall) with one to sev-eral erect stems rising from a basal rosette of leaves. It is widely distributed through our area and can be found in disturbed soils, grassy areas, and in partial shade.

Fern-like in appearance, the alternate leaves are two to three times pinnately divided and are 1–12″ long. The longer leaves are part of the basal rosette. Going up the stem, the leaves are gen-erally less than 4″ long.

The numerous white flower heads are carried in a flat-topped, corymb-like arrangement. Each head has 5–12 rays and is approximately ¼″ wide by ⅛″ high. Yarrow is an aromatic plant with a strong but pleasant odor. It belongs to a tribe of the Compositae that con-tains several plants with medicinal qualities, such as Camomile and a type of Wormwood from which absinthe is made. Perennial.

Bloom Period: March to June.
*Georgetown, Williamson Co.*

## Golden Groundsel
*Senecio obovatus*

Golden Groundsel is found on moist, shaded, calcareous soils of canyons and stream valleys in the southern half of the Hill Country. It grows 6–18″ tall, with an unbranched stem.

Both stems and leaves are essentially glabrous. At the base of the plant, the leaf blades are round to oval (with un-lobed, toothed margins) on narrow pe-tioles 2–4 times as long as the blades. There are only a few leaves along the stem. They tend to be narrowly oblan-ceolate to lanceolate in outline, and are usually deeply pinnately lobed.

The numerous yellow flower heads are ½–¾″ wide. Mature achenes have a pappus of soft, silky bristles. Perennial.

Bloom Period: March to May.
*River Hills Rd., Travis Co.*

## Texas Groundsel
*Senecio ampullaceus*

Texas Groundsel grows 1–2½′ high on sandy soils and is found locally in the Llano Uplift region.

Its stems and leaves may be densely covered in extremely fine, woolly, white hairs or may be essentially glabrous. The lanceolate to oblanceolate leaves are 1–6″ long and may be entire or toothed. They reduce in size going up the stem and (at midstem and above) have truncate, clasping bases.

The yellow flower heads are ½–¾″ in diameter and ¼–⅜″ high. Annual.

Bloom Period: April.
*Bend, San Saba Co.*

## Butterweed
*Senecio imparipinnatus*
*(Senecio tampicanus)*

Butterweed is a well-branched plant 6–24″ high. It grows on seasonally moist soils on the eastern edge of our area along a line from Hays to McLennan counties.

The leaves are evenly distributed over the plant and are 1–5″ long. They are deeply pinnately divided. The lateral lobes of the leaf are wedge-shaped (broadest at the tip) and are often lobed again.

The yellow flower heads are typical of the genus, but are only about ½″ in diameter. *S. imparipinnatus* is closely related and similar to *S. glabellus* and *S. Greggii*. Annual.

Bloom Period: March to May.
*Waco, McLennan Co.*

## Indian Plaintain
*Cacalia plantaginea*
*(Arnoglossum plantaginea)*

In our area, Indian Plaintain is found east of a line drawn between Kendall and Bosque counties. It grows 1½–4′ tall in partial shade on rich, moist soils.

Most of its leaves are basal. They are alternate, glabrous, and broadly lanceolate to elliptic, with long petioles and shallowly dentate margins. A few small leaves are carried on the stem, reducing in size as they approach the flower heads.

The white to cream-colored flower heads are clustered in a corymb-like arrangement. Perennial.

Bloom Period: May and June.
*Meridian Creek, Bosque Co.*

## Basket-Flower
*Centaurea americana*

Under favorable conditions, Basket-Flower forms large, dense colonies, particularly along roadsides. It grows 2–5′ tall on dry soils throughout the Hill Country.

The stout stems are simple to few-branched. All of the leaves are sessile and entire, with the exception of a few reduced leaves near the flower head that may be short-petiolate. At the base of the plant, the leaves are obovate. They become lanceolate going up the stem, where they average 1–2½″ long.

The solitary flower heads are 2–3½″ in diameter and consist of numerous pink and cream-colored disk flowers. There are no ray flowers present, but the outer disk flowers are larger and brighter than the inner disk flowers and apparently serve the same function as the absent rays. Individual outer disk flowers are large (about 1½″ long), with a corolla deeply incised into 4 or 5 linear lobes. Each of the lanceolate phyllaries is lined with several bristle-like lobes in its upper third to half. Annual.

Bloom Period: May and June.
*Temple, Bell Co.*

## Malta Star-Thistle
*Centaurea melitensis*

Introduced from Europe, Malta Star-Thistle is rapidly advancing and becoming an abundant pest throughout our area. It grows 6–24″ tall, branching into several ascending stems in its upper portion.

At the base of the plant, the oblanceolate, pinnately lobed leaves are 2–4″ long. Farther up the stem, the leaves become linear and smaller (up to 1¼″ long), with entire margins that extend down onto the stems, making them winged.

The yellow flower heads are ½–⅝″ high, including the globe-like involucre with its spine-tipped phyllaries. Annual to biennial.

Bloom Period: April to June.
*New Braunfels, Comal Co.*

## Musk-Thistle
*Carduus nutans*

Musk-Thistle is another species introduced from Europe that can become a problem. It is a stout, coarse, spiny plant with mostly simple stems growing 2–6′ tall. In the Hill Country area, it currently is pretty much confined to Gillespie, Kerr, and Kimble counties.

The alternate leaves are pinnately divided into spiny-toothed lobes. At the base of the leaf, the margins run down onto the stem, causing it to be winged.

The flower heads (2¼–3½″ wide) are composed of pinkish-red disk flowers and several rows of lanceolate, spine-tipped phyllaries. Biennial.

Bloom Period: May to July.
*Junction, Kimble Co.*

## Plumed Thistle
*Cirsium undulatum*

Plumed Thistle grows 1–3' tall and may be found in small colonies or as individuals. It is much less common than Texas Thistle and is found in scattered locations on dry soils throughout our area.

Pinnately divided and spiny-toothed, the lanceolate to oblanceolate leaves are almost, but not quite, as woolly on the upper surface as they are on the lower surface. The upper leaves have broad bases (not petiolate) and are either not or only slightly decurrent.

The disk flowers range in color from creamy-white to salmon to bright pink, with a range of shades between. Note that the 1–2" high involucre tends to be conical, that is, taller than wide. A sticky resin is exuded from the phyllaries, often trapping small insects. Perennial.

Bloom Period: May to July.
*Near Brady, McCulloch Co.*

## Texas Thistle
*Cirsium texanum*

Though most common in the southern half of our area, Texas Thistle can be found on dry soils in fields and prairies throughout the Hill Country. It grows 2–4½' tall, and may be single-stemmed or multi-branched.

At the midstem and above, the leaves are narrowly obovate in outline, and are pinnately divided into 3–9 spiny-toothed lobes on each side of the blade. Woolly hairs densely coat the underside of the leaf.

Pink disk flowers fan out from the slightly flattened, globe-shaped involucre. The linear phyllaries have spiny tips that bend outward from the involucre, possibly as a protective measure. Biennial to weak perennial.

Bloom Period: April to July.
*McNeil, Travis Co.*

## Peonia
*Perezia runcinata*
*(Acourtia runcinata)*

This tough little plant grows 3–12″ tall on dry desert or rocky soils in the southern half of the Hill Country.

Its leaves are in a basal rosette and may either all lay flat or range from flat to nearly upright. The narrowly obovate leaves are pinnately incised almost to the midrib. Each lobe is rounded to obovate and has several bristle-tipped teeth.

Separate designations of "ray" and "disk" flowers are inappropriate here as the pink heads consist of numerous two-lipped flowers, all of which are similar.

On some plants, the flower heads nestle among the rosette leaves, but on others they may be carried on naked peduncles up to 8″ long. The linear-lanceolate phyllaries have short, pointed tips. A little digging will expose the numerous tuberous roots which make this plant so hardy in xeric situations. Perennial.

Bloom Period: April to June.
*Medina Lake, Bandera Co.*

## Silver-Puff
*Chaptalia nutans*
*(Chaptalia texana)*

Silver-Puff is a shade-loving plant that sends up scapes 6–12" tall from a flattened basal rosette of leaves. It is most common on dry calcareous soils in the southern third of the Hill Country but can be found throughout our area.

The rosette leaves are 2½–5" long and ¾–1¼" wide. They are shallowly lobed with a lyrate or undulate margin, narrowing to a subpetiolar base. The upper leaf surface is essentially glabrous, while the lower leaf surface is densely woolly.

Naked peduncles 3–12" long carry the nodding, cylindrical flower heads. The heads are ½–1" long and remain tightly compacted until it is time to release the mature seed, at which time they expand into globe-like seedheads. Perennial.

Bloom Period: March to May.
*Fischer Hall, Comal Co.*

## White Rock-Lettuce
*Pinaropappus roseus*

Adapted to dry, rocky, calcareous soils, White Rock-Lettuce displays good ornamental qualities and is worthy of cultivation. It is a few-branched plant 6–12″ tall found throughout the Hill Country area.

Most of its leaves are crowded at the base, but a few narrowly lanceolate to linear leaves 1–3″ long advance up the stem. They may be entire or sparsely shallowly toothed.

The white to lavender-white flower heads are about 1½″ in diameter and are solitary and terminal on scape-like branches. They have linear-lanceolate phyllaries, which often have lavender margins and dark tips. Perennial.

Bloom Period: April and May.
*Concan, Uvalde Co.*

## Chicory
*Cichorium Intybus*

Currently, Chicory is uncommon in the Hill Country, but, for better or worse, is being included in commercially available wildflower seed mixes and promises to become more prevalent. It is an erect, much-branched plant 8–32″ tall that has been introduced from Europe.

Near the base, the leaves are lyrate or pinnately divided. Advancing up the stem, they become lanceoloate (or oblanceolate) with toothed margins. The uppermost leaves are bract-like and entire.

Some of the pale-blue flower heads (1–1¾″ wide) are sessile at the nodes, while others are solitary at the end of thickened, peduncle-like branches. Perennial.

Bloom Period: Spring to Fall.
*Austin, Travis Co.*

## Texas Dandelion
*Pyrrhopappus multicaulis*

Texas Dandelion grows 6–18" tall on calcareous soils throughout our area, with the exception of the Llano Uplift.

Most of its leaves are crowded at the base. Though generally 3–8" long and oblanceolate, they may vary widely in appearance since their margins can be entire, toothed, or pinnately lobed. A few reduced leaves extend 1–3 nodes up the stem and are usually deeply pinnatifid, with linear lobes.

The yellow flower heads are ¾–1¼" in diameter. Texas Dandelion is easily distinguished by the sprinkling of black to dark purple anther tubes scattered across the center of the head. Annual.

Bloom Period: March to June.
*Blanco, Blanco Co.*

## Goat's Beard
*Tragopogon dubius*

Introduced from Europe, Goat's Beard is a low, bushy plant 1–2' high, with one or a few tough stems. Common nowhere, *T. dubius* seems to be scattered through the northern half of our area.

Its alternate, linear-lanceolate leaves have a long tapering tip and are 1–7" long.

When open (most of the time they are closed), the flower heads are yellow. Each head has about 13 bract-like phyllaries that are 2" long and narrowly lanceolate. The large, globe-shaped seedhead may reach 4" in diameter. Biennial.

Bloom Period: April to June.
*Near Troy, Bell Co.*

## Skeleton-Plant
*Lygodesmia texana*

Skeleton-Plant derives its common name from its appearance of being leafless. Actually, there are a few narrow, entire to pinnately lobed leaves 4–6" long at the base of the plant, but these often dry and fall away before flowering time. Going up the stem from the base, there are a few short, linear leaves ¼–¾" long. Above the midstem, the leaves are reduced to the point of being scale-like.

An erect plant with only a few branches, *L. texana* grows 10–24" tall on dry rocky soils throughout the Hill Country.

The pink to lavender flower heads are 1–2" in diameter, and each one is composed of about 11 ray-like flowers (each true flower looks like one petal on the flower head). An equivalent number of dark purple to black anther tubes rise from the middle of the head. A light purple, velvety-looking two-parted style emerges from the center of each anther tube. In fruit, *L. texana* forms a typical dandelion-type seedhead made of achenes ⅜–⅝" long with simple pappus bristles of about the same length. Perennial.

Bloom Period: April to August.
*Marble Falls, Burnet Co.*

## Sow-Thistle
*Sonchus* sp.

Sow-Thistle grows 6–24″ tall, with an erect, few-branched stem. We have two species, *S. oleraceus* and *S. asper*, which were introduced from Europe and have become widespread on lawns and disturbed soils throughout the Hill Country.

Both species have clasping, pinnately incised, spiny-lobed leaves. The leaves reduce in size going up the stem, becoming lanceolate-deltoid near the flower heads, but remaining spiny and clasping.

For all practical purposes, the two species are identical. Both have yellow flower heads and an involucre ¼–½″ high. *S. oleraceus* has achenes 3.5–4 times longer than broad, which are broadest above the middle. *S. asper* has achenes 2–2.5 times longer than broad, which are broadest near the middle. Annual.

Bloom Period: All year.
*Henly, Hays Co.*

## Dandelion
*Taraxacum officinale*

Dandelion is a frequent pest species in lawns and disturbed soils. On the other hand, it is attractive. After all, who hasn't enjoyed blowing on one of its seedheads and watching the seeds float away? It is another introduced species from Europe, and has advanced widely through Texas.

Its leaves are in a basal rosette and are 2–6″ long. They are pinnately incised, with lobes that are slightly broadened at the tips and swept back, giving the leaves a "barbed" look.

The yellow flower heads, solitary on naked scapes 1–10″ long, are ½–1″ in diameter. Annual to perennial.

Bloom Period: All year.
*Meridian Creek, Bosque Co.*

Abbott, Carroll. *How to Know and Grow Texas Wildflowers.* Kerrville, Tex.: Green Horizons Press. 1982.

Ajilvsgi, Geyata. *Wild Flowers of the Big Thicket, East Texas, and Western Louisiana.* College Station: Texas A&M University Press. 1979.

Ajilvsgi, Geyata. *Wildflowers of Texas.* Bryan, Tex.: Shearer Publishing. 1984.

Correll, D. S., and Marshall Johnston. *Manual of the Vascular Plants of Texas.* Renner, Tex.: Texas Research Foundation. 1970.

Cronquist, Arthur. *An Integrated System of Classification of Flowering Plants.* New York: Columbia University Press. 1981.

Geiser, Samuel Wood. *Naturalists of the Frontier.* Dallas: Southern Methodist University. 1948.

Gillett, James B. *Six Years With the Texas Rangers.* Lincoln, Nebraska: University of Nebraska Press. 1976.

Grant, Verne. *Plant Speciation.* New York: Columbia University Press. 1971.

Hartmann, Hudson T., and Dale E. Kester. *Plant Propagation, Principles and Practices.* Englewood Cliffs, New Jersey: Prentice-Hall, Inc. 1959.

Loughmiller, Lynn, and Campbell Loughmiller. *Texas Wildflowers.* Austin: University of Texas Press. 1984.

McCoy, Doyle. *Roadside Flowers of Oklahoma.* Lawton, Oklahoma: Published by the author. 1976.

Nokes, Jill. *How to Grow Native Plants of Texas and the Southwest.* Austin: Texas Monthly Press. 1986.

Radford, Albert E., with William C. Dickison, Jimmy R. Massey, and C. Ritchie Bell. *Vascular Plant Systematics.* New York: Harper and Row, Publishers. 1974.

Recenthin, C. A. *Native Flowers of Texas.* Temple, Tex.: U. S. Dept. of Agriculture, Soil Conservation Service. 1972.

Rickett, Harold William. *Wildflowers of the United States,* Vol. 3, *Texas.* New York: McGraw-Hill. 1969.

Roemer, Ferdinand. *Texas.* Waco, Texas: Texian Press. 1967.

Schulz, Ellen D. *Texas Wild Flowers.* Chicago and New York: Laidlaw Brothers, Publishers. 1928.

Stearn, William T. *Botanical Latin.* London: David and Charles. 1966.

Stiff, Edward. *The Texan Emigrant.* Waco, Tex.: Texian Press. 1968.

Turner, B. L. *The Legumes of Texas*. Austin: University of Texas Press. 1959.

Vines, Robert A. *Trees, Shrubs, and Woody Vines of the Southwest*. Austin: University of Texas Press. 1960.

Warnock, Barton H. *Wildflowers of the Big Bend Country, Texas*. Alpine, Tex.: Sul Ross University. 1970.

Warnock, Barton H. *Wildflowers of the Guadalupe Mountains and the Sand Dune Country, Texas*. Alpine, Tex.: Sul Ross University. 1974.

Warnock, Barton H. *Wildflowers of the Davis Mountains and Marathon Basin, Texas*. Alpine, Tex.: Sul Ross University. 1977.

Wasowski, Sally, and Julie Ryan. *Landscaping with Native Texas Plants*. Austin: Texas Monthly Press. 1985.

Weniger, Del. *Cacti of Texas and Neighboring States*. Austin: University of Texas Press. 1984.

Whitehouse, Eula. *Texas Flowers in Natural Colors*. Austin: Published by the author. 1936.

Wills, Mary Motz, and Howard S. Irwin. *Roadside Flowers of Texas*. Austin: University of Texas Press. 1961.

Wood, Carroll E. *A Student's Atlas of Flowering Plants: Some Dicotyledons of Eastern North America*. New York: Harper and Row. 1974.

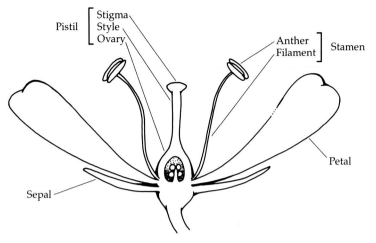

Pistil [ Stigma, Style, Ovary

Anther, Filament ] Stamen

Petal

Sepal

CROSS-SECTION OF A HYPOTHETICAL FLOWER.

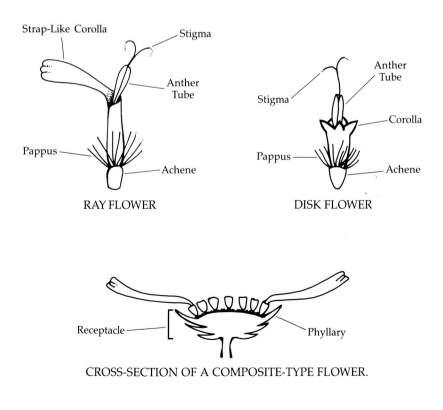

Strap-Like Corolla        Stigma

Anther Tube

Pappus

Achene

RAY FLOWER

Stigma

Anther Tube

Corolla

Pappus

Achene

DISK FLOWER

Receptacle

Phyllary

CROSS-SECTION OF A COMPOSITE-TYPE FLOWER.

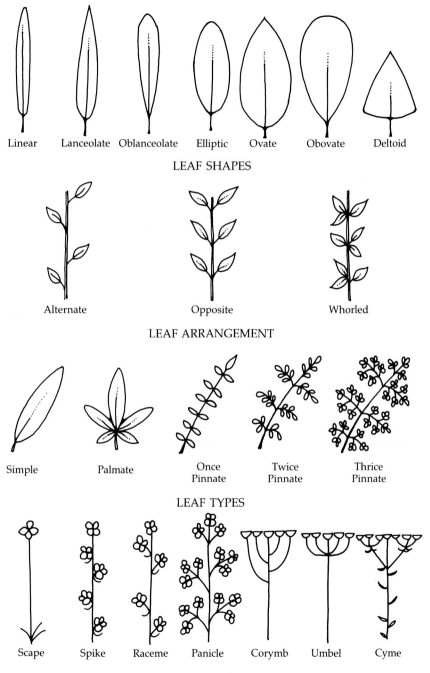

Linear    Lanceolate   Oblanceolate   Elliptic   Ovate   Obovate   Deltoid

LEAF SHAPES

Alternate          Opposite          Whorled

LEAF ARRANGEMENT

Simple     Palmate     Once       Twice      Thrice
                       Pinnate    Pinnate    Pinnate

LEAF TYPES

Scape     Spike     Raceme     Panicle     Corymb     Umbel     Cyme

INFLORESCENCE TYPES

*Achene*  a small, dry, one-seeded indehiscent fruit.

*Alternate*  any leaf arrangement along the axis other than opposite or whorled.

*Annual*  a plant completing its life cycle within a single year or season.

*Antrorse*  directed upward or forward, usually parallel to a plane or axis.

*Apex*  tip of a plant part.

*Appressed*  pressed parallel to or against another structure.

*Areole*  in cactus, a raised or depressed spot on the surface through which spines or leaves grow.

*Aromatic*  fragrant, spicy-pungent; usually in reference to a scent given off by crushed leaves.

*Ascending*  rising or curving upward.

*Awn*  a terminal bristle on an organ.

*Axil*  the angle formed between a leaf and the stem it attaches to.

*Axillary*  born or carried in the axil.

*Biennial*  a plant completing its life cycle in two years.

*Bract*  a reduced or modified leaf subtending a flower or flower cluster.

*Bulb*  underground bud enclosed in numerous overlapping thickened leafy scales; the common onion.

*Calcareous*  consisting of a large percentage of calcium carbonate; in reference to soils, those derived from limestone.

*Caliche*  a white to cream-colored carbonate soil; decomposed limestone.

*Calyx*  collectively, the outer whorl of flower parts, usually green.

*Campanulate*  bell-shaped.

*Capitate*  head-like, or aggregated into dense heads.

*Capsule*  a dry, dehiscent fruit consisting of two or more carpels.

*Carpel*  the ovule-bearing portion of a flower; a simple pistil or one part of a compound pistil.

*Catkin*  a scaly deciduous spike.

*Ciliate*  fringed with hairs on the margin.

*Cleistogamous*  refers to small, non-opening, self-fertilizing flowers.

*Conduplicate*  folded lengthwise.

*Connate*  united at the base; usually refers to the joining of the basal part of the blades of opposite leaves.

*Cordate*  heart-shaped.

*Corolla*  the inner, colored whorl of flower parts; the petals collectively.

*Corymb*  a flat-topped or convex flower cluster with the outer pedicels longest, the outer flowers opening first.

*Crenate*  a margin with rounded teeth.

*Cuneate*  wedge-shaped, often in reference to the base of a leaf.

*Cyathium*  the specialized inflorescence of Euphorbia, consisting of a flower-like, cup-shaped involucre which carries the several true flowers within.

*Decumbent*   lying down with the tip ascending.

*Decurrent*   extending beyond normal placement, as the margin of a leaf sometimes extends past the leaf node and down the stem.

*Deltoid*   triangular.

*Dentate*   a margin with teeth that point outward but not forward.

*Dichotomous*   repeatedly branching in pairs.

*Disk Flower*   a small tubular flower found on the central disk of a composite-type flower head.

*Drupe*   a fleshy, one-seeded, indehiscent fruit; stone-fruits such as peach and plum.

*Elliptic*   narrowly oval, usually twice as long as broad.

*Endemic*   restricted in range to a given area that may be defined politically or geographically.

*Entire*   a margin that is linear and unbroken.

*Exsert*   beginning within and projecting beyond.

*Fascicle*   a compact bundle or cluster.

*Filament*   slender, threadlike stalk supporting the anther; any threadlike structure.

*Filiform*   threadlike.

*Follicle*   a dry, one-carpelled, dehiscent fruit which opens along one line.

*Form*   a rank below subvariety (subvariety is one rank below variety).

*Glabrous*   lacking hairs.

*Gland*   a structure on or beneath a surface that secretes a sticky or aromatic fluid.

*Glandular*   bearing glands.

*Glaucous*   covered or tinted with a whitish or colored blush, like cabbage.

*Globose*   spherical, rounded.

*Grus*   a loose, gravelly soil consisting of weathered,decomposed granite.

*Hastate*   usually refers to a leaf with basal lobes that turn outwards.

*Head*   a dense cluster of flowers that rise from a common point on a peduncle.

*Herbaceous*   herb-like, usually leafy and green, non-woody.

*Incised*   cut, often deeply.

*Indehiscent*   not opening of itself, tending to remain closed.

*Inflorescence*   the flower cluster or flower head of a plant.

*Infructescence*   the inflorescence in its fruiting or seed stage.

*Internode*   the section of stem between two nodes.

*Involucel*   a secondary involucre.

*Involucre*   the whorl of bracts (or phyllaries) subtending a flower or flower cluster.

*Laciniate*   cut into slender lobes.

*Lateral*   on the side of.

*Linear*   long and narrow.

*Lyrate*   lyre-shaped; pinnately, sinuately lobed, the terminal lobe often largest.

*Margin*   edge; refers to the outer edge of a leaf.

*Marl*   a friable calcareous deposit characterized by numerous limestone nodules in a matrix of loose lime mud.

*Merous*   when preceded by a numeral (2-, 3-, 5-, etc.), indicates that the flower parts are equal to or in multiples of that number.

*Morphology*   the form and structure of an object.

*Mucronate*   having a small, short projection at the tip.

*Mycelium*   the filament-like structure of a fungus.

*Nerve*   the vein or rib of a leaf blade.

*Node*   the point on a stem from which leaves arise.

*Oblong*   much longer than broad, with nearly parallel sides.

*Orbicular*   more or less round.

*Ovary*   the ovule-bearing part of the pistil.

*Panicle*   a compound, raceme-like inflorescence.

*Pappus*   a crown of scales or bristles on an achene.

*Parasite*   a plant that derives its nourishment from another living plant.

*Pedicel*   the stem of a single flower or of one flower in a group of flowers.

*Peduncle*   the stalk of a single flower or a group of flowers.

*Peltate*   a type of leaf having its petiole attached to the center of the lower surface of the blade, as in *Hydrocotyle.*

*Pendulous*   hanging.

*Perennial*   a plant of indefinite life span that renews itself each year.

*Perfoliate*   a condition with the stem apparently piercing a leaf, or surrounded by basally joined opposite leaves.

*Perianth*   collectively, the inner and outer whorls of flower parts; used when the distinction between the two whorls is vague or difficult to determine.

*Petiole*   the leaf stalk.

*Phyllary*   in the Compositae, one bract of the involucre.

*Pinna*   one leaflet or primary division of a pinnately divided leaf.

*Pinnate*   a compound leaf with the leaflets symmetrically arranged on both sides of a common petiole.

*Pinnatifid*   pinnately incised into lobes which may reach almost, but not quite, to the midrib.

*Pistil*   collectively, the stigma, style, and ovary; the ovule-bearing portion of a flower.

*Pleiochasium*   each main axis of a cyme producing more than two flowers.

*Plicate*   folded.

*Plumose*   featherlike.

*Pod*   a dry, dehiscent fruit; the fruit of a legume.

*Prickle*   a sharp outgrowth of the bark or epidermis of a plant.

*Procumbent*   trailing on the ground without rooting.

*Prostrate*   lying flat.

*Pubescent*   covered with hairs.

*Punctate*   dotted; either by punctures, depressions, or translucent glands.

*Raceme*   a simple, elongate inflorescence, with the pedicels of the flowers all nearly the same length.

*Rachis*   the axis of a spike, raceme, or compound leaf.

*Ray Flower*   the outer, petal-like flowers surrounding the disk of a member of the Compositae.

*Reniform*   kidney-shaped.

*Reticulate*   having a net-like pattern.

*Retrorse*   directed downward or backward, usually parallel to a plane or axis.

*Retuse*   notched at the apex.

*Rhizome*   an underground stem capable of producing new stems or plants at its nodes.

*Rugose*   wrinkled or bumpy.

*Sagittate*   shaped like an arrowhead.

*Samara*   an indehiscent winged fruit.

*Scape*   a flower stalk rising from the ground and carrying one or more flowers; it may bear scales or bracts, but no leaves.

*Scorpioid*   curled; as the shape of a scorpion's tail.

*Sepal*   a leaf-like segment of the calyx.

*Serrate*   a toothed margin, with the teeth pointing forward.

*Sessile*   a condition in which the blade of a leaf attaches directly to the stem, without a petiole.

*Sigmoid*   double-curved, S-shaped.

*Silique*   a type of capsule found in the Cruciferae, either half of which peels away from a central, transparent, dividing membrane.

*Simple*   undivided, not branched, not compound.

*Sinuate*   strongly or deeply wavy, usually in reference to a leaf margin.

*Spadix*   the flowering spike enveloped by a spathe.

*Spathe*   a sheath-like bract enclosing a spadix.

*Spatulate*   shaped like a spatula; wide and rounded at the apex, but narrow at the base.

*Spike*   an elongate inflorescence of sessile flowers.

*Spine*   a sharp-pointed rigid structure, usually a highly modified leaf or stipule.

*Ssp.*   subspecies.

**Stamen**  the male (pollen-bearing) organ of a flower; anther and filament collectively.

**Staminode**  a sterile stamen.

**Stellate**  having radiating arms, or shaped like a star.

**Stigma**  the pollen-receptive part of the pistil.

**Stipules**  pairs of much-reduced leaflike appendages found at the base of the petiole.

**Striate**  having fine ridges, grooves, or lines along the axis.

**Strigose**  covered with rough, stiff, sharp hairs that run more or less parallel to a given surface.

**Subtend**  to be closely below or adjacent to.

**Subulate**  awl-shaped.

**Succulent**  fleshy; soft and juicy.

**Tendril**  a coiling or twining organ with which a plant climbs.

**Tepals**  a collective term for petals and sepals, used when they cannot readily be differentiated.

**Ternate**  in sets of three, as a leaf composed of three leaflets.

**Thorn**  a sharp-pointed modified branch.

**Throat**  in a corolla composed of fused petals, the central opening of the flower.

**Tribe**  a subdivision of a Family which is higher than genus rank.

**Trifoliolate**  having three leaflets.

**Truncate**  abruptly ending; in reference to a leaf, one whose blade contracts sharply, in a very short distance, at the base.

**Tuber**  a short, thickened underground stem which bears numerous buds.

**Tubercle**  a knoblike protrusion from a surface; in the Cactaceae, a protrusion that bears an areole on or near its tip.

**Umbel**  a flat-topped or convex flower cluster in which the pedicels arise from a common point.

**Undulate**  wavy, usually in reference to a surface or margin.

**Unifoliolate**  with one leaf or leaflet.

**Var.**  variety.

**Vesicle**  a bladder or cavity.

**Whorl**  a ring-like arrangement of like parts (often leaves).

**Wing**  a ribbon-like membrane bordering plant parts, as along stems, around seeds, etc.

**Xeric**  pertaining to arid or desert conditions, implying minimal water supply.

*Abutilon incanum,* 99
Acacia, Catclaw, 54
*Acacia Farnesiana,* 54
  *Greggii,* 54
  *Roemeriana,* 54
*Acalypha hederacea,* 87
  *Lindheimeri,* 87
  *monostachya,* 87
  *radians,* 87
Acanthaceae, 193–196
Acanthus Family, 193–196
Acanthus, Flame, 195
*Achillea millefolium,* 243
*Acleisanthes longiflora,* 20
*Acourtia runcinata,* 249
*Aesculus arguta,* 92
  *glabra,* 92
  *Pavia,* 93
*Agalinis edwardsiana,* 188
  *heterophylla,* 188
Agalinis, Plateau, 188
  Prairie, 188
*Agaloma marginata,* 90
Agarita, 33
*Ageratina havanensis,* 209
Alamo Vine, 145
*Allium canadense,* 8
  *Drummondii,* 8
Almond, Texas, 51
Aloe, American, 12
*Aloysia gratissima,* 159
Amaranth Family, 18
Amaranthaceae, 18
Amaryllidaceae, 12
Amaryllis Family, 12
American Aloe, 12
*Amblyolepis setigera,* 238
Amole Plant, 12
*Amoreuxia Wrightii,* 103
*Amorpha fruticosa,* 68
*Amphiachyris amoenum,* 215
*Amsonia ciliata,* 134
Anacardiaceae, 91
Anacua, 153
*Anagallis arvensis,* 128
*Androstephium coeruleum,* 10
*Anemone edwardsiana,* 29
  *heterophylla,* 28
Anemone, Two-Flower, 29
Angel Hair, 146
Angel Trumpets, 20

*Anisacanthus Wrightii,* 195
Antelope-Horns, 135
Anthemideae, 243
*Aphanostephus ramosissimus,* 219
  *skirrhobasis,* 219
Apocynaceae, 134
*Apocynum cannabinum,* 134
*Aquilegia canadensis,* 25
*Arabis petiolaris,* 37
Araceae, 1
*Arbutus xalapensis,* 127
*Argemone albiflora,* 35
  *mexicana,* 35
*Arisaema Dracontium,* 1
*Arnoglossum plantaginea,* 245
Arum Family, 1
Asclepiadaceae, 135–141
*Asclepias asperula,* 135
  *incarnata,* 139
  *oenotheroides,* 136
  *texana,* 138
  *tuberosa,* 137
  *viridiflora,* 137
  *viridis,* 136
*Aster ericoides,* 218
  *patens,* 217
  *praealtus,* 217
  *subulatus,* 218
  *texanus,* 217
Aster, Dwarf White, 218
  Spread-Leaf, 217
  Tall, 217
  Texas, 217
  White, 218
Asterae, 210–219
*Astragulus crassicarpus,* 76
  *Lindheimeri,* 75
  *lotiflorus,* 74
  *Nuttallianus,* 75
Astragulus, Lindheimer's, 75
Avens, White, 49

Baby Blue-Eyes, 151
Baby's Breath, 197
*Baccharis neglecta,* 210
Balsam-Gourd, 203
Barbara's Buttons, 234
Barberry Family, 32–33
Barberry, Texas, 32
Basket-Flower, 246

*Bauhinia congesta*, 58
   *lunarioides*, 58
Beautyberry, American, 161
Beaver Poison, 120
Beebalm, Basil, 172
   Lemon, 173
   Spotted, 172
Bee-Brush, 159
Bee-Brush, 68
Beggar's Ticks, 125
Bellflower, Basin, 204
Berberidaceae, 32–33
*Berberis Swaseyi*, 32
   *trifoliolata*, 33
*Berlandiera texana*, 223
*Bifora americana*, 121
Bignoniaceae, 191
Bindweed, Purple, 145
   Texas, 143
Bishop's-Weed, Prairie, 121
Bitterweed, Brown, 237
   Slender-Stem, 239
   Yellow, 237
Black Cherry, Escarpment, 50
Black-Haw, Rusty, 199
   Southern, 199
Bladderpod, Engelmann's, 40
   Fendler's, 41
   Low, 42
   Silver, 40
Blazing Star, 208
Bluebell Family, 204–206
Bluebell Gentian, 133
Bluebell, Texas, 204
Bluebonnet, Texas, 63
Blue-Curls, 152
Blue-Eyed Grass, 13
Bluehearts, 190
Blue-Star, 134
Bluets, 197
Bluets, Small, 197
*Boerhaavia coccinea*, 20
Boneset, White, 209
Borage Family, 153–156
Boraginaceae, 153–156
Brazoria, Prairie, 164
*Brazoria scutellarioides*, 164
Briar, Sensitive, 57
Brickell-Bush, 208
*Brickellia cylindraceae*, 208
Broom-Wood, 101

Brown-Eyed Susan, 226
*Buchnera floridana*, 190
Buckeye Family, 92–93
Buckeye, Mexican, 94
   Red, 93
   Texas, 92
   White, 92
Buckthorn Family, 95
Buckwheat, Wild, 17
Bull Nettle, 89
Bundleflower, Illinois, 56
Buffalo Bur, 179
*Bupleurum rotundifolium*, 122
Bush-Clover, Tall, 78
Buttercup, Large, 26
Butterfly-Weed, 137
Butterweed, 245
Buttonbush, 198

*Cacalia plantaginea*, 245
Cacao Family, 101
Cactaceae, 109–110
Cactus Family, 109–110
Cactus, Hedgehog, 110
   Lace, 109
   Nipple, 110
   Strawberry, 110
Calico Bush, 160
*Callicarpa americana*, 161
*Callirhoe digitata*, 98
   *involucrata*, 97
   *leiocarpa*, 98
   *pedata*, 98
*Calylophus Berlandieri*, 113
   *Drummondianus*, 113
   *Hartweggii*, 112
*Calyptocarpus vialis*, 234
Camas, Death, 6
*Camassia scilloides*, 10
*Campanula Reverchonii*, 204
Campanulaceae, 204–206
Camphor Weed, 121
*Campsis radicans*, 191
Caper Family, 43
Capparidaceae, 43
Caprifoliaceae, 199–200
Cardinal Feather, 87
Cardinal Flower, 206
*Carduus nutans*, 247
Carrot, Wild, 124

Caryophyllaceae, 24
*Cassia fasciculata*, 60
*Lindheimeri*, 60
*pumilio*, 59
*Roemeriana*, 59
*Castilleja indivisa*, 190
*purpurea*, 189
Catalpa Family, 191
*Ceanothus americanus*, 95
*herbaceus*, 95
Celestials, 13
Cenizo, 182
*Centaurea americana*, 246
*melitensis*, 247
*Centaurium Beyrichii*, 132
*calycosum*, 132
*texense*, 133
Centaury, Lady Bird's, 133
*Cephalanthus occidentalis*, 198
*Cercis canadensis*, 59
*Cevallia sinuata*, 107
Cevallia, Stinging, 107
*Chilopsis linearis*, 191
Cichorieae, 251–254
*Cichorium Intybus*, 251
*Cicuta maculata*, 120
*mexicana*, 120
*Cirsium texanum*, 248
*undulatum*, 248
Cistaceae, 102
Citrus Family, 84
*Chaetopappa bellidifolia*, 218
*Chamaecrista fasciculata*, 60
*Chamaesaracha coniodes*, 177
*sordida*, 177
*Chaptalia nutans*, 250
*texana*, 250
Cherry, Escarpment Black, 50
Chickweed, 24
Chicory, 251
*Chrysactina mexicana*, 241
Clammy-Weed, 43
*Clematis Drummondii*, 29
*Pitcheri*, 31
*texensis*, 30
*Cleomella angustifolia*, 43
Clover, Pin, 80
Clover, Sour, 64
White, 65
*Cnidoscolus texanus*, 89
Cochlospermaceae, 103

Cochlospermum Family, 103
*Coldenia canescens*, 154
Columbine, 25
*Commelina erecta*, 4
Commelinaceae, 3–5
*Commelinantia anomala*, 3
Compositae, 207–254
Coneflower, Clasping-Leaf, 226
Cone-Flower, Purple, 225
*Conium maculatum*, 120
*Conoclinium coelestinum*, 209
Convolvulaceae, 142–146
*Convolvulus equitans*, 143
*Cooperia Drummondii*, 12
*pedunculata*, 12
*Cordia podocephala*, 153
Cordia, White, 153
*Coreopsis basalis*, 232
*tinctoria*, 232
Cornaceae, 126
Corn-Salad, 201
*Cornus Drummondii*, 126
Corona de Cristo, 106
*Corydalis curvisiliqua*, 36
*Coryphantha sulcata*, 110
*Cotinus obovatus*, 91
Crabapple, Blanco, 47
Crassulaceae, 44
*Crataegus*, 48
*Croptilon divaricatum*, 210
*Hookerianum*, 210
Crowfoot Family, 25–31
Crow-Needles, 122
Crow-Poison, 7
Cruciferae, 37–42
*Cucurbita foetidissima*, 202
Cucurbitaceae, 202–203
*Cuscuta*, 146
Cymopterus, Big-Root, 123
*Cymopterus macrorhizus*, 123
*Cynanchum barbigerum*, 141
Cynareae, 246–248

Daisy, Black-Foot, 221
Cowpen, 231
Engelmann, 224
Granite, 210
Lazy, 219
Lindheimer, 223
Pincushion, 236
Rock, 239

Saw-Leaf, 214
Scratch, 210
Straggler, 234
*Dalea aurea*, 70
  *compacta*, 72
  *frutescens*, 69
  *Hallii*, 71
  *lasiathera*, 69
  *multiflora*, 72
  *nana*, 71
Dalea, Black, 69
  Dwarf, 71
  Golden, 70
  Hall's, 71
  Purple, 69
  Pussy-Foot, 70
Damianita, 241
Dandelion, 254
Dandelion, Texas, 252
*Datura inoxia*, 180
*Daucosma laciniatum*, 121
*Daucus pusillus*, 124
Day Flower, 4
Day Flower, False, 3
Death Camas, 6
*Delphinium carolinianum*, 27
  *vimineum*, 27
  *virescens*, 27
*Descurania pinnata*, 38
Desert Willow, 191
*Desmanthus illinoensis*, 56
Devil's Claw, 192
Dewberry, 49
Dodder, 146
Dogbane, 134
Dogbane Family, 134
Dog's Ear, 154
Dog's-Tooth-Violet, White, 9
Dogweed, 240
Dogwood Family, 126
*Draba cuneifolia*, 39
*Dracopis amplexicaulis*, 226
Dragon-Head, Beautiful False, 166
Dragon-Head, False, 166
Dutchman's Breeches, 84
*Dyschoriste linearis*, 193
*Dyssodia pentachaeta*, 240
  *tagetoides*, 240

*Echinacea angustifolia*, 225
*Echinocactus setispinus*, 110

*Echinocereus caespitosas*, 109
  *Reichenbachii*, 109
  *triglochidiatus*, 110
*Ehretia anacua*, 153
Elder-Berry, 199
*Engelmannia pinnatifida*, 224
*Ephedra antisyphylitica*, 2
Ephedraceae, 2
Ephedra Family, 2
*Epipactis gigantea*,14
Ericaceae, 127
*Erigeron modestus*, 219
  *philadelphicus*,219
*Eriogonum annuum*, 17
*Erodium cicutarium*, 80
  *texanum*, 80
*Eryngium Leavenworthii*, 125
Eryngo, 125
*Erythronium albidum*, 9
Eupatorieae, 208–209
*Eupatorium coelestinum*, 209
  *havanense*, 209
  *serotinum*, 209
Euphorbiaceae, 87–90
*Euphorbia cyathophora*, 90
  *marginata*, 90
  *Roemeriana*, 89
*Eustoma grandiflorum*, 133
Evening Primrose Family, 112–119
Eve's Necklace, 61
*Evolvulus Nuttallianus*, 142
  *sericeus*, 142
Evolvulus, Shaggy, 142
  Silky, 142
  White, 142
*Eysenhardtia texana*, 68

*Ferocactus setispinus*, 110
Figwort Family, 181–190
Firewheel, 235
Flame Acanthus, 195
Flame-Flower, 23
Flax Family, 82–83
Flax, Hudson, 83
  Meadow, 82
  Rock, 82
  Yellow, 83
Fleabane, Marsh, 220
  Philadelphia, 219
  Plains, 219

Four-O'Clock, 19
Four-O'Clock Family, 19–20
Fox-Glove, 182
*Froelichia gracilis,* 18
Frog-Fruit, 161
Frostweed, 231
Fumariaceae, 36
Fumitory Family, 36
Funnel-Flower, 10

*Gaillardia pulchella,* 235
  *suavis,* 236
*Galactia heterophylla,* 76
Garlic, Wild, 8
*Gaura calcicola,* 113
  *coccinea,* 114
  *suffulta,* 115
Gaura, False, 119
  Limestone, 113
  Scarlet, 114
Gay-Feather, 208
Gentianaceae, 131–133
Gentian, Bluebell, 133
Gentian Family, 131–133
Geraniaceae, 80
*Geranium carolinianum,* 80
Geranium Family, 80
Geranium, Wild, 80
Germander, American, 162
  Cut-Leaf, 162
*Geum canadense,* 49
Gilia, Blue, 148
  Cut-Leaf, 147
*Gilia incisa,* 147
  *rigidula,* 148
*Glandularia bipinnatifida,* 158
  *pumila,* 159
Goat's Beard, 252
Golden-Aster, Gray, 211
Golden-Eye, 227
Goldenrod, Tall, 216
  Prairie, 216
Golden-Wave, 232
Gourd Family, 202–203
Gourd, Buffalo, 202
  Speckled, 202
  Stinking, 202
Granite-Daisy, Sticky, 212
Grass, Blue-Eyed, 13
Green Dragon, 1
Green-Eyes, Texas, 223

Green Lily, 7
Greenthread, 233
*Grindelia lanceolata,* 213
  *microcephala,* 213
  *squarrosa,* 213
Gromwell, False, 156
Ground Cherry, Purple, 176
  Yellow, 177
Ground Plum, 76
Groundsel, Golden, 244
  Texas, 244
Gumweed, 213
Gumweed, Fall, 213
*Gutierrezia Sarothrae,* 215
*Gymnosperma glutinosum,* 214

Hamamelidaceae, 46
*Hamamelis virginiana,* 46
Hawthorn, 48
Heath Family, 127
*Hedeoma acinoides,* 175
  *Drummondii,* 175
Hedge-Parsley, 125
  Knotted, 124
*Hedyotis crassifolia,* 197
  *nigricans,* 197
Helenieae, 235–242
*Helenium amarum,* 237
  *autumnale,* 237
  *badium,* 237
  *microcephalum,* 236
  *quadridentatum,* 236
Heliantheae, 221–234
*Helianthemum georgianum,* 102
*Helianthus annuus,* 229
  *hirsutus,* 228
  *Maximiliani,* 228
Heliotrope, White, 155
*Heliotropium indicum,* 154
  *tenellum,* 155
Hellebore, Giant, 14
Hemlock, Poison, 120
  Water-, 120
Hemp, Indian, 134
Henbit, 167
*Hermannia texana,* 101
*Heterotheca canescens,* 211
  *latifolia,* 211
  *stenophylla,* 212
Hierba del Marrano, 218
Hierba de Zizotes, 136

Hippocastanaceae, 92–93
Honeysuckle Family, 199–200
Honeysuckle, Texas, 200
White, 200
Honeysuckle, Wild, 115
Horehound, Common, 174
Horsemint, Purple, 173
Horse-Nettle, Western, 178
*Houstonia crassifolia*, 197
*nigricans*, 197
Huisache, 54
Huisache-Daisy, 238
Hyacinth, Wild, 10
*Hydrocotyle umbellata*, 123
Hydrophyllaceae, 151–152
*Hymenopappus scabiosaeus*, 242
*Hymenoxys linearifolia*, 240
*scaposa*, 239
Hymenoxys, Slender-Leaf, 240

*Ibervillea Lindheimeri*, 203
Indian Apple, 180
Indian Blanket, 235
Indian-Turnip, 67
Indigo, False, 68
*Indigofera miniata*, 65
Inuleae, 220
*Ipomoea Lindheimeri*, 144
*pandurata*, 143
*sinuata*, 145
*trichocarpa*, 145
*Ipomopsis rubra*, 147
Iridaceae, 13
Iris Family, 13
Ironweed, Western, 207
Woolly, 207

*Jatropha dioica*, 88
Jimson-Weed, 180
Joint-Fir, 2
*Justicia americana*, 196
*pilosella*, 196

Kidney Wood, 68
Knock-Away, 153
Knotweed Family, 17
*Krameria lanceolata*, 79
Krameriaceae, 79

Labiatae, 162–175
Ladies' Tresses, 14

*Lamium amplexicaule*, 167
*Lantana horrida*, 160
Lantana, Texas, 160
Larkspur, Prairie, 27
Lauraceae, 34
Laurel Family, 34
Lead-Tree, Golden-Ball, 55
Leatherflower, Scarlet, 30
Purple, 31
Leather Stem, 88
Legume Family, 54–78
Leguminosae, 54–78
*Lepidium virginicum*, 39
*Lespedeza Stuevei*, 78
*Lesquerella argyraea*, 40
*densiflora*, 42
*Engelmannii*, 40
*Fendleri*, 41
*Leucophyllum frutescens*, 182
*Liatris mucronata*, 208
Liliaceae, 6–11
Lily Family, 6–11
Lily, Green, 7
Linaceae, 82–83
*Linaria texana*, 186
*Lindera Benzoin*, 34
*Lindheimera texana*, 223
*Linum hudsonioides*, 83
*pratense*, 82
*rigidum*, 83
*rupestre*, 82
*Lithospermum incisum*, 155
Loasaceae, 107–108
*Lobelia cardinalis*, 206
*Lonicera albiflora*, 200
Loosestrife, California, 111
Stream, 111
Loosestrife Family, 111
Low Milk-Vetch, 74
*Ludwigia octovalvis*, 119
*Lupinus texensis*, 63
*Lygodesmia texana*, 253
Lythraceae, 111
*Lythrum californicum*, 111
*ovalifolium*, 111

Madder Family, 197–198
Madrone, Texas, 127
Mallow Family, 96–100

Mallow, Globe, 99
Indian, 99
Mexican, 101
Rose, 96
Velvet-Leaf, 98
Malpighiaceae, 85
Malpighia Family, 85
Malvaceae, 96–100
*Malvaviscus arboreus*, 96
*Drummondii*, 96
*Mammillaria sulcata*, 110
*Manfreda maculosa*, 12
Marble-Seed, 156
*Marrubium vulgare*, 174
*Marshallia caespitosa*, 234
Martyniaceae, 192
*Matelea bifora*, 139
*edwardsensis*, 140
*reticulata*, 140
*Maurandya antirrhiniflora*, 186
*Melampodium leucanthum*, 221
Mejorana, 170
*Melilotus albus*, 64
*indicus*, 64
*officinalis*, 64
*Melochia pyramidata*, 101
Meloncito, 202
*Melothria pendula*, 202
*Menodora heterophylla*, 130
*longiflora*, 130
Menodora, Showy, 130
*Mentha spicata*, 174
*Mentzelia oligosperma*, 108
*Reverchonii*, 108
Mercury, Three-Seeded, 87
*Merremia dissecta*, 145
Mexican Hat, 227
Milfoil, 243
Milkpea, 76
Milk-Vetch, Low, 74
Nuttall's, 75
Milkvine, Plateau, 140
Milkweed Family, 135–141
Milkweed, Climbing, 141
Green, 136
Orange, 137
Pearl, 140
Pink, 139
Texas, 138
Wand, 137
White, 138

Milkweed Vine, Green, 140
Purple, 139
Wavy-Leaf, 141
Milkwort Family, 86
Milkwort, Purple, 86
White, 86
*Mimosa biuncifera*, 56
*borealis*, 56
Mimosa, Pink, 56
*Mimulus glabrata*, 181
Mint Family, 162–175
*Mirabilis linearis*, 19
Mist-Flower, Blue, 209
Mock-Orange, Canyon, 45
*Monarda citriodora*, 173
*clinopodioides*, 172
*punctata*, 172
Monkey-Flower, 181
Moraceae, 15
Mormon-Tea, 2
Morning Glory Family, 142–146
Morning Glory, Lindheimer's, 144
*Morus microphylla*, 15
Mountain Laurel, Texas, 62
Mountain Pink, 132
Mulberry Family, 15
Mulberry, Littleleaf, 15
Texas, 15
Mullein, Common, 181
Musk-Flower, Scarlet, 19
Musk-Thistle, 247
Mustard Family, 37–42
Mutisieae, 249–250

*Nama hispidum*, 152
Navajo Tea, 233
*Nemastylis geminiflora*, 13
*Nemophila phacelioides*, 151
*Neptunia lutea*, 57
Nerve-Ray, 224
*Nicotiana repanda*, 180
*trigonophylla*, 180
Nightshade Family, 176–180
Nightshade, False, 177
Silver-Leaf, 178
Texas, 179
*Nothoscordum bivalve*, 7
Nuttall's Milk-Vetch, 75
Nyctaginaceae, 19–20
*Nyctaginia capitata*, 19

Obedient-Plant, 165
*Oenothera Jamesii*, 115
  *laciniata*, 118
  *macrocarpa*, 116
  *missouriensis*, 116
  *rhombipetala*, 117
  *speciosa*, 116
  *triloba*, 118
Old Man's Beard, 29
Old Plainsman, 242
Oleaceae, 130
Olive Family, 130
Onagraceae, 112–119
Onion, Canada, 8
  Wild, 8
*Onosmodium Helleri*, 156
  *molle*, 156
*Opuntia compressa*, 109
  *leptocaulis*, 109
  *macrorhiza*, 109
Orchidaceae, 14
Orchid, Chatterbox, 14
Orchid Family, 14
Orchid Tree, Anacacho, 58
Oreja de Perro, 154
Orpine Family, 44
Oxalidaceae, 81
*Oxalis Dillenii*, 81
  *Drummondii*, 81

Paintbrush, Prairie, 189
  Texas, 190
*Palafoxia callosa*, 242
Paloverde, 61
Papaveraceae, 35
*Parkinsonia aculeata*, 61
*Paronychia virginica*, 24
Parralena, 240
Parsley Family, 120–125
Partridge Pea, 60
*Passiflora affinis*, 105
  *foetida*, 106
  *lutea*, 105
  *tenuiloba*, 105
Passifloraceae, 105–106
Passion-Flower Family, 105–106
Passionflower, Slender-Lobe, 105
  Yellow, 105
*Pavonia lasiopetala*, 96
Pavonia, Rose, 96

Pea, Hoary, 73
  Scarlet, 65
Peach Bush, 52
Pennyroyal, Annual, 175
  Mock, 175
*Penstemon baccharifolius*, 183
  *Cobaea*, 182
  *guadalupensis*, 184
  *Helleri*, 185
  *laxiflorus*, 184
  *triflorus*, 185
Penstemon, Cut-Leaf, 183
  Loose-Flowered, 184
  Scarlet, 185
  White, 184
Peonia, 249
Peppergrass, 39
*Perezia runcinata*, 249
*Perityle Lindheimeri*, 239
*Persicaria bicornis*, 17
*Petalostemum multiflorum*, 72
  *pulcherrimum*, 72
*Philadelphus Ernestii*, 45
  *texensis*, 45
*Physalis cinarescens*, 177
  *lobata*, 176
  *viscosa*, 177
Pigeon-Berry, 21
*Pilostyles Thurberi*, 16
Pimpernel, Scarlet, 128
Pin Clover, 80
*Pinaropappus roseus*, 251
Pink Family, 24
Pink, Mountain, 132
*Phacelia congesta*, 152
  *patuliflora*, 151
Phacelia, Blue, 151
Phlox Family, 147–150
*Phlox Drummondii*, 149
  *pilosa*, 150
  *Roemeriana*, 150
Phlox, Drummond, 149
  Golden-Eye, 150
  Prairie, 150
*Phyla incisa*, 161
  *nodiflora*, 161
*Physostegia angustifolia*, 166
  *intermedia*, 165
  *pulchella*, 166
Phytolaccaceae, 21

Plaintain, Indian, 245
*Pluchea odorata*, 220
  *purpurescens*, 220
Plum, Creek, 52
  Mexican, 53
  Texas, 52
*Poinsettia cyathophora*, 90
Poison Hemlock, 120
Pokeweed Family, 21
*Polanisia dodecandra*, 43
Polemoniaceae, 147–150
*Polianthes maculosa*, 12
Polygalaceae, 86
*Polygala alba*, 86
  *Lindheimeri*, 86
Polygonaceae, 17
*Polygonum bicorne*, 17
Poppy Family, 35
Poppy, Mexican, 35
  White Prickly, 35
Portulacaceae, 22–23
*Portulaca umbraticola*, 22
Potato, Wild, 143
Poverty Weed, 210
Prairie Clover, Purple, 72
  White, 72
Prickly Pear, 109
Primrose Family, 128
Primrose, Cut-Leaf Evening, 118
  Four-Point Evening, 117
  Missouri, 116
  Pink Evening, 116
  Square-Bud, 113
  Stemless Evening, 118
  River, 115
  Western, 112
Primulaceae, 128
*Prionopsis ciliata*, 214
*Proboscidea louisianica*, 192
*Prunus mexicana*, 53
  *minutiflora*, 51
  *rivularis*, 53
  *serotina*, 50
  *texana*, 52
*Psoralea cuspidata*, 67
  *cyphocalyx*, 66
  *latestipulata*, 66
  *rhombifolia*, 67
Psoralea, Brown-Flowered, 67
  Wand, 66

*Ptelea trifoliata*, 84
Puccoon, 155
Purple Sage, 182
Purslane, 22
Purslane Family, 22–23
Pussy-Foot Dalea, 70
Pyramid Flower, 101
*Pyrrhopappus multicaulis*, 252
*Pyrus ionensis*, 47

Queen's Delight, 88

Rafflesia Family, 16
Rafflesiaceae, 16
Rain-Lily, 12
Ranunculaceae, 25–31
*Ranunculus macranthus*, 26
Ratany, 79
Ratany Family, 79
*Ratibida columnaris*, 227
Rattlesnake-Weed, 124
Redbud, 130
Redbud, Texas, 59
Redroot, 95
Retama, 61
Rhamnaceae, 95
*Rhus microphylla*, 91
*Rivina humilis*, 21
Rock-Cress, 37
Rock-Lettuce, White, 251
Rockrose, 102
Rockrose Family, 102
Roosevelt Weed, 210
*Rorippa Nasturtium-aquaticum*, 38
Rosaceae, 47–53
Rose Family, 47–53
Rose-Gentian, 131
Rosin-Weed, Simpson, 222
  White, 222
Rosita, 132
Rough-Leaf Dogwood, 126
Rubber Plant, 88
Rubiaceae, 197–198
*Rubus trivialis*, 49
*Rudbeckia amplexicaulis*, 226
  *hirta*, 226
*Ruellia Drummondiana*, 193
  *humilis*, 195
  *nudiflora*, 194
Rutaceae, 84

*Sabatia campestris*, 131
Sage, Blue, 168
Cedar, 169
Giant Blue, 171
Lyre-Leaf, 167
Mealy, 170
Shrubby Blue, 170
Tropical, 171
*Salvia azurea*, 171
*ballotaeflora*, 170
*coccinea*, 171
*Engelmannii*, 168
*farinacea*, 170
*lyrata*, 167
*Roemeriana*, 169
*texana*, 168
Salvia, Engelmann's, 168
*Sambucus canadensis*, 199
Sand Bells, 152
Sapindaceae, 94
*Sarcostemma crispum*, 141
*cynanchoides*, 141
Saxifragaceae, 45
Saxifrage Family, 45
*Scandix Pecten-Veneris*, 122
*Schrankia*, 57
*Schoenocaulon texanum*, 7
Scrambled Eggs, 36
Scrophulariaceae, 181–190
Scurf-Pea, 66
*Scutellaria Drummondii*, 163
*ovata*, 164
*resinosa*, 163
*Wrightii*, 163
*Sedum Nuttallianum*, 44
*Senecio ampullaceus*, 244
*glabellus*, 245
*Greggii*, 245
*imparipinnatus*, 245
*obovatus*, 244
*tampicanus*, 245
Senecioneae, 244–245
*Senna Lindheimeri*, 60
*pumilio*, 59
*Roemeriana*, 59
Senna, Lindheimer's, 60
Two-Leaved, 59
*Sida filicaulis*, 100
*Lindheimeri*, 100
*procumbens*, 100
Sida, Lindheimer's, 100

*Silphium albiflorum*, 222
*Simpsonii*, 222
Silver-Puff, 250
*Siphonoglossa pilosella*, 196
*Sisyrinchium ensigerum*, 13
Skeleton-Plant, 253
Skullcap, Bushy, 163
Drummond's, 163
Heart-Leaf, 164
Sleepy-Daisy, 212
Smartweed, Pink, 17
Smoke-Tree, 91
Snake-Apple, 203
Snake-Cotton, 18
Snake Herb, 193
Snakeweed, Broom, 215
Snapdragon Vine, 186
Sneezeweed, 236
Sneezeweed, Fall, 237
Snow Bell, Sycamore-Leaf, 129
Soap-Berry Family, 94
Solanaceae, 176–180
*Solanum citrullifolium*, 179
*dimidiatum*, 178
*eleagnifolium*, 178
*rostratum*, 179
*triquetrum*, 179
*Solidago altissima*, 216
*canadensis*, 216
*nemoralis*, 216
*Sonchus asper*, 254
*oleraceus*, 254
*Sophora affinis*, 61
*secundiflora*, 62
Sow-Thistle, 254
Spearmint, 174
Speedwell, Persian, 187
Water, 187
*Sphaeralcea angustifolia*, 99
Spicebush, 34
Spiderling, Scarlet, 20
Spiderwort Family, 3–5
Spiderwort, Giant, 4
Granite, 5
Western, 5
*Spiranthes cernua*, 14
Spurge Family, 87–90
Spurge, Roemer's, 89
Standing Cypress, 147
Star-Thistle, Malta, 247
*Stellaria media*, 24

*Stenosiphon linifolius,* 119
Sterculiaceae, 101
Stick-Leaf, 108
    Reverchon's, 108
Stick-Leaf Family, 107-108
Sticky Granite-Daisy, 212
*Stillingia texana,* 88
Stonecrop, Yellow, 44
Storax Family, 129
Stork's Bill, 80
*Streptanthus bracteatus,* 37
Styracaceae, 129
*Styrax platanifolia,* 129
Sumac, Desert, 91
Sumac Family, 91
Sunflower, Bush, 230
    Common, 229
    Maximilian, 228
    Rough, 228
Sunflower Family, 207-254
Swamp-Milkweed, 139
Sweet Clover, White, 64

*Talinum auranticum,* 23
    *parviflorum,* 22
Tansy-Mustard, 38
*Taraxacum officinale,* 254
Tasajillo, 109
Tatalencho, 214
*Tephrosia Lindheimeri,* 73
*Tetragonetheca texana,* 224
*Teucrium canadense,* 162
    *cubense,* 162
    *laciniatum,* 162
Texas Almond, 51
Texas-Parsley, 124
Texas Plume, 147
Texas Star, 223
*Thamnosma texana,* 84
*Thelesperma filifolium,* 233
    *simplicifolium,* 233
Thistle, Plumed, 248
    Texas, 248
Thoroughwax, 122
*Thryallis angustifolia,* 85
*Tinantia anomala,* 3
*Tiquilia canescens,* 154
*Tithymalus Roemerianus,* 89
Toad-Flax, Texas, 186
Tobacco, Desert, 180
    Fiddle-Leaf, 180

*Torilis arvensis,* 125
    *nodosa,* 124
*Tradescantia gigantea,* 4
    *humilis,* 5
    *occidentalis,* 5
    *pedicellata,* 5
*Tragopogon dubius,* 252
*Trifolium repens,* 65
*Triodanis coloradoensis,* 205
    *perfoliata,* 205
Trumpet Creeper, 191
Tube-Tongue, 196
Turk's Cap, 96
Turnsole, 154
Twin-Pod, 130
Twine-Vine, 141
Twist-Flower, Bracted, 37
Two-Flower Anemone, 29

Umbelliferae, 120-125
*Ungnadia speciosa,* 94
Unicorn-Plant Family, 192

Valerian Family, 201
Valerianaceae, 201
*Valerianella amarella,* 201
Venus' Comb, 122
Venus' Looking Glass, 205
*Verbascum Thapsus,* 181
*Verbena bipinnatifida,* 158
    *canescens,* 157
    *Halei,* 157
    *pumila,* 159
Verbena, Low, 159
    Prairie, 158
Verbenaceae, 157-161
*Verbesina encelioides,* 231
    *virginica,* 231
*Vernonia Baldwinnii,* 207
    *Lindheimeri,* 207
    *guadalupensis,* 207
Vernonieae, 207
*Veronica Anagallis-aquatica,* 187
    *persica,* 187
Vervain Family, 157-161
Vervain, Dakota, 158
    Gray, 157
    Pink, 159
    Texas, 157
Vetch, Deer Pea, 78
*Viburnum rufidulum,* 199

*Vicia ludoviciana,* 78
*Viguiera dentata,* 227
*Viola missouriensis,* 104
   *Langloisii,* 104
Violaceae, 104
Violet Family, 104
Violet, Missouri, 104
Viperina, 77

Wafer-Ash, 84
Water-Cress, 38
Water-Hemlock, 120
Waterleaf Family, 151–152
Water-Pennywort, 123
Water-Primrose, 119
Water-Willow, American, 196
*Wedelia hispida,* 229
Western Venus' Looking Glass, 205
White-Brush, 159
Whitlow-Grass, 39
Whitlow-Wort, 24
Widow's Tears, 4
Wild Petunia, Common, 194
   Drummond's, 193
   Low, 195
Wind-Flower, 28
Winecup, 97
   Standing, 98
*Wissadula holosericea,* 98
Witch-Hazel, 46
Witch-Hazel Family, 46
Wood Sage, 162
Wood-Sorrel, 81
Wood-Sorrel Family, 81
Wood-Sorrel, Yellow, 81
Woolly-White, 242

*Xanthisma texanum,* 212
*Xanthocephalum dracunculoides,* 215
   *Sarothrae,* 215

Yarrow, 243
Yellow-Puff, 57
Yellow-Show, 103
*Yucca rupicola,* 11
Yucca, Twist-Leaf, 11

*Zexmenia hispida,* 229
*Zigadenus Nuttallii,* 6
*Zornia bracteata,* 77